ENGINEERING MATHEMATICS
WITH MATHEMATICA

International Series in Pure and Applied Mathematics

Ahlfors: *Complex Analysis*
Bender and Orszag: *Advanced Mathematical Methods for Scientists and Engineers*
Boas: *Invitation to Complex Analysis*
Brown and Churchill: *Fourier Series and Boundary Value Problems*
Buchanan and Turner: *Numerical Methods and Analysis*
Buck: *Advanced Calculus*
Chartrand and Oellerman: *Applied and Algorithmic Graph Theory*
Colton: *Partial Differential Equations*
Conte and de Boor: *Elementary Numerical Analysis: An Algorithmic Approach*
Edelstein-Keshet: *Mathematical Models in Biology*
Farlow: *An Introduction to Differential Equations and Their Applications*
Goldberg: *Matrix Theory with Applications*
Gulick: *Encounters with Chaos*
Hill: *Experiments in Computational Matrix Algebra*
Kurtz: *Foundations of Abstract Mathematics*
Lewin and Lewin: *An Introduction to Mathematical Analysis*
Morash: *Bridge to Abstract Mathematics: Mathematical Proof and Structures*
Parzynski and Zipse: *Introduction to Mathematical Analysis*
Pinsky: *Partial Differential Equations and Boundary-Value Problems with Applications*
Pinter: *A Book of Abstract Algebra*
Ralston and Rabinowitz: *A First Course in Numerical Analysis*
Ritger and Rose: *Differential Equations with Applications*
Robertson: *Engineering Mathematics with Mathematica*
Rudin: *Functional Analysis*
Rudin: *Principles of Mathematical Analysis*
Rudin: *Real and Complex Analysis*
Simmons: *Differential Equations with Applications and Historical Notes*
Small and Hosack: *Calculus: An Integrated Approach*
Small and Hosack: *Explorations in Calculus with a Computer Algebra System*
Vanden Eynden: *Elementary Number Theory*
Walker: *Introduction to Abstract Algebra*

ENGINEERING MATHEMATICS WITH MATHEMATICA

John S. Robertson
Professor of Applied Mathematics
United States Military Academy

McGraw-Hill, Inc.

New York   St. Louis   San Francisco   Auckland   Bogotá   Caracas
Lisbon   London   Madrid   Mexico   Milan   Montreal   New Delhi
San Juan   Singapore   Sydney   Tokyo   Toronto

ENGINEERING MATHEMATICS
WITH MATHEMATICA

 This book is printed on recycled, acid-free paper containing 10% postconsumer waste.

1 2 3 4 5 6 7 8 9 0   DOC   DOC   9 0 9 8 7 6 5 4

ISBN 0-07-053171-4

The editors were Maggie Lanzillo and Jack Shira; the production supervisor was Denise L. Puryear. R.R. Donnelley & Sons was printer and binder.

The illustration shown on the cover was generated by *Mathematica* and depicts the surface created by rotating the graph of the Bessel function of the first kind of order zero about the z-axis. In particular,

$$z = J_0(\sqrt{x^2 + y^2})$$

with $-15 < x < 15$ and $-15 < y < 15$.

This manual was typeset by the author with LaTeX, the document preparation system by Leslie Lamport built atop the TeX engine of Donald Knuth. Special design macros were provided by ETP Services. The illustrations were prepared on a Macintosh IIci with *Mathematica* and MacDraw Pro.

Library of Congress Cataloging-in-Publication Data

ABOUT THE AUTHOR

John S. Robertson is a Professor of Applied Mathematics at the United States Military Academy. He received his Ph.D. in Mathematics from Rensselaer Polytechnic Institute. Since 1991 he has been a full professor at West Point. He is an active researcher in computational acoustics and computer applications to mathematics education. His work has been supported by the Office of Naval Research, the National Aeronautics and Space Administration, and a number of Army research agencies. He is a member of the Acoustical Society of America and the Society for Industrial and Applied Mathematics.

To the memory of Don Alvaro del Portillo
1914–1994
Deo omnia gloria!

CONTENTS

Preface   xiii

1 Introduction   1

1.1   Goals   1
1.2   About *Mathematica*   1
1.3   Basic Algebra and Calculus Operations   2
1.4   Two-Dimensional Graphics   5
1.5   Three-Dimensional Graphics   7
      Exercises   11

2 Vector Algebra   14

2.1   Laboratory Goals   14
2.2   Building Vectors   14
2.3   Vector Products   17
2.4   Determining Direction Cosines   18
2.5   Applications   19
      Exercises   22

3 Manipulating Discrete Data   25

3.1   Laboratory Goals   25
3.2   Lists   25
3.3   Reading Lists of Data   27
3.4   Multidimensional Lists   32
      Exercises   34

4 Matrices   37

4.1   Laboratory Goals   37
4.2   Products, Transposes, and Inverses   37

4.3   Powers, Eigenvalues, and Eigenvectors   40
4.4   Transition Probabilities   42
4.5   Application to Cryptography   44
      Exercises   47

5   Linear and Nonlinear Equations   49
5.1   Laboratory Goals   49
5.2   Linear Equations   49
5.3   Nonlinear Equations   52
5.4   Graphical and Numerical Solutions   54
      Exercises   56

6   First-Order ODEs   58
6.1   Laboratory Goals   58
6.2   First-Order Linear ODEs   58
6.3   Separable Equations   61
6.4   Homogeneous Equations   61
6.5   Special First-Order Equations   61
      Exercises   63

7   Second-Order Constant-Coefficient ODEs   65
7.1   Laboratory Goals   65
7.2   General Solutions   65
7.3   Using Initial Conditions   69
7.4   Damped Motion   70
7.5   Forced Motion   73
      Exercises   78

8   Laplace Transforms   79
8.1   Laboratory Goals   79
8.2   Simple Transforms   79
8.3   Application to Differential Equations   82
8.4   A Circuit Analysis Problem   83
      Exercises   86

9   The Simple Pendulum   87
9.1   Laboratory Goals   87
9.2   Model Formulation   87
9.3   A Special Case—The Inverted Pendulum   88
9.4   Periodic Oscillations of the Pendulum   90
      Exercises   91

10 Systems of ODEs   93
10.1 Laboratory Goals   93
10.2 Homogeneous Linear Systems   93
10.3 Nonhomogeneous Linear Systems   96
10.4 Chemical Mixing   99
      Exercises   102

11 Numerical Solutions of ODEs   104
11.1 Laboratory Goals   104

11.2	Second-Order Equations	104
11.3	Manipulating Multiple Solutions	106
11.4	Systems of ODEs	108
	Exercises	110

12 Variable Coefficient ODEs   **112**

12.1	Laboratory Goals	112
12.2	Cauchy-Euler Equations	112
12.3	Other Special Equations	114
12.4	Applications	117
	Exercises	119

13 Fourier Series   **122**

13.1	Laboratory Goals	122
13.2	Fourier Sine Series	122
13.3	Fourier Cosine Series	126
13.4	The `FourierTransform` Package	128
13.5	Fourier Series	129
	Exercises	133

14 The Heat Equation   **135**

14.1	Laboratory Goals	135
14.2	One-Dimensional Solution	135
14.3	Asymmetric Initial Temperature	136
14.4	Displaying Heat Flow Dynamics	139
14.5	Discussion	140
	Exercises	141

15 The Vibrating Bar   **143**

15.1	Laboratory Goals	143
15.2	Vibrating Bar	143
15.3	Separation of Variables	144
15.4	The Hinged-Hinged Bar	145
15.5	The Hinged-Clamped Bar	150
15.6	Examining Many Eigenvalues	156
	Exercises	160

16 The Vibrating Annulus   **161**

16.1	Laboratory Goals	161
16.2	Description of the Annulus	161
16.3	Separation of Variables Solution	162
16.4	Determination of the Eigenvalues	163
16.5	Sketching the Eigenmodes	165
	Exercises	167

17 Approximating Eigenvalues   **168**

17.1	Laboratory Goals	168
17.2	Motivation	168
17.3	Using Difference Equations	169
17.4	Generating the Coefficient Matrix	171

17.5   Application to Vibrating String 173
Exercises 175

18   Vector Differentiation 177
18.1   Laboratory Goals 177
18.2   The Gradient, Divergence, and Curl 177
18.3   Other Vector Differentiation Operators 180
18.4   Establishing Vector Identities 181
Exercises 182

19   Coordinate Systems 184
19.1   Laboratory Goals 184
19.2   Setting The Coordinate System 184
19.3   Changing Coordinates 186
19.4   Vector Multiplication in Other Systems 187
19.5   Vector Differentiation in Other Systems 188
19.6   Plotting in Other Coordinates 189
Exercises 191

20   Vector Functions of a Single Variable 192
20.1   Laboratory Goals 192
20.2   Three-Dimensional Particle Motion 192
20.3   The TNB Coordinate System 195
20.4   Curvature and Torsion 196
Exercises 198

21   Vector Integration 199
21.1   Laboratory Goals 199
21.2   The Divergence Theorem 199
21.3   Stoke's Theorem 201
Exercises 204

22   Multi-Variable Optimization 205
22.1   Laboratory Goals 205
22.2   Description of the Trough 205
22.3   Locating Critical Points 206
22.4   The Second Derivative Test 209
22.5   Discussion 209
Exercises 211

23   Visualizing Fields 213
23.1   Laboratory Goals 213
23.2   Gradient Fields 213
23.3   Divergence of a Vector Field 215
Exercises 218

24   Complex Arithmetic 219
24.1   Laboratory Goals 219
24.2   Manipulating Complex Numbers 219
24.3   Complex Functions 222
Exercises 224

25   Taylor and Laurent Series   225
    25.1 Laboratory Goals   225
    25.2 Taylor Series   225
    25.3 Laurent Series   229
         Exercises   235

26   Residues   236
    26.1 Laboratory Goals   236
    26.2 Determining Residues   236
    26.3 Integrating with Residues   238
    26.4 Evaluating Real Integrals   239
         Exercises   240

27   Visualizing Complex Mappings   241
    27.1 Laboratory Goals   241
    27.2 Mapping Rectangular Regions   241
    27.3 The Exponential Map   242
    27.4 The Sine Map   243
    27.5 The Logarithm Map   245
    27.6 Other Mappings   248
         Exercises   248

28   Conformal Mappings   250
    28.1 Laboratory Goals   250
    28.2 Linear Fractional Transformations   250
    28.3 Equilibrium Temperatures   254
    28.4 Flow in a Corner   256
         Exercises   258

A   Summary of Functions and Operators   260

B   Unit Conversions and Constants   268
    B.1 Physical Constants   270
    B.2 Chemical Data   271

C   Enhancing Graphics   273
    C.1 Two-Dimensional Plots   273
    C.2 Three-Dimensional Plots   275

D   Generating FORTRAN and C Code   278
    D.1 FORTRAN Example   278
    D.2 C Example   279

    Bibliography   281

    Index   282

PREFACE

This book is intended for use as a supplemental tool for courses in engineering mathematics, applied ordinary and partial differential equations, vector analysis, applied complex analysis, and other advanced courses in which *Mathematica*[1] is used. My goal in writing this text was to prepare a supplementary book that could be used to guide students through a series of laboratory exercises that would do the following:

- present cogent applications of the mathematics
- demonstrate the effective uses of the computational tool (in this case, *Mathematica*) to do the mathematics
- provide discussion of the results obtained by using *Mathematica*
- stimulate thought about and analysis of additional applications

Each chapter has been written so that the material it contains may be covered in a typical laboratory session of about 1-1/2 to 2 hours. The goals for every laboratory are stated at the beginning of each chapter. Mathematical concepts are then discussed within a framework of abundant engineering applications and problem-solving techniques using *Mathematica*. I have tried to keep the *Mathematica* instruction *per se* to a minimum, but have included enough material to get students up and running quickly.

Each chapter is followed by a set of exercises. Many of these are exploratory in nature and are intended to serve as a starting point for a student's mathematical experimentation. In addition, since most of the exercises can be solved

---

[1] *Mathematica* is a registered trademark of Wolfram Research, Inc.

in more than one way, I have not provided an answer key for the student or instructor. Students should be encouraged to develop their own problem-solving skills with *Mathematica* and not just look for the "correct" answer.

Colleges and universities across the nation have been carefully re-examining the ways in which undergraduate mathematics is taught and done. The advent of computer algebra systems such as *Mathematica*, which can perform elaborate symbolic calculations, in conjunction with the rapidly expanding power of computers to function as graphic visualization devices have forced a critical rethinking of how much of what is called higher mathematics ought to be taught and done.

The calculus reform movement has already borne much fruit. As it matures, the same style of innovative thinking must subsequently be brought to bear on virtually all the mathematics courses taken by upperclassmen. While core mathematics has been the object of substantial national attention, less emphasis has been placed on adapting advanced courses to the technology and the student expectations it brings with it.

For these reasons, one of the most promising areas in which to exploit computation is in "engineering mathematics," a rubric which covers applied ordinary and partial differential equations, vector analysis, and applied complex analysis in courses normally taken junior and senior year. One approach to this problem is to write new textbooks with clearly-woven computational threads. I have taken a different approach by presenting discussion that is compatible with a broad range of engineering mathematics texts, as well as smaller, more specialized texts in differential equations and complex variables.

Although it might be desirable to make such a laboratory text independent of any particular software package, this goal is not yet in sight. There are simply too many differences in package front-ends and capabilities. In my view, a laboratory text must deal concretely with the details of a specific package. For a number of reasons, I have selected *Mathematica* as the computer algebra package for this text. *Mathematica* possesses a wealth of features which make it an excellent laboratory tool for engineering mathematics. In addition, *Mathematica* is available on a broad array of platforms—386 PCs, Macintoshes, Sun Sparcstations, IBM RS/6000s, etc.—and is found at many universities.

I would like to thank many, many people for their help while I prepared this book. My wife Julia alternately encouraged and cajoled me during the many months of its writing. Colonel Frank Giordano provided numerous useful insights and kept more than one wolf at bay. Dr. Norbert Carballo provided timely advice regarding the true purpose of the effort. Prof. Heidi A. Pattee of Oregon State University carefully read the manuscript and offered a myriad of suggestions which substantially improved the book. My editor, Maggie Lanzillo, was simply wonderful.

John S. Robertson

ENGINEERING MATHEMATICS
WITH MATHEMATICA

CHAPTER
1

INTRODUCTION

1.1 GOALS

a. To become familiar with the basic syntax of *Mathematica*.
b. To plot two-dimensional graphs.
c. To plot three-dimensional surfaces.

1.2 ABOUT *Mathematica*

Mathematica is a powerful symbolic algebra tool that provides an extraordinarily rich variety of symbolic, graphical and numerical capabilities to anyone working with engineering mathematics.

Mathematica

FIGURE 1.1
Clicking on this (or a similar) icon starts *Mathematica* on the Macintosh.

    Mathematica sessions are started differently on different machines. For example, on the Macintosh, you can click on a *Mathematica* icon, as shown in Fig. 1.1. This will open a *Mathematica* notebook into which you can start typing.

1

On a UNIX-based workstation, such as an IBM RISC System 6000, you would type `math` at the command prompt. In this case you will see the following text in your window:[1]

```
Mathematica 2.0 for IBM RISC System 6000
Copyright 1988-91 Wolfram Research, Inc.
  -- X11 windows graphics initialized --

In[1]:=
```

Refer to the *Local Guide* that came with your *Mathematica* implementation on starting *Mathematica* on other computer systems.[2]

    Mathematica syntax, while initially a bit strange, is fairly easy to learn and remarkably consistent. As you work with it, keep the following rules in mind:

- *Mathematica* is case-sensitive.
- All *Mathematica* functions are capitalized.
- Function arguments are always delineated with square brackets, i.e. [...].
- Lists are always delineated with curly brackets, i.e. {...}.
- Variable ranges (for integration, plotting, and counting) are always built with lists.
- A double question mark ?? followed by the *Mathematica* function name will elicit a short help message. This is useful only if you already understand the command. There is no substitute for referring to the *Mathematica* book[3] for definitive guidance on a particular function or operation.

1.3 BASIC ALGEBRA AND CALCULUS OPERATIONS

There are a few fundamental operations which must be mastered early on if the power of *Mathematica* is to be put to good use in the laboratory exercises. Consider the following expression:

---

[1] As of this writing, notebooks are available for major UNIX platforms. With the release of *Mathematica* Version 2.2, you can also obtain a window directly to the *Mathematica* kernel on the Macintosh. Notebooks, though, are easier to manage, and their use should be *de rigeur* when available.

[2] In this and all subsequent chapters, input and output will be confined between the upward- and downward-facing horizontal brackets as shown in the above example. In addition, within a section, statements will always be consecutively numbered beginning with 1, e.g. In[1]:= and Out[1]=.

[3] Stephen Wolfram, *Mathematica: A system for doing mathematics by computer*, Addison-Wesley, Redwood City, CA, 1991.

```
In[1]:= (x + y)^2

              2
Out[1]= (x + y)
```

In this example, x and y are variables and the ^ operator denotes exponentiation. *Mathematica* returns the result in so-called display form, not unlike the way we would write the result down on paper. Input lines are always numbered like In[n] and output lines like Out[n] where n is the sequential number of the line beginning with the n = 1 for the current *Mathematica* session.

    Mathematica can be directed to expand the result with the Expand[] function:

```
In[2]:= Expand[%]

            2         2
Out[2]= x   + 2 x y + y
```

The % symbol stands for the output of the immediately previous calculation. In this example, % is equivalent to Out[1]. This result of the last command can be further manipulated, say, by subtracting 4 x y from it:

```
In[3]:= % - 4 x y

            2         2
Out[3]= x   - 2 x y + y
```

Note that spaces between symbols designates *implied* multiplication. The use of the asterisk * makes the intention to multiply explicit, i.e., 4*x*y is equivalent to 4 x y.

    In any case, to factor the result shown in Out[3] we use the Factor[] function:

```
In[4]:= Factor[%]

               2
Out[4]= (-x + y)
```

Mathematica contains many powerful functions for performing basic algebra operations. Many of these will be introduced in subsequent chapters of this book. A complete listing of all the *Mathematica* operators, functions, and special symbols is given in Appendix A.

Mathematica can perform a variety of calculus operations. For example, let $f(x) = x/(x^2 + 1)$. Then the derivative $f'(x)$ can be determined with the `D[]` function, which takes two arguments. The first is the function to be differentiated while the second is the variable of differentiation:[4]

```
In[5]:= f[x_] := x / (x^2 + 1)

In[6]:= D[f[x], x]

                2
           -2 x            1
Out[6]=  --------- + ------
            2 2           2
         (1 + x )     1 + x
```

In line `In[5]` we *defined* a *Mathematica* function `f[x]`. This method of defining functions will be discussed in more detail later in this book. (Note that this command generated no output line.)

The indefinite integral is obtained with the `Integrate[]` function. The arguments are the same as those of `D[]`:

```
In[7]:= Integrate[f[x], x]

                2
         Log[1 + x ]
Out[7]=  -----------
              2
```

where `Log[]` denotes the natural logarithm function.[5]

Definite integrals may also be evaluated with the `Integrate[]` function, although the function syntax is slightly different. The second argument is a list with three components: the first is the variable of integration, while the second and third correspond to the lower and upper limits of integration, respectively. For example, to calculate the expression $\int_0^4 f(x)\, dx$, we enter:

---

[4]`D[]` can take partial derivatives of a function of several variables, since *Mathematica* normally treats all symbols as independent variables.

[5]*Mathematica* knows all about the analytical and numerical properties of all the elementary functions, and an impressive menagerie of special functions, too. The nomenclature and syntax of these will be introduced as they appear in later chapters. See Appendix A.

```
In[8]:= Integrate[f[x], {x, 0, 4}]

            Log[17]
Out[8]= -------
               2
```

We emphasize that this is a *symbolic* result: *Mathematica* has calculated this result *exactly*. *Mathematica* can also perform numerical integrations with the `NIntegrate[]` function. The arguments used are identical to those for definite integration:

```
In[9]:= NIntegrate[f[x], {x, 0, 4}]

Out[9]= 1.41661
```

To check this against the symbolic result obtained previously, we can force a numerical evaluation of that symbolic result with the `N[]` function:

```
In[10]:= N[%%]

Out[10]= 1.41661
```

where the symbol `%%` designates the next-to-last result.[6]

1.4   TWO-DIMENSIONAL GRAPHICS

Two-dimensional plotting is straightforward in *Mathematica*. The `Plot[]` function generally takes two arguments. The first is the function to be plotted, while the second is a 3-element list which denotes the domain of the independent variable. Thus, to plot the graph of the function $\sin x$ on the interval $[0, 2\pi]$, you give the following command to *Mathematica*:

```
In[11]:= Plot[Sin[x], {x, 0, 2 Pi}]

Out[11]= -Graphics-
```

---

[6]The `%` can be chained together as many times as necessary. Thus, if we are at `Out[10]`, `%` is equivalent to `Out[9]`, `%%` is equivalent to `Out[8]`, `%%%` is equivalent to `Out[7]`, and so forth.

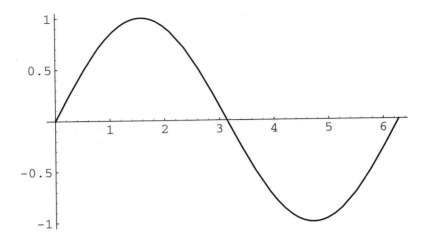

FIGURE 1.2
A plot of the sine function on $[0, 2\pi]$.

The keyword −Graphics− in Out[11] means that the plot appears elsewhere. If you are using a notebook, the plot is entered immediately above the Out[11] line. On a workstation without a notebook, a new graphics window appears somewhere on the screen, and the plot is located within *that* window. Pi is a symbol used by *Mathematica* to denote the exact value of π.[7] The result of this command is shown in Fig. 1.2. *Mathematica* normally scales the x- and y-axes in a natural way, typically to show as much of the plot as possible. Occasionally, the default choices *Mathematica* makes are inadequate. The scaling can be modified with additional arguments to the Plot[] function.

As another example, consider the graph of the function $\cos x$ on the interval $\pi/2 \leq x \leq 5\pi/2$. The command to generate the graph of this in *Mathematica* is:

```
In[12]:= Plot[Cos[x], {x, Pi/2, 5 Pi/2}]

Out[12]= -Graphics-
```

with the result shown in Fig. 1.3. Note how *Mathematica* shifted the scale on the x-axis to accommodate the domain for this plot.

It is often desirable to combine two or more graphs on the same set of axes. *Mathematica* has a powerful facility for this kind of operation. If you are using a notebook, make a note of the number assigned to your plot in the output list. If

---

[7]Other special symbols are E, which is e, is the base of the natural logarithm, and I, which is $i = \sqrt{-1}$.

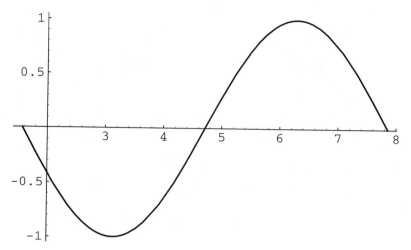

FIGURE 1.3
A plot of the sine function on $[\pi/2, 5\pi/2]$.

you are using a workstation without a notebook, make a note of the number in the title bar of each separate graph. For example, the sine curve may be titled `Out[11]` and the cosine curve `Out[12]`.[8] The `Show[]` function can be used to overlay both graphs with automatic axis scaling:

```
In[13]:= Show[%11, %12]

Out[13]= -Graphics-
```

Note that the symbols `%11` and `%12` stand for `Out[11]` and `Out[12]` respectively. The result of this command is shown in Fig. 1.4. Note that each curve is displayed only over the domain for which it was defined. In addition, the `Show[]` function works with the stored graphic, not with the underlying computation that was used by `Plot[]` to make the graphic. Thus, plot manipulation with `Show[]` is very efficient. *Mathematica* permits an arbitrary number of curves to be combined in this way. To make complicated pictures easier to understand, *Mathematica* also has the ability to change line patterns and thicknesses and to add all sorts of other information to the plot. See Appendix C for some hints on how to do this.

---

[8]These are just example numbers. Your figures may well have different titles. Use the ones on *your* screen.

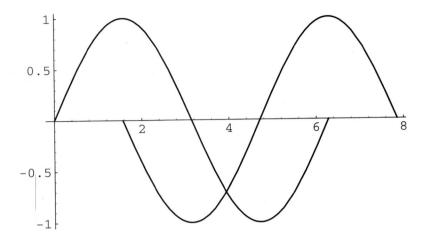

FIGURE 1.4
A plot of both sine and cosine functions on $[0, 5\pi/2]$. Note that the correct range is shown for each curve.

1.5   THREE-DIMENSIONAL GRAPHICS

One of *Mathematica*'s most powerful features is its ability to manipulate three-dimensional information. The surface plot is one way this is done. The appropriate *Mathematica* function is `Plot3D[]`, which takes three arguments: a function of two variables, and two variable domains. For example, consider the surface generated by the function $z = \cos x \sin y$, with $x \in [0, 4\pi]$ and $y \in [0, 4\pi]$. This surface is plotted with the command

```
In[14]:= Plot3D[Cos[x] Sin[y], {x, 0, 4 Pi}, {y, 0, 4 Pi},
         PlotPoints -> 30]

Out[14]= -SurfaceGraphics-
```

with the result shown in Fig. 1.5. The option `PlotPoints->30` forces the surface to be plotted over a 30 by 30 mesh.[9] The default value of `PlotPoint` is 15 by 15, too coarse for this example.

Once this figure is constructed, there are several other simple ways to visualize the characteristic behavior of the surface. For example, a density plot can be generated by the `DensityGraphics[]` function:

---

[9]The other operator -> can be read as "takes the value of." Thus `PlotPoint -> 30` means that `PlotPoint` takes the value of 30. The -> operator is used extensively in this book.

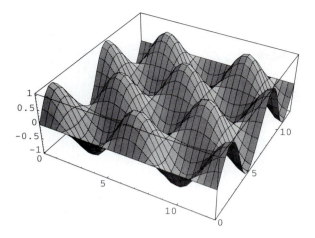

FIGURE 1.5
A surface plot of $z = \cos x \sin y$ on $x \in [0, 4\pi]$ and $y \in [0, 4\pi]$.

```
In[15]:= Show[DensityGraphics[%14]]

Out[15]= -DensityGraphics-
```

with the result shown in Fig. 1.6. In this example, we assumed that the title of graph was Out[14]. Density plots give a more precise way of locating specific surface features with regard to the their locations in the coordinated plane. The darkest areas correspond to the smallest value of z while the lightest areas correspond to the largest value of z.[10] We can see that the maximum and minimum values of z in this example are evenly spaced in both the horizontal and vertical directions.

A different way to visualize three dimensional information is by superimposing contour lines over the density shadings with the including contour lines with the ContourGraphics[] function:

```
In[16]:= Show[ContourGraphics[%15]]

Out[16]= -ContourGraphics-
```

The result of this function call is shown in Fig. 1.7. As in the previous figure, the darkest areas correspond to regions of minimum z-values while the lightest

---

[10]There is a function called DensityPlot[] which generates the same result without the need of calling Plot3D[] and Show[]. It takes the same arguments as Plot3D.

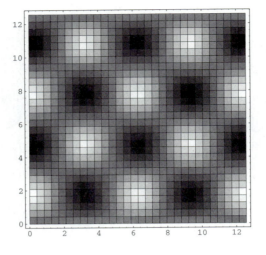

FIGURE 1.6
Density plot of the surface in Fig. 1.5.

regions correspond to the largest z-values. The slightly jagged appearance of the contour lines is a consequence of the resolution of the original surface. The contours can be further smoothed by raising the resolution with a larger value of `PlotPoints`.

It is also possible to overlay multiple surfaces in *Mathematica* in much the same way as discussed in the previous section. To illustrate the point, we now generate a second surface with $z = \sin(y/2)$, with $x \in [0, 4\pi]$ and $y \in [0, 4\pi]$. This is done with the command

```
In[17]:= Plot3D[Sin[y/2], {x, 0, 4 Pi}, {y, 0, 4 Pi}, PlotPoints -> 30]

Out[17]= -SurfaceGraphics-
```

and the resulting surface is illustrated in Fig. 1.8. Note that this surface does not vary with x since z depends only on y. Both Fig. 1.5 and Fig. 1.8 can be overlain with the `Show[]` command as follows:

```
In[18]:= Show[%14, %17]

Out[18]= -SurfaceGraphics-
```

where we have assumed that `Out[17]` is the title of the second surface. This new surface may take a few additional moments to generate. When the figure does

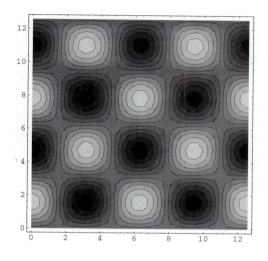

FIGURE 1.7
Contour plot of the surface shown in Fig. 1.5

appear on the screen, it will look like the one shown in Fig. 1.9.   As a final
note to this section, *Mathematica* allows you to change your viewpoint of the
surface with the `ViewPoint` option. This is equivalent to "walking around" the
surface in 3-space. Many other options can be altered to produce interesting,
even stunning, visual effects. See Appendix C for more details on how this is
done.

EXERCISES

1.1. Use *Mathematica* to verify the well-known formulas for factoring the sum and
difference of two cubes. Determine all integers $3 < n \leq 15$ such that $x^n + 1$ has
more than two factors.

1.2. Let $f(x) = x^x$. Plot $f(x)$ and $f'(x)$ on the interval $(0, 2]$ and graphically estimate
the minimum value of $f(x)$. Can you determine an analytical expression for this
value?

1.3. Let $g(x) = 1/\ln(x)$. Plot $\int g(x)\,dx$ on $(0, 3)$.

1.4. Let $h(x, y) = x/(x^2 + y^2)$. Plot the surface represented by $z = h(x, y)$ with
$-1 \leq x \leq 1$ and $-1 \leq y \leq 1$. What is happening at the origin?

1.5. For many gases, viscosity μ is computed with Sutherland's formula:[11]

$$\mu = C_1 \frac{T^{1.5}}{T + C_2},$$

where T is the temperature in degrees Kelvin and both C_1 and C_2 are em-
pirically-determined constants. For hydrogen, $C_1 = 0.649 \times 10^{-6}$ and $C_2 = 70.6$,

---

[11] John J. Bertin, *Engineering Fluid Mechanics*, Prentice-Hall, Englewood Cliffs, 1984, pp.
12–13.

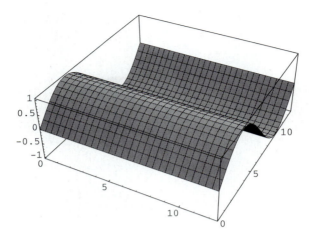

FIGURE 1.8
Plot of the surface $z = \sin(y/2)$ on $x \in [0, 4\pi]$ and $y \in [0, 4\pi]$.

while for nitrogen, $C_1 = 1.39 \times 10^{-6}$ and $C_2 = 102$. (Units for C_1 and C_2 are kg $s^{-1}m^{-1}K^{-0.5}$ and K respectively.) Plot the viscosity of both gases for the temperature range -20 to 120 degrees Celsius.

1.6. Burger's equation is a nonlinear parabolic partial differential equation which can be used to model certain types of viscous fluid flows. One form of this equation is

$$\frac{\partial u}{\partial t} + (c + bu)\frac{\partial u}{\partial x} = \mu \frac{\partial^2 u}{\partial x^2}.$$

Surprisingly, this equation has the *exact* solution (when the flow is stationary) u given by[12]

$$u = -\frac{c}{b}\left[1 + \tanh \frac{c(x - x_0)}{2\mu}\right].$$

(a) Show by direct computation that the given form of u is actually a solution to Burger's equation.

(b) Let $c = 1$ and $\mu = 1/4$. Plot the surface corresponding to u as a function of both b and $(x - x_0)$. Experiment with values of b around -1 and a range of $x - x_0$ within three units either side of the origin.

1.7. When plane electromagnetic waves pass through a small circular aperture at an oblique angle, the transmission coefficients for the two states of polarization are given by:

$$T_\parallel = \frac{64}{27\pi^2}(ka)^4\left(\frac{4 + \sin^2 \alpha}{4\cos \alpha}\right),$$

---

[12]Dale A. Anderson, John C. Tannehill, and Richard H. Pletcher, *Computational Fluid Mechanics and Heat Transfer*, Hemisphere Publishing, Washington, 1984, p. 155.

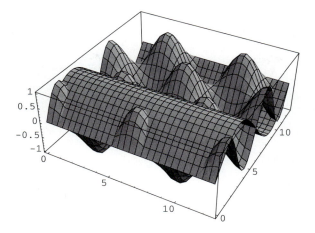

FIGURE 1.9
Intersection of the surfaces shown in Fig. 1.5 and Fig. 1.8. Note that *Mathematica* correctly hides masked portions of the surfaces.

and

$$T_\perp = \frac{64}{27\pi^2}(ka)^4 \cos\alpha,$$

where $T_\parallel$ and $T_\perp$ are the transmission coefficients for parallel and transverse polarization, a is the radius of the hole, k is the wave number, and α is the angle of incidence. Plot $T_\parallel$ and $T_\perp$ as functions of α and graphically determine values of α, if any, for which they are equal.

1.8. One result from the theory of special relativity is the parallel-velocity addition law:

$$v = \frac{v_1 + v_2}{1 + v_1 v_2/c^2},$$

where c is the speed of light. Plot v as a function of v_1 and v_2 and interpret the figure. [Hint: You may find it easier to use the dimensionless velocities $u_1 = v_1/c$ and $u_2 = v_2/c$.]

CHAPTER
2

VECTOR ALGEBRA

2.1 LABORATORY GOALS

a. To create vectors and perform basic algebraic manipulations of them.

b. To take dot products, cross products, and scalar triple products of vectors.

2.2 BUILDING VECTORS

Before proceeding further, the `VectorAnalysis` package should be loaded:[1]

```
In[1]:= <<Calculus`VectorAnalysis`
```

Packages are collections of *Mathematica* functions and routines which must be loaded individually. Several dozen packages come with the *Mathematica* distribution. They are described in *Guide to Standard Mathematica Packages*.[2]

    Mathematica uses the notion of a *list* to build and manipulate vectors. A list is built by placing objects inside a a pair of curly braces, {}. For example,

---

[1] In the input line, the symbols ` are called *backquotes*. On most keyboards the backquote is on the same key as the tilde ~.

[2] Phil Boyland, *Guide to Standard Mathematica Packages*, Wolfram Research, Champaign, Ill., 1991, which comes with the distribution.

consider the three-dimensional vector $\mathbf{v}_1 = 3\mathbf{i} + 2\mathbf{j} - \mathbf{k}$.[3] This vector would be represented in *Mathematica* as a three-component list:

```
In[2]:= v1 = {3, 2, -1}

Out[2]= {3, 2, -1}
```

This object behaves just like we would expect a vector to behave. For example, scalar multiplication has the obvious effect:

```
In[3]:= 3 v1

Out[3]= {9, 6, -3}
```

Moreover, vector addition is also done as expected. Let $\mathbf{v}_2 = 4\mathbf{i} + 5\mathbf{j} + \mathbf{k}$. Then

```
In[4]:= v2 = {4, 5, 1}

Out[4]= {4, 5, 1}
```

and the sum $\mathbf{v}_1 + \mathbf{v}_2$ is found by:

```
In[5]:= v1 + v2

Out[5]= {7, 7, 0}
```

Mathematica provides a variety of functions to manipulate the contents of a list. For example, to access a component of a list, we use the name of the list together with the [[]] construct. This operator gives us a way of grabbing on to the components of a list.[4] Thus to extract the second element of $\mathbf{v}_1$, we give the following command:

```
In[6]:= v1[[2]]

Out[6]= 2
```

[3]$\mathbf{i}$, $\mathbf{j}$, and $\mathbf{k}$ represent the three coordinate unit vectors in cartesian coordinates.

[4]Think of it as a form of subscripting.

To replace any component of a vector, the same construct is used. For example, to change the third component of $\mathbf{v}_2$ from $\mathbf{k}$ to $-3\mathbf{k}$, we do the following:

```
In[7]:= v2[[3]] = -3

Out[7]= -3

In[8]:= v2

Out[8]= {4, 5, -3}
```

The number of components, or length, of a vector is obtained with the `Length[]` function:[5]

```
In[9]:= Length[v2]

Out[9]= 3
```

Vectors may also be displayed in column form with the `ColumnForm[]` function:

```
In[10]:= ColumnForm[v1]

Out[10]= 3
         2
         -1
```

It is also possible to extract multiple components of vectors. For example, to pull out the first and third components of $\mathbf{v}_1$ we use the following command:

```
In[11]:= v1[[{1, 3}]]

Out[11]= {3, -1}
```

Mathematica contains many other functions for manipulating the contents of lists. Some of these are useful when working with vectors and will be used later on in this manual.

---

[5]`Length[]` actually returns the number of components of the list given as its argument.

2.3   VECTOR PRODUCTS

Mathematica contains functions for computing the dot product, the cross product, and the scalar triple product.

For example, to compute $\mathbf{v}_1 \cdot \mathbf{v}_2$, we use the DotProduct[] function:[6]

```
In[12]:= DotProduct[v1, v2]

Out[12]= 25
```

The norm of a vector is easily determined using the formula $|\mathbf{v}| = \sqrt{\mathbf{v} \cdot \mathbf{v}}$:

```
In[13]:= Sqrt[DotProduct[v1, v1]]

Out[13]= Sqrt[14]
```

Recalling that $\mathbf{v}_1 \cdot \mathbf{v}_2 = |\mathbf{v}_1||\mathbf{v}_2|\cos\theta$ where θ is the angle between the two vectors, we can find that angle as follows:

```
In[14]:= ArcCos[DotProduct[v1, v2] /
             (Sqrt[DotProduct[v1, v1]] Sqrt[DotProduct[v2, v2]])]

                      5
Out[14]= ArcCos[---------]
                  2 Sqrt[7]
```

The result in degrees is obtained with:

```
In[15]:= N[180 % / Pi]

Out[15]= 19.1066
```

Cross products are easily computed with the CrossProduct[] function:[7]

---

[6]The dot product here assumes that the vector is expressed in cartesian coordinates. See Chapter 19 for a discussion of other coordinate systems.

[7]Also assuming cartesian coordinates for now.

```
In[16]:= v3 = CrossProduct[v1, v2]

Out[16]= {-1, 5, 7}
```

Note the result obtained for $\mathbf{v}_1 \cdot \mathbf{v}_2$:

```
In[17]:= DotProduct[v1, v3]

Out[17]= 0
```

This is the well-known result that the cross product is orthogonal to both its factors.

The scalar triple product is given by the formula $\mathbf{v}_1 \cdot (\mathbf{v}_2 \times \mathbf{v}_3)$. It is computed with the `ScalarTripleProduct[]` function:[8]

```
In[18]:= ScalarTripleProduct[v1, v2, v3]

Out[18]= 75
```

2.4   DETERMINING DIRECTION COSINES

As an application of these vector abilities of *Mathematica* we will now develop expressions for the direction cosines of a vector. The direction cosines are the cosines of the angles a given vector makes with the three unit vectors each of which are parallel to the cartesian coordinate axes. If α is the direction cosine from $\mathbf{v}$ to $\mathbf{i}$, then $\cos \alpha = (\mathbf{v} \cdot \mathbf{i})/(|\mathbf{v}||\mathbf{i}|)$. But $\mathbf{v} \cdot \mathbf{i}$ is just the first component of $\mathbf{v}$ and $|\mathbf{i}| = 1$. Using similar arguments for the other two direction cosines, we can determine the three direction cosines for $\mathbf{v}_1$:

```
In[19]:= dcosalpha = v1[[1]] / Sqrt[DotProduct[v1, v1]]


                    3
Out[19]= --------
              Sqrt[14]
```

---

[8] Also in cartesian coordinates.

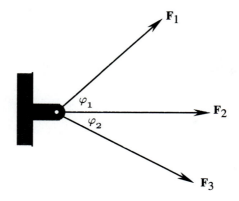

FIGURE 2.1
Three wires under tension pull on a hook attached to a wall. The net force on the hook is sought.

```
In[20]:= dcosbeta = v1[[2]] / Sqrt[DotProduct[v1, v1]]

                2
Out[20]= Sqrt[-]
                7

In[21]:= dcosgamma = v1[[3]] / Sqrt[DotProduct[v1, v1]]

                 1
Out[21]= -(--------)
             Sqrt[14]
```

Note that the sum of the squares of the three direction cosines is one:

```
In[22]:= dcosalpha^2 + dcosbeta^2 + dcosgamma^2

Out[22]= 1
```

2.5 APPLICATIONS

Consider the situation as depicted in Fig. 2.1. Three cables are attached to a fastening as indicated. The tensions on the wires are $F_1 = 500$ N, $F_2 = 400$ N, and $F_3 = 700$ N. The angles are $\varphi_1 = 30°$ and $\varphi_2 = 50°$. We need to determine the magnitude and direction of the resultant force. First, we write each force as a vector:

```
In[23]:= f1 = 500 {Cos[30 Pi / 180], Sin[30 Pi / 180]}

Out[23]= {250 Sqrt[3], 250}

In[24]:= f2 = 400 {1, 0}

Out[24]= {400, 0}

In[25]:= f3 = 700 {Cos[50 Pi / 180], Sin[50 Pi / 180]}


                    5 Pi              5 Pi
Out[25]= {700 Cos[----], 700 Sin[----]}
                     18                18
```

The resultant is obtained by adding the three forces:

```
In[26]:= fr = f1 + f2 + f3

                                       5 Pi                5 Pi
Out[26]= {400 + 250 Sqrt[3] + 700 Cos[----], 250 + 700 Sin[----]}
                                        18                  18
```

The magnitude of the resultant is given by the norm of `fr`:

```
In[27]:= N[Sqrt[fr . fr]]

Out[27]= 1504.71
```

In the previous calculation, we have used the . operator to take the dot product between two vectors. To determine the direction of the resultant, we compute the angle between its two components:

```
In[28]:= ArcTan[fr[[2]]/fr[[1]]]


                                      5 Pi
                          250 + 700 Sin[----]
                                       18
Out[28]= ArcTan[---------------------------------]
                                           5 Pi
                  400 + 250 Sqrt[3] + 700 Cos[----]
                                            18
```

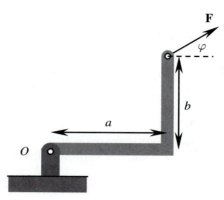

FIGURE 2.2
A force **F** produces a moment about the point O.

We can express this as a result in degrees with the following operation:

```
In[29]:= N[% 180 / Pi]

Out[29]= 31.501
```

Since both components of `fr` are positive, we know that the resultant force direction is 31.5° above the horizontal reference line.

Now consider the bracket shown in Fig. 2.2. A force of magnitude 10 N is applied at angle of $\varphi = 40°$ at the indicated point. The two sides of the bracket are $a = 4$ cm and $b = 3$ cm respectively. We seek the magnitude of the moment generated by the force about the point O.

First, we write the force as a vector. Since we will take cross products, we include the z-component of the force:

```
In[30]:= f = 10 {Cos[40 Pi / 180], Sin[40 Pi / 180], 0}

                2 Pi            2 Pi
Out[30]= {10 Cos[----], 10 Sin[----], 0}
                 9               9
```

The moment arm length is 5 cm (by inspection), and the cosine moment arm angle is 4/5 while the sine is 3/5. Thus the moment arm is written in vector form as

```
In[31]:= r = 5 {4/5, 3/5, 0} / 100


          1     3
Out[31]= {--, ---, 0}
          25   100
```

where we have divided by 100 in order to convert the result to meters. The moment is given by $\mathbf{M} = \mathbf{r} \times \mathbf{F}$, which is expressed in *Mathematica* as

```
In[32]:= m = CrossProduct[r, f]


                    2 Pi          2 Pi
            -3 Cos[----]    2 Sin[----]
                     9             9
Out[32]= {0, 0, ------------ + -----------}
                    10              5
```

The magnitude of the moment is then found to be

```
In[33]:= N[Sqrt[DotProduct[m ,m]]]

Out[33]= 0.0273017
```

Thus, $|M| = 2.73 \times 10^{-2}$ N-m.

EXERCISES

2.1. Write a sequence of *Mathematica* statements which reverses the components of a given three-dimensional vector.

2.2. Determine the angle between the vectors $(3, 7, 1)$ and $(9, -3, -3)$. [With this notation, $(3, 7, 1) = 3\mathbf{i} + 7\mathbf{j} + \mathbf{k}$.]

2.3. Determine the direction cosines of the following vectors:
   (a) $(2, 3, 1)$
   (b) $(-1, -1, -2)$

2.4. Evaluate the cross products:
   (a) $(3, 2, 1)$ with $(1, 2, 3)$
   (b) $(2, 2, 1)$ with $(-4, -4, -2)$

2.5. A block of weight W is placed on a plane inclined at an angle of 25° as shown in Fig. 2.3. The coefficient of friction is $\mu = 0.32$. What is the largest mass that can be placed on the plane without slippage?

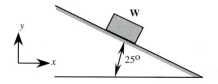

FIGURE 2.3
The block is at rest on the inclined plane.

2.6. A mass weighing 5 N is suspended from two cables as shown in Fig. 2.4.
   (*a*) Determine the tension in the cables if $\varphi_1 = \varphi_2 = 20°$.
   (*b*) Determine the tension in the cables if $\varphi_1 = \varphi_2 = 10°$.

2.7. A force with magnitude 11 kN is applied to the links pinned together at C as shown in Fig. 2.5. The length of each link is 2.5 m. Determine the moments $\mathbf{M}_A$ and $\mathbf{M}_B$.

2.8. Evaluate the scalar triple product of $(2, 0, 1)$, $(3, 2, 1)$, and $(a, -2, -1)$. For what value of a does the triple product vanish?

2.9. A pick-up truck has been stranded in a ditch, but the driver has a coil of rope in the back of the vehicle. He ties one end of the rope to the front of the truck and the other end tightly to a telephone pole about 12 meters from the truck. He then pushes on the middle of the rope with a force of about 500 N, displacing the center of the rope 1 meter from its equilibrium position. What force is exerted on the truck? Assuming this force were sufficient to move the truck and that the driver pushed the midpoint of the rope an additional 1 meter, how far would the truck move? Would you conclude that this is a practical method for getting a vehicle out of a ditch?

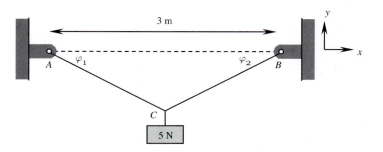

FIGURE 2.4
The weight is at rest.

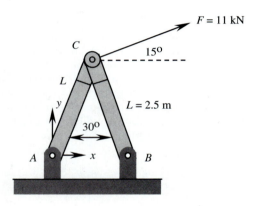

FIGURE 2.5
The force is applied in the indicated direction to a pair of identical pinned links.

CHAPTER
3

MANIPULATING DISCRETE DATA

3.1 LABORATORY GOALS

a. To perform basic manipulations on lists of numbers.

b. To read discrete data from a file into a *Mathematica* list.

c. To construct interpolating functions to discrete data sets.

d. To plot discrete data sets.

3.2 LISTS

Mathematica provides a variety of useful functions for the manipulation of discrete sets of data. The most basic form used is that of the list. Lists are simply arrays of objects separated by commas and delineated by curly brackets. Thus

```
In[1]:= a = {-1, 2, 0, 1/2}

                   1
Out[1]= {-1, 2, 0, -}
                   2
```

a is a list containing four numbers. The elements of a list can be anything: numbers, variables, functions, and even other lists. In this laboratory we are concerned primarily with lists of numbers.

There are many ways to manipulate lists. For example, each element of the list a can be incremented by 1 by just adding 1 to the list. Thus,

```
In[2]:= a + 1

                 3
Out[2]= {0, 3, 1, -}
                 2
```

Lists can also be scaled by multiplying them by a scaling factor. For example,

```
In[3]:= b = 2 a

Out[3]= {-2, 4, 0, 1}
```

Lists can also be used as arguments to many functions. In most cases, the result obtained is that the function is applied to each element of the list which, of course, produces a new list:

```
In[4]:= Sqrt[Abs[b]]

Out[4]= {Sqrt[2], 2, 0, 1}
```

Two lists may be added, subtracted, multiplied, or divided, and the result is a new list whose components are obtained by applying the operation term-by-term to the elements of the two lists:

```
In[5]:= a + b

                 3
Out[5]= {-3, 6, 0, -}
                 2

In[6]:= a / b

                              1
      Power::infy: Infinite expression - encountered.
                              0
```

```
Infinity::indet:
    Indeterminate expression 0 ComplexInfinity encountered.

         1   1                     1
Out[6]= {-,  -,  Indeterminate,  -}
         2   2                     2
```

The warning message was generated because the third element of b is 0. Since division by 0 is undefined, *Mathematica* places the special symbol **Indeterminate** in the new list at the appropriate place.

Attempts to operate on two lists with different numbers of elements will also generate a warning message:

```
In[7]:= c = {2, 1, 2, 1, -2}

Out[7]= {2, 1, 2, 1, -2}

In[8]:= a + c

        Thread::tdlen:
            Objects of unequal length in
                          1
            {-1, 2, 0, -} + {2, 1, 2, 1, -2} cannot be combined.
                          2

                  1
Out[8]= {-1, 2, 0, -} + {2, 1, 2, 1, -2}
                  2
```

Note that the final result is listed as the sum of both lists, but that each is left in its proper form.

3.3   READING LISTS OF DATA

Mathematica has the ability to read data into a list structure. This is useful when discrete data are available from, say, an experiment or data table. For example, consider the data in Table 3.1, which indicate the reduction in percent of rated pump speed for different liquid viscosities. Suppose these data are contained in the file with name **PumpData**, with each viscosity and reduction entry on a separate line. The first three lines in this file might look like this:

```
600     2
800     6
1000    10
```

We can use the **ReadList[]** function to read the contents of this file into a *Mathematica* list. **ReadList[]** takes two arguments in general. The first is the

TABLE 3.1
Rotary Pump Speed Reduction

Fluid Viscosity	Percentage Reduction of Pump Speed
600	2
800	6
1000	10
1500	12
2000	14
4000	20
6000	30
8000	40
10000	50
20000	55
30000	57
40000	60

name of the file to be read, entered as string delineated with double quotes ("),
and the second tells *Mathematica* what kind of data types to expect. In this
instance, all the data are of type **Number**. We also want to have *Mathematica*
interpret each line of data from the file as a sublist. To do this, we set the
RecordLists option to **True**. The file is read in with the following command:

```
In[9]:= pumpdata = ReadList["PumpData", Number,
            {RecordLists -> True}]

Out[9]= {{600, 2}, {800, 6}, {1000, 10}, {1500, 12}, {2000, 14},

            {4000, 20}, {6000, 30}, {8000, 40}, {10000, 50},

            {20000, 55}, {30000, 57}, {40000, 60}}
```

We can now plot these data with the **ListPlot[]** function:

```
In[10]:= ListPlot[pumpdata]

Out[10]= -Graphics-
```

with the result shown in Fig. 3.1.   Note that *Mathematica* has automatically
scaled the two axes to conform to the range of data corresponding to each axis. In
this example, it may be more natural to think of the pump reduction percentage

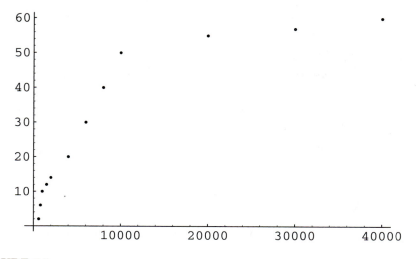

FIGURE 3.1
Discrete plot of the data contained in Table 3.1.

as a function of fluid viscosity. This involves transposing the two coordinate axes. In order to do this in *Mathematica* we will have to switch the data in each pair of coordinates contained in **pumpdata**. The first step involves determining the transpose of the **pumpdata** data set. This is done with the **Transpose[]** function:

```
In[11]:= Transpose[pumpdata]

Out[11]= {{600, 800, 1000, 1500, 2000, 4000, 6000, 8000, 10000,

           20000, 30000, 40000},

          {2, 6, 10, 12, 14, 20, 30, 40, 50, 55, 57, 60}}
```

The result of this calculation is now an array of just two lists. The first list corresponds to the viscosities, while the second represents the pump reduction rates. Next we interchange these two lists of data by accessing each with the subscript symbol **[[]]**:

```
In[12]:= {%[[2]], %[[1]]}

Out[12]= {{2, 6, 10, 12, 14, 20, 30, 40, 50, 55, 57, 60},

          {600, 800, 1000, 1500, 2000, 4000, 6000, 8000,
```

```
                    10000, 20000, 30000, 40000}}
```

Finally, we transpose this back to the original form of the data set with **Transpose[]**:

```
In[13] := pumpdatatr = Transpose[%]

Out[13]= {{2, 600}, {6, 800}, {10, 1000}, {12, 1500}, {14, 2000},

          {20, 4000}, {30, 6000}, {40, 8000}, {50, 10000},

          {55, 20000}, {57, 30000}, {60, 40000}}
```

We can see from this *Mathematica* expression that the data has the desired form, i.e. a list of lists each of which contains two numbers. To verify our work, we plot this last list with **ListPlot[]**:

```
In[14] := ListPlot[pumpdatatr]

Out[14]= -Graphics-
```

The result is shown in Fig. 3.2.

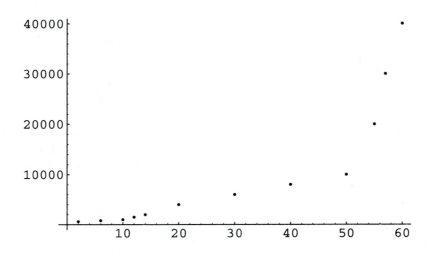

FIGURE 3.2
Discrete transposed plot of the data contained in Table 3.1.

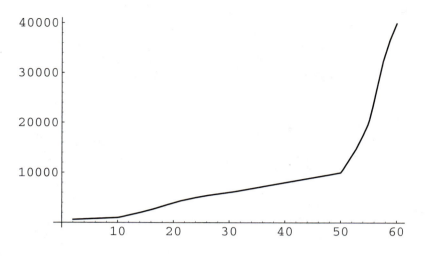

FIGURE 3.3
Continuous approximation to the discrete transposed plot of the data contained in Table 3.1.

We can also use *Mathematica* to construct functions which approximate discrete data sets. This is done with the `Interpolation[]` function. This function takes one argument, which is the list of data points to be interpolated. The format of this list is identical to that required by the `ListPlot[]` function. Optional arguments specify the interpolation order. In the following example, we set the `InterpolationOrder` option to 2:[1]

```
In[15]:= pump = Interpolation[pumpdatatr,
                              InterpolationOrder -> 2]

Out[15]= InterpolatingFunction[{2, 60}, <>]
```

Mathematica always returns the interpolating function in so-called *short* form. This is indicated by the appearance of the angle brackets `<>` in the output above. Interpolating functions can be very long and convoluted—their actual form is rarely of interest. At any rate, we can now plot this function using a call to `Plot[]`. Note that we must force *Mathematica* to evaluate the interpolating function with a call to `Evaluate[]` before plotting the result:[2]

```
In[16]:= Plot[Evaluate[pump[x]], {x, 2, 60}]
```

[1]For a more complete discussion of how the interpolation function works, see the *Mathematica* Book.

[2]Failure to do so will result in numerous error messages from the call to `Plot[]`.

```
Out[16]= -Graphics-
```

The result is shown in Fig. 3.3. Compare this result to that shown in Fig. 3.2. The approximation is excellent. This function could now be used to provide estimates of the reduction rate for different viscosities, to obtain mean values of selected ranges, and for other purposes as well.

3.4   MULTIDIMENSIONAL LISTS

Discrete data are also frequently available for cases in which there are more than one independent variable. *Mathematica* has additional function which construct three-dimensional list plots and generate multidimensional interpolating functions. For example, consider the data given in the following *Mathematica* expression:

```
In[17]:= surf = {{1, 2, 3, 4}, {1, 2, 1, 2}, {2, 2, 3, 3},
               {4, 3, 2, 1}}

Out[17]= {{1, 2, 3, 4}, {1, 2, 1, 2}, {2, 2, 3, 3}, {4, 3, 2, 1}}
```

The list `surf` contains four lists containing four data values. In this example, we omit specific reference to the two independent variables, and *Mathematica* assumes the respective ranges if each are 1 through 4. These data can be taken to represent a surface, and the `ListPlot3D[]` function will construct that surface:

```
In[18]:= ListPlot3D[surf]

Out[18]= -SurfaceGraphics-
```

The resulting surface is displayed in Fig. 3.4.

To generate an interpolating function, we must construct a list of coordinates for each of the data points. One way to do this is with the `Table[]` function. This rather ponderous expression constructs a table of three-element lists. The first and second element of each list correspond to the variables j and k. The third element corresponds to the appropriate data point for that set of coordinates, and is obtained by picking the right value from the set of data in `surf`.[3]

---

[3]Facility with multidimensional data sets requires a great deal of practice!

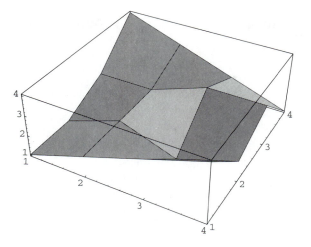

FIGURE 3.4
Approximation of example three-dimensional data set.

```
In[19]:= tabsurf = Table[{j, k, surf[[k]][[j]]}, {j, 1, 4},
                    {k, 1, 4}]

Out[19]= {{{1, 1, 1}, {1, 2, 1}, {1, 3, 2}, {1, 4, 4}},

          {{2, 1, 2}, {2, 2, 2}, {2, 3, 2}, {2, 4, 3}},

          {{3, 1, 3}, {3, 2, 1}, {3, 3, 3}, {3, 4, 2}},

          {{4, 1, 4}, {4, 2, 2}, {4, 3, 3}, {4, 4, 1}}}
```

We now pass this list to the `Interpolation[]` function. We must remove the extra curly brackets from `tabsurf` and this is done with the `Flatten[]` function:[4]

```
In[20]:= sm = Interpolation[Flatten[tabsurf, 1]]

Out[20]= InterpolatingFunction[{{1, 4}, {1, 4}}, <>]
```

The result is again given in short form, with the range of the two independent variable being explicitly listed. We can use `Plot3D` to visualize the interpolating function:

---

[4]`Flatten[]` takes two arguments in this context. The first is the list to be flattened, and the second represents the level to which flattening is applied. In our example, we want to flatten the list to the first level. See the *Mathematica* book for a more comprehensive discussion of this kind of list manipulation.

```
In[21]:= Plot3D[Evaluate[sm[x, y], {x, 1, 4}, {y, 1, 4}]]

Out[21]= -SurfaceGraphics-
```

The resulting surface is displayed in Fig. 3.5. Compare this result to Fig. 3.4.

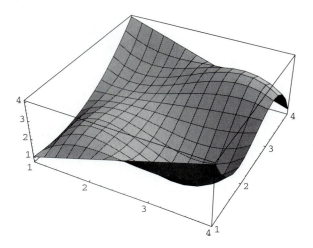

FIGURE 3.5
Interpolated approximation of example three-dimensional data set.

EXERCISES

3.1. Use the `Table[]` function to build a list containing the function $f(x) = (\sin x)/x$ evaluated at the points $x = n\pi/10$, with $n = 1, 2, \ldots, 10$. Build an interpolating function using different values for `InterpolatingOrder`. Which choice gives the best approximation? Which choices give poorer approximations? Can you think of some reasons why?

3.2. The required minimum fire flow rates for municipalities with indicated populations are listed in Table 3.2. Plot the flow rates as a function of population. Determine an interpolating polynomial for the flow rate and estimate the required rate for a city of population 115,000.

3.3. In a certain North American City, the average monthly percentages of sunshine and total insolation (the total amount of energy arriving in that city from the sun) is given in Table 3.3.

    (*a*) Plot the percentage of sunshine and total insolation as a function of the month.

    (*b*) If a certain solar collector has a total surface area of 1.2m^2, and operates with an efficiency of 41%, determine the average monthly energy output of the collector.

TABLE 3.2
Required Fire Flow Rates

Population Thousands	Flow Rate liter/(second)
22	284
28	315
40	379
60	442
80	505
100	568
125	631
150	694
200	757

(*c*) Determine the average annual energy output of the collector.

TABLE 3.3
Solar Energy Availability

Month	Mean Sunshine Percent	Total Insolation $W/(m^2 day)$
Jan	49	4662.9
Feb	54	6220.1
Mar	55	7025.5
Apr	57	7150.1
May	60	7044.4
Jun	64	6955.7
Jul	72	6939.5
Aug	69	6940.4
Sep	60	6675.7
Oct	54	5870.6
Nov	40	4565.5
Dec	40	3941.2

3.4. The cross-sectional temperature distribution (in relative degrees) of a rectangular plate is given in Table 3.4. The plate dimensions are 4 cm and 5 cm respectively. Temperatures are provided at equi-spaced nodes as indicated in the table.
   (*a*) Plot the temperature distribution as a function of both dimensions.
   (*b*) Determine the average value of the temperature distribution.

TABLE 3.4
Temperature Distribution of Plate.

	0	1	2	3	4
0	0	0	0	0	0
1	0	0.07	0	−0.2	−0.38
2	0	0.083	0	−0.25	−0.47
3	0	−0.12	0	0.37	0.71
4	0	−0.27	0	0.81	1.52
5	0.1	0	−0.11	0	0.09

CHAPTER
4

MATRICES

4.1 LABORATORY GOALS

a. To learn the syntax of matrix manipulation with *Mathematica*.

b. To compute eigenvalues and eigenvectors of square matrices.

c. To use matrices to compute n-step transition probabilities.

4.2 PRODUCTS, TRANSPOSES, AND INVERSES

Matrices and matrix manipulation methods are used extensively throughout engineering mathematics. Models of many systems and approximations to many models can assume the form of a matrix.

Consider the matrix A with

$$A = \begin{bmatrix} 1 & 2 \\ 3 & 4 \end{bmatrix}. \tag{4.1}$$

This matrix can be entered into *Mathematica* as a list of lists. Thus each row of the matrix is in the form of a list. For example,

```
In[1]:= A = {{1, 2}, {3, 4}}

Out[1]= {{1, 2}, {3, 4}}
```

Mathematica contains a number of functions for manipulating matrices, especially square matrices. For example, let $B = A^{-1}$. To determine the inverse B, we can use the **Inverse[]** function:

```
In[2]:= B = Inverse[A]

                  3    1
Out[2]= {{-2, 1}, {-,  -(-)}}
                  2    2
```

Note that *Mathematica* uses exact arithmetic in calculating the inverse of this matrix.[1] To demonstrate that B is in fact the inverse of A, we can multiply the two together with the . operator:[2]

```
In[3]:= A . B

Out[3]= {{1, 0}, {0, 1}}
```

which you may recognize as the identity matrix. Matrix multiplication can be done with matrices of any size, provided the dimensions are compatible.

It is also straightforward to determine the transpose of A, A^T and the determinant of A, $|A|$. Each is returned by the **Transpose[]** and **Det[]** functions respectively:

```
In[4]:= Transpose[A]

Out[4]= {{1, 3}, {2, 4}}

In[5]:= Det[A]

Out[5]= -2
```

Mathematica can also print a matrix in the more familiar array format with the **MatrixForm[]** command:

---

[1]Whenever *Mathematica* encounters expressions containing symbols (such as **Pi**), variables, integers and rational numbers (explicit ratios of integers), the arithmetic is done exactly.

[2]The . operator will also yield the dot product between two vectors.

```
In[6]:= MatrixForm[A]

Out[6]= 1   2

        3   4
```

For example, consider the matrix A with

$$A = \begin{bmatrix} 1 & 2 & 1 \\ 1 & -1 & 5 \\ a & 2 & -1 \end{bmatrix} \tag{4.2}$$

For what values of a is this matrix singular? First, enter A into *Mathematica*:

```
In[7]:= A = {{1, 2, 1}, {1, -1, 5}, {a, 2, 1}}

Out[7]= {{1, 2, 1}, {1, -1, 5}, {a, 2, 1}}
```

Now, compute A^{-1}:

```
In[8]:= B = Inverse[A]

               1                1
Out[8]= {{-(------), 0, ------},
             -1 + a         -1 + a

           -1 + 5 a       1 - a          -4
         {-----------, -----------, -----------},
          11 (-1 + a)   11 (-1 + a)  11 (-1 + a)

            2 + a        -2 + 2 a        -3
         {-----------, -----------, -----------}}
          11 (-1 + a)   11 (-1 + a)  11 (-1 + a)
```

from which we see that the inverse exists if and only if $a \neq 1$. A specific value of a can be used to get a particular result. Suppose we want to let $a = 2$. This substitution is made with the /. and -> operators:

```
In[9]:= B /. a -> 2

                    9    1     4      4   2    3
Out[9]= {{-1, 0, 1}, {--, -(--), -(--)}, {--, --, -(--)}}
                   11   11    11     11  11    11
```

The /. operator tells *Mathematica* to use the substitution rule which follows it everywhere in the expression.[3]

4.3   POWERS, EIGENVALUES, AND EIGENVECTORS

Additional *Mathematica* functions allow you to compute matrix powers, eigenvalues, and eigenvectors. For example, the eigenvalues of A can be found with the EigenValues[] function:

```
In[10]:= Eigenvalues[A]

            1
Out[10]= {- + (40 + 3 a) /
            3

                                       3/2
              (3 (-89 + 153 a + 3

                                            2    3  1/3
                 Sqrt[-2077 - 1542 a + 827 a  - a ])   ) +


                 .
                 .
                 .


                                       3/2
                  (-89 + 153 a + 3

                                            2    3  1/3
                 Sqrt[-2077 - 1542 a + 827 a  - a ])    / 3) / 2}
```

an exact, if somewhat unwieldy list containing the eigenvalues. Note that we have eliminated all but the first and last two lines of the output expression, indicating the missing parts by the three vertical dots. The result you see on your screen will be about 25 lines long.[4] Components of a list (remember, every vector and matrix can be thought of as a list of something) can be obtained through the use of double square brackets. Thus, the first eigenvalue of A is the first element of the list in the last expression:

[3]The more natural-appearing a = 2 won't work in the obvious way. If you give this expression, and then re-evaluate B, the value of B will be changed and a will always be equal to 2. In our example, the value of a doesn't change, and neither does B. The substitution affected only Out[9].

[4]There are two ways to shorten the form of an output expression. The first is to terminate the *Mathematica* statement with a semicolon (;). This suppresses the appearance of the usual Out[] line. The second way is by embedding the expression within the Short[] function. This function lists just a piece of the head and tail of an expression, enough to fit on one line of text.

```
In[11]:= %[[1]]

          1
Out[11]= - + (40 + 3 a) /
          3

                                3/2
            (3 (-89 + 153 a + 3

                                                2   3  1/3
                    Sqrt[-2077 - 1542 a + 827 a  - a ])   ) +

                    3/2                         2   3  1/3
        (-89 + 153 a + 3    Sqrt[-2077 - 1542 a + 827 a  - a ])
        ------------------------------------------------------------
                                    3
```

One benefit to symbolic manipulation of matrices is apparent from this example. The eigenvalue list above provides one simple and direct way to study how that eigenvalue depends upon the parameter *a*. There is, in general, no simple and direct way to do this.

Eigenvectors are computed with the `EigenVectors[]` function. We use this function together with the substitution operators to obtain the following formidable results:

```
In[12]:= Eigenvectors[A /. a -> 2]

                                           1/3
Out[12]= {{(-12696 + 759 (217 + I Sqrt[50247])    -

                                              1/3
            23 I Sqrt[50247] (217 + I Sqrt[50247])    +

            .
            .
            .

                                          2/3
            63 Sqrt[1861] (217 + I Sqrt[50247])    +

                                            2/3
            7 I Sqrt[50247] (217 + I Sqrt[50247])    ) / 76176, 1}}
```

The actual output expression is about 40 lines long. Again we have omitted all but the first and last pair of lines for brevity. Calculating eigenvectors for such a matrix by hand would be unthinkable, yet *Mathematica* makes this kind of computation effortlessly.[5] Even more, the tedious additional work sometimes required for eigenvectors corresponding to eigenvalues of multiplicity greater than one is obviated.

It is also possible to generate the powers of a matrix using the `Matrix-Power[]` function. For example, let

$$B = \begin{bmatrix} -1 & 1 & 0 & 0 \\ 2 & 0 & 0 & 1 \\ 0 & 1 & 0 & 0 \\ 0 & -1 & 0 & -3 \end{bmatrix}, \tag{4.3}$$

and suppose we require B^5. First, enter B into *Mathematica*:

```
In[14]:= B = {{-1,1,0,0}, {2,0,0,1}, {0,1,0,0},
             {0,-1,0,-3}}

Out[14]= {{-1, 1, 0, 0}, {2, 0, 0, 1}, {0, 1, 0, 0}, {0, -1, 0, -3}}

In[15]:= MatrixPower[B,5]

Out[15]= {{-11, -5, 0, -43}, {-10, 27, 0, 81}, {-2, -6, 0, -29},

          {86, -81, 0, -130}}

In[16]:= MatrixForm[%]

Out[16]= -11    -5     0     -43

         -10    27     0      81

          -2    -6     0     -29

          86   -81     0    -130
```

As you can see, the ability of *Mathematica* to manipulate matrices is extraordinary, making the exploration of matrix applications in engineering mathematics an exciting possibility.

4.4   TRANSITION PROBABILITIES

Consider a two-player game in which each player starts with $2. A coin is flipped and player A calls it. If the call is correct, player A wins $1 from B, else he loses $1 to B. Assuming that the coin is fair, the probability of gaining or losing a dollar on each turn is $1/2$, unless either player is bankrupt. This situation is

---

[5]Effortless in the sense that the machine does all the work. The actual determination of these eigenvalues can take some time. The eigenvectors of A took many minutes to find on the author's Macintosh IIci.

modeled mathematically by saying that there are five possible states for player A (and thus for player B), S_{i+1}, $i = 0, \ldots, 4$ where i represents the amount of money in the possession of A. If A has one, two, or three dollars, the probability of gaining or losing a dollar is $1/2$, i.e. the probability $p_{i(i\pm1)}$ of moving from state S_i to $S_{i\pm1}$ is $1/2$ if $i = 1, 2, 3$. If A is bankrupt, the probability of remaining so is 1 and of changing to any other state is 0. Thus $p_{11} = 1$ and $p_{1j} = 0$ if $j > 1$. Similarly if B is bankrupt, the probability that A gains or loses any money is 0 while the probability that A remains with all the money is 1. Thus $p_{55} = 1$ and $p_{5j} = 0$ if $j < 5$. This set of probabilities can be described by the probability transition matrix P:

$$P = \begin{bmatrix} 1 & 0 & 0 & 0 & 0 \\ 1/2 & 0 & 1/2 & 0 & 0 \\ 0 & 1/2 & 0 & 1/2 & 0 \\ 0 & 0 & 1/2 & 0 & 1/2 \\ 0 & 0 & 0 & 0 & 1 \end{bmatrix}, \tag{4.4}$$

This matrix is entered in *Mathematica* as follows:

```
In[17]:= P = {{1, 0, 0, 0, 0},
             {1/2, 0, 1/2, 0, 0},
             {0, 1/2, 0, 1/2, 0},
             {0, 0, 1/2, 0, 1/2},
             {0, 0, 0, 0, 1}}

               1    1              1    1
Out[17]= {{1, 0, 0, 0, 0}, {-, 0, -, 0, 0}, {0, -, 0, -, 0},
               2    2              2    2

            1    1
   {0, 0, -, 0, -}, {0, 0, 0, 0, 1}}
            2    2
```

The probabilities of two-step transitions are merely components of the square of this matrix, and the n-step transition probabilities are given in P^n. For example, what is the probability that A is bankrupt after 4 turns? First, we calculate P^4:

```
In[18]:= MatrixForm[MatrixPower[P, 4]]

Out[18]= 1   0   0   0   0

         5   1       1   1
         -   -       -   -
         8   8   0   8   8
```

$$\begin{bmatrix} \frac{3}{8} & 0 & \frac{1}{4} & 0 & \frac{3}{8} \\ \frac{1}{8} & \frac{1}{8} & 0 & \frac{1}{8} & \frac{5}{8} \\ 0 & 0 & 0 & 0 & 1 \end{bmatrix}$$

This probability corresponds to the transition from S_3 (that A has two dollars) to S_1 (A has nothing), or $p_{31}^{(4)}$. Note that the superscript $^{(4)}$ denotes that the element is taken from P^4. From the *Mathematica* result, we see that $p_{31}^{(4)} = 3/8$.

4.5 APPLICATION TO CRYPTOGRAPHY

Another interesting application of matrices is to the encoding and decoding of information. There are many ways to attack this problem, but we will use one based on an interesting property of matrices with integer coefficients. If a matrix A has integer coefficients, then its inverse A^{-1} will have integer coefficients if and only if $|A| = \pm 1$. Suppose we have such a pair of matrices. Let **b** be an n-component vector with all integer entries. **b** is called the *plaintext*. The product $A\mathbf{b}$ is called the *ciphertext*. The ciphertext is decode by multiplying it by A^{-1}. The reason for insisting on integer coefficients for both A and its inverse is straightforward: integer arithmetic is exact, that is, it can be performed by machines without introducing any round-off errors. This guarantees that the ciphertext will produce an exact copy of the plain text when the matrix multiplication is performed.

Suppose we want to encipher the message "Meet noon" using this method. Our approach will be to take the plaintext and convert it into nine integers using the standard ASCII codes.[6] Then we construct a 3x3 array containing these nine integers. We produce the ciphertext by multiplying the plaintext by the *key* matrix, and demonstrate how the process is reversed.

The first requirement is a key matrix, a 3x3 array of integers whose inverse also consists of all integers. We begin by guessing a matrix A as follows:

$$A = \begin{bmatrix} 1 & b & 6 \\ 4 & 9 & 11 \\ a & -4 & 3 \end{bmatrix} \tag{4.5}$$

where a and b are two integers to be determined. In *Mathematica*, we represent this as

---

[6]Each upper and lower case letter of the alphabet, as well as all common punctuation, is represented as an integer between 32 and 127. It is the most common scheme in use for representing English text in computers and other digital devices.

```
In[19]:= key = {{1, b, 6}, {4, 9, 11}, {a, -4, 3}}

Out[19]= {{1, b, 6}, {4, 9, 11}, {a, -4, 3}}
```

Now we compute the determinant of A:

```
In[20]:= detkey = Det[key]

Out[20]= -25 - 54 a - 12 b + 11 a b
```

Next, we set this equal to 1 and use the `Solve[]` function to solve for a in terms of b:

```
In[21]:= Solve[detkey == 1, a]

                 2 (13 + 6 b)
Out[21]= {{a -> ------------}}
                 -54 + 11 b
```

We then use the substitution operator `/.` to isolate the expression for a:

```
In[22]:= a = a /. %[[1]]

          2 (13 + 6 b)
Out[22]= ------------
          -54 + 11 b
```

It is not immediately clear what values (if any) for b yield integer results for this expression. We therefore use the time-honored engineering approach of trying a few guesses. In particular we try values of b from 1 to 10 and see what happens. This is done with the `Table[]` function:

```
In[23]:= Table[%, {b, 1, 10}]

             38     25     62     37        49  110  61  134  73
Out[23]= {-(--), -(--), -(--), -(--), 86, --, ---, --, ---, --}
             43     16     21      5         6   23  17   45  28
```

and we can see that $b = 5$ works. We will use this value now to determine a:

```
In[24]:= a /. b -> 5

Out[24]= 86
```

We can now obtain the matrix A by substituting these values for a and b into the expression we had for **key**:

```
In[25]:= key = key /. {a -> 86, b -> 5}

Out[25]= {{1, 5, 6}, {4, 9, 11}, {86, -4, 3}}
```

To verify that A has the desired property, we compute its inverse:

```
In[26]:= keyinv = Inverse[key]

Out[26]= {{71, -39, 1}, {934, -513, 13}, {-790, 434, -11}}
```

We now use the **Characters[]** function to convert the string "Meet noon" into a list of nine characters:

```
In[27]:= Characters["Meet noon"]

Out[27]= {M, e, e, t,  , n, o, o, n}
```

Another *Mathematica* function, **ToCharacterCode[]** will convert these letters to their corresponding ASCII codes:

```
In[28]:= ToCharacterCode["Meet noon"]

Out[28]= {77, 101, 101, 116, 32, 110, 111, 111, 110}
```

To convert this list of nine integers into a 3x3 array, we use the **Take[]** function. **Take[]** takes two arguments. The first is the list to be used, and the second is the range of the list to be extracted. Thus,

```
In[29]:= plaintext = {Take[%, 3], Take[%, {4, 6}], Take[%, -3]}

Out[29]= {{77, 101, 101}, {116, 32, 110}, {111, 111, 110}}
```

The expression `Take[%, 3]` takes the first three elements of the list. `Take[%, 4, 6]` take the fourth through the sixth elements of the list, while `Take[%, -3]` takes the last three elements of the list. The result is the matrix `plaintext`. Finally we produce the ciphertext by multiplying the key and plaintext together:

```
In[30]:= ciphertext = key . plaintext

Out[30]= {{1323, 927, 1311}, {2573, 1913, 2604}, {6491, 8891, 8576}}
```

Note that the ciphertext consists of integers that happen to all lie outside the ASCII range of 32 to 127.

To reverse the process, we multiply the ciphertext by the inverse of the key, and use `Flatten[]` to restore the plaintext to a flat list:

```
In[31]:= keyinv . ciphertext

Out[31]= {{77, 101, 101}, {116, 32, 110}, {111, 111, 110}}

In[32]:= Flatten[%]

Out[32]= {77, 101, 101, 116, 32, 110, 111, 111, 110}
```

This can be converted back into an ASCII string with the `FromCharacterCode[]` function:

```
In[33]:= FromCharacterCode[%]

Out[33]= Meet noon
```

EXERCISES

4.1. What *Mathematica* expression would you use to extract a single element from a matrix? A whole row? An entire column?

4.2. Consider the matrix A with

$$\cdot\, A = \begin{bmatrix} 1 & 2 & 1 \\ 1 & -1 & 0 \\ 0 & 2 & -1 \end{bmatrix} \tag{4.6}$$

(a) Determine the eigenvalues of A.
(b) Determine the eigenvectors of A.
(c) Determine the characteristic polynomial of A. Use the `Solve[]` function[7] to find the roots of this polynomial and show that they are the eigenvalues of A.
(d) Show that A itself satisfies its characteristic polynomial.
(e) Show by direct computation that the eigenvectors of A are orthogonal.

4.3. Regarding Section 4.4, what is the probability that A will be bankrupted at the fourth turn but not at the third turn?

4.4. Regarding Section 4.4, what is the probability that A will bankrupt B at the twentieth turn?

4.5. Construct a 3x3 key matrix of your own. Make your initial guess different from the one in the text, and apply the procedure described there. Verify that the inverse has the correct property.

4.6. Describe a strategy for using a 3x3 key matrix to encrypt a message consisting of more than nine characters. For example, encrypt the message "Attack at dawn".

4.7. Suppose you had both the plaintext and the ciphertext, but not the key. Could you deduce the key? What does this imply about security requirements for the key and the ciphertext?

---

[7]You may peek ahead to the next chapter.

CHAPTER 5

LINEAR AND NONLINEAR EQUATIONS

5.1 LABORATORY GOALS

a. To solve simultaneous linear equations.
b. To obtain numerical solutions to transcendental equations.
c. To become familiar with the `Solve[]` and `FindRoot[]` functions.

5.2 LINEAR EQUATIONS

The solution of simultaneous linear equations occurs frequently in applications of engineering mathematics. Consider the pair of equations given by

$$x + 3y = 1 \tag{5.1}$$

$$2x - 4y = 3. \tag{5.2}$$

In *Mathematica* this system is represented by

```
In[1]:= x + 3y == 1

Out[1]= x + 3 y == 1

In[2]:= 2x - 4y == 3

Out[2]= 2 x - 4 y == 3
```

In this context the symbol == is used to construct a symbolic equation rather than as an assignment operator. Symbolic equations are passed as arguments to functions which determine analytical as well as numerical solutions.[1] The `Solve[]` function determines the solution to this system:

```
In[3]:= Solve[{%1, %2}, {x, y}]

              13            1
Out[3]= {{x -> --, y -> -(--)}}
              10           10
```

Note that the equations to be solved are given as a list (in this case using the % symbol). The variables to be determined, x and y, are also specified as a list. The result as given above is set in a form which permits substitution of the solutions into general expressions involving either x or y. For example, suppose that $f(x, y) = x^3 - y^3$, so that

```
In[4]:= f[x_, y_] := x^3 - y^3
```

In order to evaluate this function at the values specified by `Out[3]`, we use the `/.` operator which causes the substitutions $x = 13/10$ and $y = -1/10$ to be made only for that one expression:

```
In[5]:= f[x,y] /. %3

            1099
Out[5]= {----}
            500
```

There is in principal no limit to the size of systems that can be solved in this way.

If the system is underdetermined, we would normally expect to obtain infinitely many solutions. Consider the system

$$x + y = 2 \qquad (5.3)$$

$$2x + 2y = 4. \qquad (5.4)$$

This system is solved with the following sequence of *Mathematica* statements:

---

[1] More accurately, the == operator performs a logical comparison between the left- and right-hand sides. Readers familiar with the C programming language will recognize this use.

```
In[6] := x + y == 2

Out[6] = x + y == 2

In[7] := 2x + 2y == 4

Out[7] = 2 x + 2 y == 4

In[8] := Solve[{%6, %7}, {x, y}]

Out[8] = {{x -> 2 - y}}
```

Note that *Mathematica* has correctly characterized the infinite family of solutions in this case, i.e. for all x such that $x = 2 - y$. If, on the other hand, the system is overdetermined or inconsistent, there may or may not be solutions. Consider this obviously inconsistent system:

```
In[9] := x + y == 1

Out[9] = x + y == 1

In[10] := x + y == 2

Out[10] = x + y == 2

In[11] := Solve[{%, %%}, {x, y}]

Out[11] = {}
```

Note that *Mathematica* reports an empty list in this instance, meaning that it could find no solution.[2]

5.3 NONLINEAR EQUATIONS

Nonlinear equations arise in a number of instances: optimization, equilibrium determination, eigenvalue calculations, etc. Let us begin with an easy example. Let $g(x) = x^2 - 5x - 6$ be a quadratic polynomial. *Mathematica* can determine the roots of this polynomial using the `Solve[]` function:

```
In[12] := y = x^2 - 5 x - 6
```

---

[2]The claim that no solution was found *may* mean that no solution exists. Some sort of double-check should be performed. This *caveat* is particularly apropos when working with nonlinear equations.

```
                                 2
Out[12]= -6 - 5 x + x

In[13]:= Solve[{y == 0}, {x}]

Out[13]= {{x -> -1}, {x -> 6}}
```

In **In[12]** we used the = symbol instead of the := sign. In this instance, the left-hand side immediately assumes the value of the right-hand expression. Thus, until changed, y literally means x^2 - 5 x - 6.

Mathematica correctly determines both roots. Either of them can be gotten for further manipulation by using double brackets [[]] to access the individual members of the list. For example, the first root is obtained with

```
In[14]:= %13[[1]]

Out[14]= {x -> -1}
```

while the second can be obtained with %13[[2]].

A more challenging problem is to seek solution to a pair of nonlinear equations. Consider the pair of quadratic polynomials $y_1 = (x - 2)^2/2$ and $y_2 = -(x+3)^2/4+9$. We represent both polynomials in *Mathematica* as follows:

```
In[15]:= y1 = (x - 1)^2 / 2

                 2
         (-1 + x)
Out[15]= ---------
             2

In[16]:= y2 = -(x + 3)^2 / 4 + 9

                  2
          (3 + x)
Out[16]= 9 - --------
              4
```

The **Solve[]** function is now invoked like this:

```
In[17]:= sols = Solve[{y1 == y2}, x]


          -2 - 4 Sqrt[19]          -2 + 4 Sqrt[19]
Out[17]= {{x -> ---------------}, {x -> ---------------}}
                 6                        6
```

In this last expression we assigned the symbolic name `sols` to `Out[17]`. Numerical approximations of this list is obtained with the `N[]` function, which renders all exact constants into floating point form:[3]

```
In[18]:= N[sols]

Out[18]= {{x -> -3.23927}, {x -> 2.5726}}
```

To visualize the location of these solutions, we can have *Mathematica* plot both y_1 and y_2:

```
In[19]:= Plot[{y1, y2}, {x, -5, 5}]

Out[19]= -Graphics-
```

The two polynomials are seen to intersect twice in Fig. 5.1. The value of the

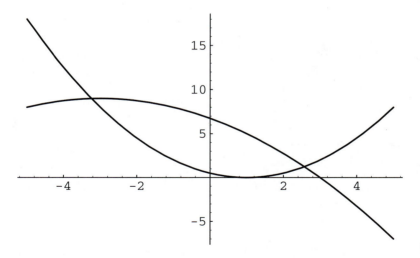

FIGURE 5.1
Plot of $y_1 = (x-1)^2/2$ and $y_2 = -(x+3)^2/4 + 9$

polynomials at the intersection points is obtained by substituting the solution list `sols` into one of the polynomials:

---

[3]Elaborate symbolic expressions are often simplified considerably this way.

```
In[20]:= y1 /. sols

                     -2 - 4 Sqrt[19] 2         -2 + 4 Sqrt[19] 2
              (-1 + ----------------)    (-1 + ----------------)
                           6                         6
Out[20]= {------------------------, ------------------------}
                      2                          2


In[21]:= N[%]

Out[21]= {8.98569, 1.23653}
```

The numerical values have also been found with the `N[]` function.

5.4 GRAPHICAL AND NUMERICAL SOLUTIONS

In many instances, exact solutions to nonlinear equations may be simply unobtainable. For example, a problem which often arises when solving boundary value problems involving homogeneous boundary conditions of the third kind[4] is to determine all solutions to equations of this form:

$$\tan \lambda = \lambda \tag{5.5}$$

The roots of this equation are related to the eigenvalues of the underlying problem. Equations such as Eq. (5.5) are called transcendental equations. Their solutions can usually only be obtained numerically. The first step in such problems is to estimate the location of solutions using graphical means, and then to use that information to calculate precise numerical approximations.

In this case, we first plot the function $f(\lambda) = \tan \lambda - \lambda$:

```
In[22]:= f = Tan[lambda] - lambda

Out[22]= -lambda + Tan[lambda]

In[23]:= Plot[f, {lambda, 0, 15}]

Out[23]= -Graphics-
```

As seen in Fig. 5.2, there are roots immediately to the left of each vertical asymptote (except the first at $x = \pi/2$).[5] Since the asymptotes occur at

---

[4]They take the form $y(\alpha) + \beta y'(\alpha)$, and are also called mixed or Robin conditions.

[5]The function $\tan x$ has singularities for all $x = \pi/2 \pm n\pi$ *Mathematica* automatically scaled the plot and skipped over the singularities. The vertical asymptotes are an artifact, albeit a handy one, of the process.

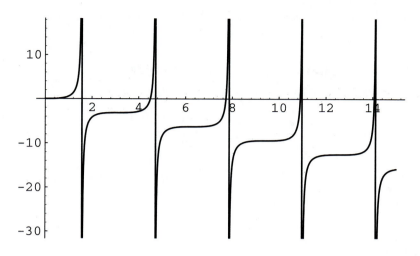

FIGURE 5.2
Plot of $f(\lambda) = \tan \lambda - \lambda$.

$\lambda = (2n - 1)\pi/2$, this gives us an estimate which can be supplied to the root-finding function **FindRoot[]**. To use this function we must provide an initial guess "sufficiently close" to the root. How close is sufficiently close? It depends very much on the function involved, but in general, the better the guess, the more likely **FindRoot[]** will converge *quickly* to the *correct* root.

As seen in Fig. 5.2, the first root is $\lambda_1 \approx 4.4$. Then we give the following *Mathematica* command:

```
In[24]:= FindRoot[Tan[lambda] - lambda == 0, {lambda, 4.4}]

Out[24]= {lambda -> 4.49341}
```

FindRoot[] takes as arguments a list of equations (in this case one), and a second list with the name of the variable to be solved for and an initial guess of the solution. The solution returned by **FindRoot[]** is correct to the indicated number of decimal places. More accuracy can be obtained (at a sometimes serious performance cost) by raising the value of the **WorkingPrecision** option. Thus

```
In[25]:= FindRoot[Tan[lambda] - lambda == 0, {lambda, 4.4},
              WorkingPrecision -> $MachinePrecision + 10]

Out[25]= {lambda -> 4.4934094579090641753078893352}
```

Since $MachinePrecision on most computers is typically set to 16 decimal digits, our result is accurate to more than 25 decimal places![6]

EXERCISES

5.1. Determine all solutions to the following linear system:

$$x + 2y + 4z = 3$$
$$3x + 4y + 5z = 7$$
$$x + 3y + 4z = 4$$

5.2. Determine all solutions to the following linear system:

$$x - y + z - 2w = -1$$
$$-3x + y - z + 2z = 3$$
$$x + y + z - w = 1$$
$$x - y - z - w = -2$$

5.3. Determine the points of intersection of the ellipse $x^2/4 + y^2/9 = 1$ and the parabola $y = x^2 - 4$.

5.4. Let $f(x) = 2\sin x - x/2$. Compute all real zeroes of $f(x)$.

5.5. Determine the first five positive roots of $\cot x = 2x$. [Hint: Some of your initial guesses must be very good!]

5.6. Consider a small sphere of radius ρ moving with speed v through air. The resistive force on the sphere is given by

$$f = 3.1 \times 10^{-4} \rho v + 0.87 \rho^2 v^2. \tag{5.6}$$

(All units are MKS). What is the terminal velocity of a raindrop with $\rho = 3$ mm falling under its own weight?

5.7. Show that[7]

$$\phi(\xi) = \alpha + \beta \mathrm{sech}^2 \sqrt{\frac{\beta\xi}{12k}}$$

is a solution to the Korteweg-deVries equation

$$\frac{\partial \psi}{\partial t} = \psi \frac{\partial \psi}{\partial x} + \nu \frac{\partial^3 \psi}{\partial x^3},$$

---

[6] *Mathematica* can generate arbitrarily accurate answers but be warned: Anything beyond $MachinePrecision on most systems forces *Mathematica* to do floating point calculations in software rather than in hardware. Software floating point manipulations are relatively slow. Moreover, in engineering computations, accuracy beyond machine hardware limits is not often needed. Demand this kind of accuracy only when the nature of the problem warrants it.

[7] $\mathrm{sech}\,(x) = \sinh(x)/\cosh(x)$ is called the *hyperbolic secant* function. The corresponding *Mathematica* expression is Sech[].

provided $\xi = x - ct$ and $c = \alpha + \beta/3$. (This equation models the propagation of waves in dispersive, nonlinear media.) Plot the solution ϕ function of x and t. This type of wave is known as a soliton.

CHAPTER
6

FIRST-ORDER ODES

6.1 LABORATORY GOALS

a. To determine the general solutions to first order linear and non-linear ordinary differential equations.

b. To manipulate the form certain types of first-order equations.

6.2 FIRST-ORDER LINEAR ODES

Consider the first-order linear ODE[1].

$$y'(x) + p(x)y(x) = f(x). \tag{6.1}$$

This differential can always be solved, and, in fact, there is a formula for the solution. *Mathematica* uses this formula to construct solutions. For example, let $p(x) = 1/x$ and $f(x) = 1$. The differential equation is solved with the `DSolve[]` function:

```
In[1]:= DSolve[y'[x] +  y[x] / x == 1, y[x], x]

                    x    C[1]
Out[1]= {{y[x]  ->  - + ----}}
                    2    x
```

[1]ODE means *ordinary differential equation*

The `DSolve[]` function determines a symbolic solution to a differential equation. As arguments, it takes the differential equation, the name of the dependent variable, and the name of the independent variable. Note that the explicit functional dependence of `y` on `x` is given. Also note that the derivative is marked with the ' operator.[2] The solution shown in `Out[1]` uses `C[1]` for the arbitrary constant. This symbol is the standard one for representing all arbitrary constants in symbolic solutions to differential equations in *Mathematica*.

The general solution to our ODE is therefore

$$y = x/2 + c_1/x \qquad (6.2)$$

where c_1 is an arbitrary constant. There are two ways to apply an initial condition to these kinds of equations. The first way is to use the `Solve[]` function to determine the constant. Suppose, for example, that we require $y(1) = -1$. Then, using the result we just obtained, we set $x = 1$, demand that $y = -1$ and solve for c_1:

```
In[2]:= Solve[(y[x] /. %[[1]]) == -1 /. x -> 1, C[1]]

                3
Out[2]= {{C[1] -> -(-)}}
                2
```

Thus $c_1 = -3/2$. A second approach is to specify the initial condition within the `DSolve[]` function. Suppose again that $y(1) = -1$. Then

```
In[3]:= DSolve[{y'[x] +  y[x] / x == 1, y[1] == -1},
               y[x], x]

              -3    x
Out[3]= {{y[x] -> --- + -}}
              2 x    2
```

Note that the initial condition was expressed as the symbolic equation `y[1] == -1`, and included with the differential equation as the element of a list. This list, i.e. the differential equation along with the initial condition, becomes the first argument to `DSolve[]`.

Even though a formula exists for the solutions to first-order linear ODEs, *Mathematica* may not always find the explicit result. Consider the innocent-looking equation

$$y' + x^2 y = x. \qquad (6.3)$$

---

[2] `y'[x]` is logically equivalent to `D[y[x], x]`.

```
In[4]:= DSolve[y'[x] +  x^2 y[x]  == x, y[x], x]

                                  3
                                 x /3
                  C[1] + Integrate[E     x, x]
Out[4]= {{y[x] -> -------------------------}}
                              3
                             x /3
                            E
```

The best that *Mathematica* can do is to present the solution in the form

$$y = \exp(-x^3/3) \left[c_1 + \int x \exp(-x^3/3) \, dx \right] \qquad (6.4)$$

6.3   SEPARABLE EQUATIONS

Another class of first-order differential equations that can be attacked with *Mathematica* has (or can be put into) the following form:

$$y'(x) = p(x)/q(y). \qquad (6.5)$$

Such a differential equation is said to be separable. For example, let $p(x) = 8x^3$ and $q(y) = 1/y^2$. Again we use `DSolve[]` to determine the general solution:

```
In[5]:= DSolve[y'[x] == 8 x^3 y[x]^2, y[x], x]

                       1
Out[5]= {{y[x] -> ------------}}
                      4
                  -2 x  - C[1]
```

Thus $y = -1/(2x^4 + c_1)$. Another example is the differential equation

$$y' = (x + y - 3)^2 - 2(x + y - 3). \qquad (6.6)$$

Mathematica easily handles this equation as follows:

```
In[6]:= DSolve[y'[x] == (x + y - 3)^2 - 2 (x + y - 3), y[x], x]

                                  3
                       2         x             2          2
Out[6]= {{y[x] -> 15 x - 4 x  + --- - 8 x y + x  y + x y  + C[1]}}
                                 3
```

6.4 HOMOGENEOUS EQUATIONS

Let $y' = f(x, y)$. If $f(\lambda x, \lambda y) = \lambda^n f(x, y)$, the differential equation is said to be homogeneous. *Mathematica* can find the general solution to most homogeneous equations. For example, let $y' = (x - y)^2$. The `DSolve[]` function produces the following result:

```
In[7]:= DSolve[y'[x] == (x - y)^2, y[x], x]

                3
               x    2       2
Out[7]= {{y[x] -> --- - x  y + x y  + C[1]}}
               3
```

A more complicated example is given by the equation

$$xy' - y = \sqrt{x^2 - y^2}, \qquad (6.7)$$

which is solved by *Mathematica* as:

```
In[8]:= DSolve[x y'[x] - y == Sqrt[x^2 - y^2], y[x], x]

                    2    2                 y
Out[8]= {{y[x] -> Sqrt[x  - y ] + y ArcTan[-------------] + C[1] +
                                          2    2
                                       Sqrt[x  - y ]

        y Log[x]}}
```

6.5 SPECIAL FIRST-ORDER EQUATIONS

Consider the differential equation

$$3xy' + y + x^2y^4 = 0, \qquad (6.8)$$

which is an example of Bernoulli's equation, whose general form is $y' + P(x)y = Q(x)y^n$. The `DSolve[]` function can handle this equation:

```
In[9]:= DSolve[3 x y'[x] + y[x] + x^2 (y[x])^4 == 0, y[x], x]

                        -(1/3)
Out[9]= {{y[x] -> (x (x + C[1]))       },
```

$$\{y[x] \;\to\; \frac{(-1)^{2/3}}{(x\,(x + C[1]))^{1/3}}\}, \;\; \{y[x] \;\to\; \frac{(-1)^{4/3}}{(x\,(x + C[1]))^{1/3}}\}\}$$

Note that *Mathematica* returns *three* forms of the solution. Which of the three is appropriate depends upon the initial value selected in a particular problem. A multiplicity of solution forms (nonuniqueness of solutions) is often seen when working with non-linear differential equations.

Another type of special equation is called the Ricatti equation, with form $y' = P(x)y^2 + Q(x)y + R(x)$. For example consider

$$y' = y^2 + (1 - 2x)y + (x^2 - x + 1). \tag{6.9}$$

Mathematica is not able to determine the general solution to this equation: [3]

```
In[10]:= ricc = y'[x] ==
             (y[x])^2 + (1 - 2 x) y[x] + (x^2 - x + 1)

                      2                          2
Out[10]= y'[x] == 1 - x + x  + (1 - 2 x) y[x] + y[x]

In[11]:= DSolve[ricc, y[x], x]

                            2                          2
Out[11]= DSolve[y'[x] == 1 - x + x  + (1 - 2 x) y[x] + y[x] , y[x], x]
```

Ricatti equations can be transformed into linear equations under certain special conditions. If a *particular* solution, call it $u(x)$, can be found, then the transformation $y = u + 1/z$ will reduce the Ricatti equation to a linear equation. For example, $u(x) = x$ is a particular solution to Eq. (6.9). We can use *Mathematica* to make the necessary transformations:

```
In[12]:= ricc = ricc /. {y[x] -> x - 1/z[x],
             y'[x] -> D[x - 1/z[x], x]}

             z'[x]            2                     1           1  2
Out[12]= 1 + ----- == 1 - x + x  + (1 - 2 x) (x - ----) + (x - ----)
                  2                                z[x]         z[x]
             z[x]
```

Note that the substitution `y[x] -> x - 1/z[x]` only affects the symbol `y[x]`.
We must explicitly make the substitution for `y'[x]`. Also note that in `In[12]`
we assigned the modified result to the symbol `ricc`. We can now use `DSolve[]`
to find the general solution:

```
    In[13]:= DSolve[ricc, z[x], x]

                     x     C[1]
                    E  + E
    Out[13]= {{z[x] -> ----------}}
                          x
                         E
```

and the general solution can be found be doing the reverse substitution:

```
    In[14]:= x - 1/z[x] /. %

                   x
                  E
    Out[14]= {-(----------) + x}
                  x     C[1]
                 E  + E
```

Mathematica can be used in this way to attack other kinds of special differential
equations of first and higher order, reducing them to forms which yield to the
known methods of solution.[4]

EXERCISES

6.1. Determine the general solution to the equation $y' = 2y/(x+1) + (x+1)^3$.

6.2. Solve the initial value problem $y' = \sec(y/x) + (y/x)$, with $y(2) = \pi$.

6.3. Determine the general solution to the equation $y' = (x+y-3)^2 - 2(x+y-3)$.
[Hint: Try the substitution $v = x - y - 3$.]

6.4. Determine the general solution to the Ricatti equation $y' = (y-1)(y+1/x)$.
[Hint: Try guessing u as a constant.]

6.5. Determine the general solution to the Ricatti equation $y' = x^3(y-x)^2 + y/x$.
[Hint: Try a monomial in x.]

6.6. Water evaporates from most porous substances at a rate proportional to the
moisture content of the substance. Suppose a towel hung on a clothesline on a
mild, windy day loses $1/3$ its moisture in a half hour. How long will it take for
the towel to be dry? (You will have to decide what "dry" means.)

---

[4]How one obtains a particular solution of the Ricatti equation in order to begin the
process is more a matter of art than science. Sometimes a contemplative study of the equation
will yield an insight. At other times, a blind guess might just work.

6.7. The police are called to the scene of a homicide, and the investigating detective determines that the temperature of the corpse is 75 degrees Farenheit. After one hour, the temperature of the body was measured at 73 degrees. He also notes that the ambient room temperature is 65 degrees. How long ago was the murder committed? (Use Newton's Law of Cooling.)

6.8. The population $p(t)$ of a small city is governed by the logistics equation

$$dp/dt = p(0.2 - 0.0000005p), \tag{6.10}$$

where t is measured in months.

(a) If the initial population is 5,000, what will be the limiting population?

(b) How many years will it take for the population to achieve one-half of the limiting value?

CHAPTER
7

SECOND-ORDER CONSTANT-COEFFICIENT ODES

7.1 LABORATORY GOALS

a. To determine the general solution to second-order linear homogeneous and nonhomogeneous constant coefficient ordinary differential equations.

b. To apply initial conditions to determine particular solutions.

c. To manipulate parts of expressions with *Mathematica* functions.

d. To analyze solutions to spring-mass problems.

7.2 GENERAL SOLUTIONS

Consider the second-order ODE

$$y''(x) + y(x) = 0. \tag{7.1}$$

This equation has constant coefficients, and is both linear and homogeneous. It is represented in *Mathematica* as a symbolic equation:

```
In[1]:= y''[x] + y[x] == 0

Out[1]= y[x] + y''[x] == 0
```

The general solution to this equation can be obtained with the `DSolve[]` function:

```
In[2]:= DSolve[%, y[x], x]

Out[2]= {{y[x] -> C[2] Cos[x] - C[1] Sin[x]}}
```

Several things about the form of the solution should be noted. First, the general solution is provided with two arbitrary constants, `C[1]` and `C[2]`. Second, the solution is provided in a form ready for substitution, simplifying subsequent substitutions into expressions in which the solution may be needed. The portion of the solution to the right of the `->` operator can be obtained with the `[[]]` operator:

```
In[3]:= %[[1, 1, 2]]

Out[3]= C[2] Cos[x] - C[1] Sin[x]
```

The first index in `In[3]` refers to the first component of the main list, which is another list, namely `{y[x] -> C[2] Cos[x] - C[1] Sin[x]}`. The second index refers to the first component of *this* list which is the expression `y[x] -> C[2] Cos[x] - C[1] Sin[x]`. The third and last index refers to the second component of this expression, which is `C[2] Cos[x] - C[1] Sin[x]`.[1]

The `DSolve[]` function can also be used to solve second-order equations with nonhomogeneous right-hand sides, for example

$$y'' + y = x. \tag{7.2}$$

The setup and solution of this equation in *Mathematica* proceeds just as it did above:

---

[1]Confused? Remember that just about all the things *Mathematica* manipulates are lists, lists of lists, and so on. The `[[]]` operator with the right sequence of indices can access just about any part of an expression. Later in this Chapter, you will learn about a few functions that exploit the list manipulation abilities of *Mathematica*.

```
In[4]:= y''[x] + y[x] == x

Out[4]= y[x] + y''[x] == x

In[5]:= DSolve[%, y[x], x]

Out[5]= {{y[x] -> x + C[2] Cos[x] - C[1] Sin[x]}}
```

More complicated nonhomogeneous terms are not as straightforward to handle. For example, the following ODE arises in the study of an undamped spring-mass system being driven by a sinusoidal driving force:

$$y''(t) + \omega_0^2 y(t) = \sin(\omega)t. \tag{7.3}$$

In *Mathematica* we have

```
In[6]:= DSolve[y''[t] + w0^2 y[t] == Sin[w t], y[t], t]

                    -I t w0          I t w0        Sin[t w]
Out[6]= {{y[t] -> E        C[1] + E        C[2] + --------- +
                                                     2    2
                                                   -w  + w0


        w Sin[t w0]
        -----------}}
          2      3
         w  w0 - w0
```

Note several things about the form of the solution computed by *Mathematica*. First, *Mathematica* has presented the results in the (inconvenient) form which uses complex exponentials instead of trigonometric functions. This expression can be converted to a more useful form by invoking the `ComplexToTrig[]` function. This must first be loaded from the **Trigonometry** package:

```
In[7]:= <<Algebra'Trigonometry'
```

We apply the `ComplexToTrig[]` function on the result in `Out[6]`:

```
In[8]:= ComplexToTrig[%%]
```

```
                            Sin[t w]
Out[8]= {{y[t] -> ---------  + C[1] (Cos[t w0] - I Sin[t w0]) +
                     2    2
                   -w  + w0

                                                  w Sin[t w0]
        C[2] (Cos[t w0] + I Sin[t w0]) +  ----------- }}
                                                   2        3
                                                  w  w0 - w0
```

Note that complex factors still appear in the coefficients; however, upon application of appropriate initial conditions, this will be converted to real-valued expressions.

Next, *Mathematica* assumed that $\omega \neq \omega_0$. In order to explicitly account for the case in which $\omega = \omega_0$, we must solve the differential equation again, but with the appropriate change made:

```
In[9]:= DSolve[y''[t] + w0^2 y[t] == Sin[w0 t], y[t], t]

                      -I t w0          2 I t w0
Out[9]= {{y[t] -> (E          (I - I E          - t w0 -

          2 I t w0           2            2 I t w0   2
         E          t w0 + 4 w0  C[1] + 4 E          w0  C[2])

               2
        ) / (4 w0 )}}

In[10]:= ComplexToTrig[%]

Out[10]= {{y[t] -> ((Cos[t w0] - I Sin[t w0])

                           2
             (I - t w0 + 4 w0  C[1] -

             I (Cos[2 t w0] + I Sin[2 t w0]) -

             t w0 (Cos[2 t w0] + I Sin[2 t w0]) +

                 2
             4 w0  C[2] (Cos[2 t w0] + I Sin[2 t w0]))) /

                2
        (4 w0 )}}
```

Recall that the general solution to a nonhomogeneous ODE consists of two parts: the complementary solution, which is the solution to the homogeneous problem, and a particular solution, which solves the nonhomogeneous problem. The particular solution represents the principal effect of the nonhomogeneous term of the solution to the differential equation. In order to examine the form of the particular solution we obtained in Out[10], we can set the arbitrary constants to zero and and call the Simplify[] function, which cleans up the result substantially:

```
In[12]:= % /. {C[1] -> 0, C[2] -> 0}

Out[12]= {{y[t] -> ((Cos[t w0] - I Sin[t w0])

                  (I - t w0 - I (Cos[2 t w0] + I Sin[2 t w0]) -

                                                                  2
                  t w0 (Cos[2 t w0] + I Sin[2 t w0]))) / (4 w0 )}}

In[13]:= Simplify[%]

                  -(t w0 Cos[t w0] - Sin[t w0])
Out[13]= {{y[t] -> ---------------------------}}
                                 2
                             2 w0
```

We can now discern more clearly the form of the particular solution. Especially important is the term proportional to $t\cos(\omega t)$. This amplitude of this term grows linearly with time, a characteristic feature of resonance occurring in undamped spring-mass systems.

7.3   USING INITIAL CONDITIONS

Consider now the equation

$$y'' + y = \sin t, \tag{7.4}$$

along with the initial conditions $y(0) = 0$ and $y'(0) = 1$. These conditions are added as components of the list which is the first argument of DSolve[]:

```
In[14]:= DSolve[{y''[t] + y[t] == Sin[t], y[0] == 0,
             y'[0] == 1}, y[t], t]

                  -(t Cos[t] - 3 Sin[t])
Out[14]= {{y[t] -> ----------------------}}
                             2
```

Since there are no arbitrary constants, this solution can be plotted directly with the Plot:

```
In[15]:= Plot[y[t] /. %, {t, 0, 4 Pi}]

Out[15]= -Graphics-
```

The linear growth in amplitude observable in Fig. 7.1 is directly attributable

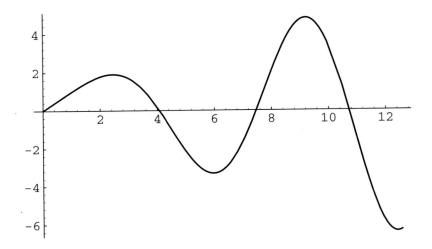

FIGURE 7.1
Solution to Eq. 7.4 over the interval $t \in [0, 4\pi]$. Note the growth in amplitude.

to the term $t \cos t$ which appears in the solution found by *Mathematica*.

7.4   DAMPED MOTION

The dynamical behavior of spring-mass systems in the presence of damping as well as forcing can lead to a variety of interesting results. As shown in Fig. 2.2, we consider a mass suspended from a vertical support to which   a driving force is imparted. The motion of the mass is damped by a device called a dashpot, shown in the figure. When properly constructed, the damping force is proportional to the instantaneous speed of the mass. The most general differential equation that describes such a system is

$$my'' + \gamma y' + ky = F(t), \tag{7.5}$$

which can also be written as

$$y'' + \beta y' + \omega_0^2 y = G(t). \tag{7.6}$$

where $\beta = \gamma/m$ and $\omega_0 = \sqrt{k/m}$.

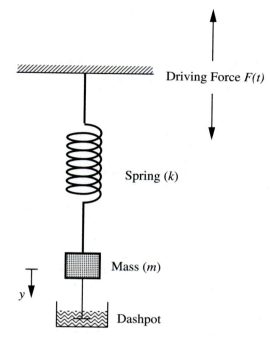

FIGURE 7.2
Spring-mass system with damping and subject to a driving force.

We first examine the behavior of this system in the absence of forcing, i.e. when $F(t) = 0$. We set up the differential equation and then apply initial conditions $y(0) = 1$ and $y'(0) = 0$. This is equivalent to releasing the system from rest:

```
In[16]:= spring1 = y''[t] + b y'[t] + w0^2 y[t] == 0

             2
Out[16]= w0  y[t] + b y'[t] + y''[t] == 0

In[17]:= sys1 = DSolve[{spring1, y[0] == 1, y'[0] == 0}, y[t], t]

                      b Sqrt[b - 2 w0] Sqrt[b + 2 w0]
               1 - -----------------------------------
                                 2      2
                                b  - 4 w0
Out[17]= {{y[t] -> ------------------------------------------------ +
                     (t (b + Sqrt[b - 2 w0] Sqrt[b + 2 w0]))/2
               2 E
```

```
      (t (-b + Sqrt[b - 2 w0] Sqrt[b + 2 w0]))/2
   (E

               b Sqrt[b - 2 w0] Sqrt[b + 2 w0]
      (1 + ---------------------------------)) / 2}}
                         2      2
                       b   - 4 w0
```

Suppose we fix $\omega_0 = 1$ and wish to examine changes in the system response for

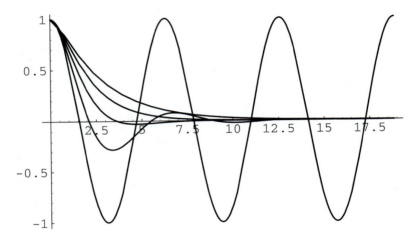

FIGURE 7.3
Solution to Eq. 7.6 for five values of β and $\omega_0 = 1$ over the interval $t \in [0, 6\pi]$.

different values of β. We are especially interested in values slightly above and below $\beta = 2$, the value for which the system is critically damped. To do this in *Mathematica*, we can use the `Table[]` function together with the `Plot[]` function to generate a series of plots with a single command. The `Table[]` function takes as arguments a list of expressions, and a list containing a variable name, start point, end point, and increment.[2] The `Table[]` function is combined with sequential substitutions, in order to generate a set of five expressions to be plotted:

```
In[18]:= Plot[Evaluate[Table[y[t] /. sys1 /. {b -> bb, w0 -> 1},
               {bb, 0, 3, 0.75}]], {t, 0, 6 Pi}]

Out[18]= -Graphics-
```

[2]The `Table[]` function functions something like a `for` loop in programming languages.

In `In[18]` we also called the `Evaluate[]` function. Without this call, `Plot[]` will be unable to properly evaluate the expressions in the list.[3] The result of this command is shown in Fig. 7.3.

7.5 FORCED MOTION

We now consider the motion of a damped spring-mass system subject to a periodic driving force as shown in Fig. 7.2. In this instance, $F(t) = \cos(\omega t)/2$. The system is described by the following initial-value problem:

$$y'' + \beta y' + y = \cos(\omega t)/2, \quad y(0) = 0, \quad y'(0) = 0. \tag{7.7}$$

In Eq. 7.7, we set $\beta = 2$ (the system's critical damping value) and we let the driving force be periodic with circular frequency ω. First, we obtain the solution to the initial value problem:

```
In[19]:= spring2 = y''[t] +  2 y'[t] + y[t]  == Cos[w t]

Out[19]= y[t] + 2 y'[t] + y''[t]  == Cos[t w]

In[20]:= DSolve[{spring2, y[0]  == 0, y'[0]  == 0}, y[t], t]

                              2     2    t
Out[20]= {{y[t] -> (-1 - t + w  - t w  + E  Cos[t w] -

            t  2              t                t      2 2
            E  w  Cos[t w] + 2 E  w Sin[t w]) / (E  (1 + w ) )}}
```

and then we examine the system response for five values of ω, again using the `Table[]`, `Plot[]`, and `Evaluate[]` functions:

```
In[21]:= Plot[Evaluate[Table[y[t] /. % /. w -> ww,
                   {ww, 0, 2, .5}]], {t, 0, 6Pi}]

Out[21]= -Graphics-
```

The result is illustrated in Fig. 7.4.

One interesting question to ask is this: What are the amplitude and phase of the steady-state solution to this problem? The desired information is contained in the solution found for us by *Mathematica*. To extract it, we first make a copy of the solution for further manipulation:

---

[3]Why? That's a good question, but the answer is beyond the scope of this manual. If you really want to know, read the *Mathematica* book.

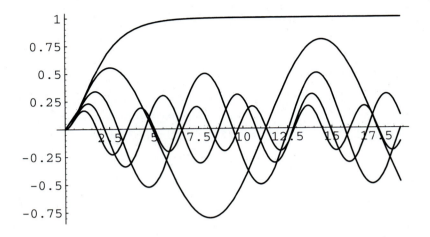

FIGURE 7.4
Solution to Eq. 7.7 for five values of $\omega_0 = 1$ over the interval $t \in [0, 6\pi]$.

```
In[22]:= s2 = %%[[1, 1, 2]]

                 2     2    t            t  2
Out[22]= (-1 - t + w  - t w  + E  Cos[t w] - E   w  Cos[t w] +

               t                t       2 2
           2 E  w Sin[t w]) / (E  (1 + w ) )
```

In order to determine the steady-state portion of the solution, we rearrange terms based on the presence of the factor e^{-t}. The `Apart[]` function will do this for us:

```
In[23]:= Apart[s2, E^t]

                  2     2                  2
         -1 - t + w  - t w    Cos[t w] - w  Cos[t w] + 2 w Sin[t w]
Out[23]= ------------------ + -------------------------------------
               t      2 2                        2 2
             E  (1 + w )                     (1 + w )
```

The steady-state solution is the second term in this result.[4] This can be extracted directly with the `Part[]` function, which grabs the indicated part of the expression given as its first argument:

[4]The transient is the portion that decays exponentially in time..

```
In[24]:= ss = Part[%, 2]

                 2
        Cos[t w] - w  Cos[t w] + 2 w Sin[t w]
Out[24]= -------------------------------------
                          2 2
                      (1 + w )
```

We further rearrange this result by separating the $\cos(\omega t)$ and $\sin(\omega t)$ terms, again using the **Apart[]** function for the necessary algebra:

```
In[25]:= ss = Apart[ss, Cos[t w]]

                 2
        (1 - w ) Cos[t w]    2 w Sin[t w]
Out[25]= -----------------  +  ------------
               2 2                 2 2
           (1 + w )             (1 + w )
```

If the steady-state solution to a spring-mass problem is given by

$$y = a_1 \cos(\omega t) + a_2 \sin(\omega t), \tag{7.8}$$

then this can be re-written as

$$y = A \cos(\omega t + \phi), \tag{7.9}$$

where $A = \sqrt{a_1^2 + a_2^2}$ and $\phi = \tan^{-1}(a_2/a_1)$. A is called the amplitude and ϕ is called the phase.

In order to compute the amplitude, we use the **Coefficient[]** function to extract the appropriate coefficients:

```
In[26]:= Coefficient[ss, Cos[t w]]

                 2
           1 - w
Out[26]= ---------
             2 2
         (1 + w )

In[27]:= Amp = Sqrt[%^2 + Coefficient[ss, Sin[w t]]]

                    2 2
             (1 - w )      2 w
Out[27]= Sqrt[--------- + ---------]
                 2 4         2 2
             (1 + w )    (1 + w )
```

We can plot A this call to `Plot[]`:

```
In[28]:= Plot[Amp, {w, 0, 3}]

Out[28]= -Graphics-
```

To determine where the maximum amplitude occurs, we can use the `NSolve[]`

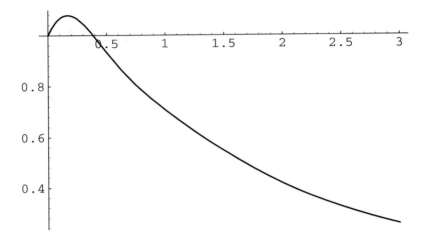

FIGURE 7.5
Amplitude of the steady-state solution to Eq. 7.7.

function:[5]

```
In[29]:= NSolve[D[Amp, w] == 0, w]

Out[29]= {{w -> -0.792258 - 1.63571 I},

          {w -> -0.792258 + 1.63571 I}, {w -> -0.745706},

          {w -> 0.167547}, {w -> 0.748004 - 0.498161 I},

          {w -> 0.748004 + 0.498161 I}}
```

---

[5]The `NSolve[]` function behaves just like `Solve[]`, except it returns numerical solutions to the passed list of equations. It is similar, though by no means equivalent to the expression `N[Solve[]]`. Since we are looking for the roots of what amounts to a fifth-degree polynomial, is is most unlikely that `Solve[]` will find symbolic roots.

When `Amp` is set to zero, the result is a sixth-degree polynomial in ω. Note that `NSolve[]` returns all six roots of this polynomial. We know from Fig. 7.5 that the value of ω we seek is real and positive. By examining the list of roots, we see that there is only one real, positive root, and so the value of ω which maximizes the amplitude of the steady-state solution is $\omega = 0.167547$.

The phase ϕ can be just as simply computed:

```
In[30]:= phi = ArcTan[Coefficient[ss, Cos[t w]] /
              Coefficient[ss, Sin[t w]]]

                   2
              1 - w
Out[30]= ArcTan[------]
               2 w
```

We can plot the phase in degrees with the following command:

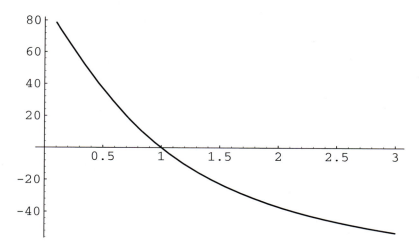

FIGURE 7.6
Phase of the steady-state solution to Eq. 7.7.

```
In[31]:= Plot[(180 / Pi) phi, {w, 0.1, 3}]

Out[31]= -Graphics-
```

From Fig. 7.6 it can be seen that the solution is in phase with the driving force only when $\omega = 1$, i.e. when the driving force is tuned to the natural frequency of the system.

EXERCISES

7.1. Find the general solution to $y'' - y = 0$.

7.2. Find the particular solution to $y'' + \omega^2 y = e^{-t}$ with $y(0) = 1$ and $y'(0) = 0$.

7.3. Consider the damped spring-mass system modeled by $y'' + \beta y + y = \sin(2t)$, $y(0) = 0$ and $y'(0) = 0$. What value of β maximizes the amplitude of the steady-state response?

7.4. Consider the damped spring-mass system of the previous problem, but with a forcing function of $\sin(2t) + \sin(4t)$. Discuss the behavior of the steady-state phase as a function of β.

7.5. Consider the RLC circuit shown in Fig. 7.7.

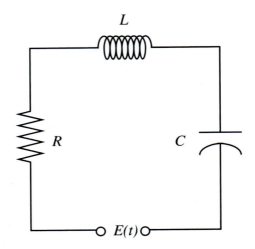

FIGURE 7.7
RLC circuit.

(a) Determine the current in this circuit assuming that the initial current and capacitor charge are both zero, and $R = 100$ ohms, $L = 1$ henry, $C = 0.005$, and $E(t) = 12\sin(20t)$ volts.

(b) Suppose instead that the applied voltage is $E(t) = 12\sin(\omega t)$ volts, and that the values of R, L, and C, as well as the initial conditions are as above. What value of ω will produce the largest current amplitude?

CHAPTER
8

LAPLACE TRANSFORMS

8.1 LABORATORY GOALS

  a. To determine the Laplace and inverse Laplace transforms of given functions.
  b. To solve linear ODEs with Laplace transforms.

8.2 SIMPLE TRANSFORMS

Before *Mathematica* can perform Laplace transforms and inverse Laplace transforms, we require the `LaplaceTransform` package, loaded with the following command:

```
In[1]:= <<Calculus'LaplaceTransform'
```

Mathematica can now determine a large variety of transforms. Direct transforms are calculated with the `LaplaceTransform[]` function. For example, let $f(t) = e^{-2t} \sin 3t$. Then the Laplace transform $\mathcal{L}\{f(t)\}$ is found with the following call:

```
In[2]:= LaplaceTransform[Exp[-2 t] Sin[3 t], t, s]

                3
Out[2]= ------------
                    2
          9 + (2 + s)
```

The `LaplaceTransform[]` takes three arguments. The first is the function to be transformed, the second is the name of the independent variable, and the third is the name of the transform variable.

Mathematica can also determine the transforms of a variety of exotic functions. For example, suppose $f(t) = J_0(t)$ where J_0 is the Bessel function of the first kind of order zero. The calculation is set up in the following way:

```
In[3]:= LaplaceTransform[BesselJ[0, t], t, s]

                1
Out[3]= ------------
                    2
          Sqrt[1 + s ]
```

In this example, `BesselJ[]` takes two arguments. The first is the order of the Bessel function, and the second is the independent variable.

Inverse Laplace transforms are found with the `InverseLaplaceTransform[]` function. For example, suppose $F(s) = s/(s^2 + 25)$.[1] Then $\mathcal{L}^{-1}\{F(s)\}$ is found by:

```
In[4]:= InverseLaplaceTransform[s/(s^2 + 25), s, t]

Out[4]= Cos[5 t]
```

The syntax for the `InverseLaplaceTransform[]` function is identical to that of the `LaplaceTransform[]` function. A wide variety of inverse transforms can be handled as well. Let $F(s) = tan^{-1}(1/s)/s$. Then the inverse transform is found with the following command:

```
In[5]:= InverseLaplaceTransform[ArcTan[1/s] / s, s, t]

Out[5]= SinIntegral[t]
```

---

[1]If $f(t)$ is the function in the time domain, then $F(s)$ is a typical representation of the transformed function.

This result is the integral $\int_0^t (\sin t)/t \, dt$, a special function built into *Mathematica*.

The `LaplaceTransform` package also contains the definition for the Dirac delta function. Thus

```
In[6]:= LaplaceTransform[Delta[t - 3], t, s]

           -3 s
Out[6]= E
```

and the `Delta[]` function will often appear in inverse transforms.[2] Unfortunately, this package does not contain full support for the Heaviside step function, a function often used in problems requiring Laplace transforms. However, the inverse transform routines can produce something that behaves like the Heaviside function. For example:

```
In[7]:= InverseLaplaceTransform[Exp[-s] / s, s, t]

Out[7]= If[1 <= t, 1, 0]
```

which is commonly written as $\mathcal{U}(t-1)$. The `If[]` takes three arguments. If the first argument is true, the function evaluates to the second argument. Otherwise, it returns the third argument.

This limitation means that some Laplace transforms, if they involve Heaviside functions, may need to be done by hand, although the inverse Transforms can be found with *Mathematica*.[3] As another example, consider the inverse transform of $F(s) = e^{-2s}/(s+1)$.:

```
In[8]:= InverseLaplaceTransform[Exp[-2 s] / (s + 1), s, t]

                    2 - t
Out[8]= If[2 <= t, E     , 0]
```

This kind of result can be plotted in a straightforward way with the `Plot[]` function:

[2]With the release of version 2.2 of *Mathematica*, the name of this function has changed to `DiracDelta[]`.

[3]A comment embedded in the `LaplaceTransform` package has this to say: "One larger (and potentially needed) area not covered is the treatment of functions that are defined differently on different regions. Implementing those in *Mathematica* (e.g., using `If[]`) is possible, but would require a wide support (e.g., `If[x<0, f1, 0] + If[x<0, 0, f2] -> If[x<0, f1, f2]`, etc.) not available now."

```
In[9]:= Plot[%, {t, 0, 3}]

Out[9]= -Graphics-
```

The result is shown in Fig. 8.1.

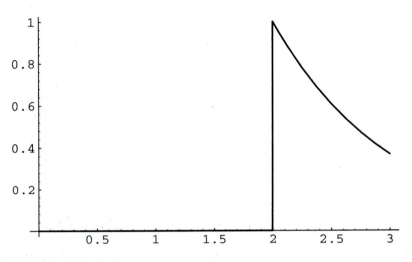

FIGURE 8.1
Plot of the function $f(t) = \mathcal{U}(t-2)\exp[-(t-2)]$ for $0 \le t \le 3$.

8.3 APPLICATION TO DIFFERENTIAL EQUATIONS

Consider the second-order differential equation

$$y'' + y = 0, \qquad (8.1)$$

with $y(0) = 1$ and $y'(0) = -1$. To solve this problem with Laplace transforms, we first enter the differential equation and then apply the **LaplaceTransform[]** function:

```
In[10]:= y''[t] + y[t] == 0

Out[10]= y[t] + y''[t] == 0

In[11]:= LaplaceTransform[%, t, s]

Out[11]= LaplaceTransform[y[t], t, s] +
```

```
       2
      s  LaplaceTransform[y[t], t, s] - s y[0] - y'[0] == 0
```

Note that *Mathematica* correctly applies the rules for taking the Laplace transform of ordinary derivatives.[4] Now, we solve this equation with the `Solve[]` function for $Y(s)$, the transform of $y(t)$ which *Mathematica* calls `LaplaceTransform[y[t], t, s]`:

```
In[12]:= Solve[%, LaplaceTransform[y[t], t, s]]

                                      -(s y[0]) - y'[0]
Out[12]= {{LaplaceTransform[y[t], t, s] -> -(-----------------)}}
                                                    2
                                               1 + s
```

We apply the initial conditions with the substitution operator `/.`:

```
In[13]:= %[[1]] /. {y[0] -> 1, y'[0] -> -1}

                                         1 - s
Out[13]= {LaplaceTransform[y[t], t, s] -> -(------)}
                                            2
                                         1 + s
```

Finally we take the inverse transform of this result:

```
In[14]:= InverseLaplaceTransform[LaplaceTransform[y[t], t, s]
         /. %, s, t]

Out[14]= Cos[t] - Sin[t]
```

Thus the solution to Eq. (8.1) satisfying the initial conditions is $y = \cos t - \sin t$.

8.4   A CIRCUIT ANALYSIS PROBLEM

Consider the electrical circuit shown in Fig. 8.2 The input voltage is a transient of unit magnitude, and this is modeled by $f(t) = \delta(t)$. The inductance is 1 henry,

---

[4]*Mathematica* can handle the usual *operational* properties of the Laplace and inverse Laplace transform.

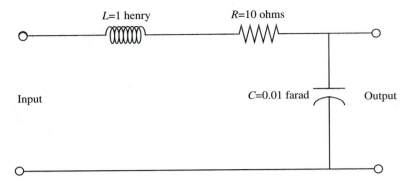

FIGURE 8.2
Sample electric circuit. The input voltage is $f(t) = \delta(t)$.

the resistance is 10 ohms, and the capacitance is 0.01 farads. We assume that at $t = 0$, there is no voltage or current present in the circuit. The differential equation which models this problem is

$$q'' + 10q' + 100q = \delta(t), \quad q(0) = q'(0) = 0, \tag{8.2}$$

where the output voltage is q/C and C is the capacitance in farads. First, we set up the differential equation in *Mathematica*:

```
In[15]:= circuit = q''[t] + 10 q'[t] + 100 q[t] == Delta[t]

Out[15]= 100 q[t] + 10 q'[t] + q''[t] == Delta[t]
```

Now we take the Laplace transform of this equation:

```
In[16]:= LaplaceTransform[circuit, t, s]

Out[16]= 100 LaplaceTransform[q[t], t, s] +

         2
        s  LaplaceTransform[q[t], t, s] +

        10 (s LaplaceTransform[q[t], t, s] - q[0]) - s q[0] -

        q'[0] == 1
```

Next, we solve for the Laplace transform itself:

```
In[17]:= Solve[%, LaplaceTransform[q[t], t, s]]

Out[17]= {{LaplaceTransform[q[t], t, s] ->

             -1 - 10 q[0] - s q[0] - q'[0]
          -(-----------------------------)}}
                                   2
               100 + 10 s + s
```

Then, apply the initial conditions and take the inverse Laplace transform:

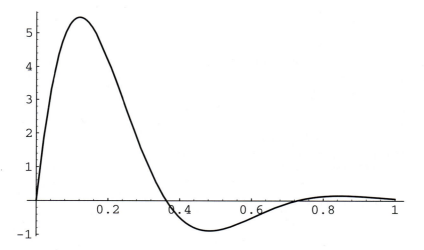

FIGURE 8.3
Output voltage of sample electric circuit.

```
In[18]:= %[[1]] /. {q[0] -> 0, q'[0] -> 0}

                                             1
Out[18]= {LaplaceTransform[q[t], t, s] -> ---------------}
                                                     2
                                          100 + 10 s + s

In[19]:= InverseLaplaceTransform[LaplaceTransform[q[t], t, s]
         /. %, s, t]

           Sin[5 Sqrt[3] t]
Out[19]= ------------------
                     5 t
          5 Sqrt[3] E
```

The output voltage can then be plotted with the `Plot[]` function. Recalling that $V = q/C$, we have:

```
In[20]:= Plot[% / 0.01, {t, 0, 1}]

Out[20]= -Graphics-
```

The result is shown in Fig. 8.3.

EXERCISES

8.1. Derive Eq. (8.2).

8.2. Find the Laplace transform of $f(t) = e^{-t}(1 - \cos t)/t$.

8.3. Find the inverse Laplace transform of $F(s) = 2e^{-3s}/[s^3(s^2 + 5)]$. Plot the result.

8.4. Determine the solution to the initial value problem $y'' + 5y' + 5y = \delta(t - 2) - 3\delta(t - 5)$ with $y(0) = y'(0) = 0$.

8.5. Determine the solution to the initial value problem $y'' + y' + 15y = 1 - \mathcal{U}(t - 2)$ with $y(0) = y'(0) = 0$. [Hint: Take the transform of the right-hand side by hand.]

8.6. Suppose a 1 kg mass stretches a spring 0.25 m. If the spring-mass system is at it's equilibrium position, determine the motion of the mass if a sinusoidal driving force of $F(t) = 0.5\sin(6\pi t)$ newtons is applied for $0 \leq t \leq \pi$ seconds.

CHAPTER
9

THE SIMPLE
PENDULUM

9.1 LABORATORY GOALS

a. To determine two analytical solutions to the simple pendulum model.

b. To become familiar with Jacobi elliptic functions.

9.2 MODEL FORMULATION

Consider the motion of a frictionless simple pendulum, as shown in Fig. 9.1. A bob of mass m hangs from a rigid, massless support of length L. We seek an expression for the angular displacement y, which measures how much the pendulum deviates from its rest position.

By applying a force balance law on the pendulum, and invoking Newton's Second law, we obtain the following equation of motion for the pendulum:

$$y'' + \omega_n^2 \sin y = 0, \qquad (9.1)$$

where $\omega_n = \sqrt{g/L}$ is called the natural frequency of the pendulum. Here, g represents the gravitational acceleration. If the angular displacements are sufficiently small, Eq. (9.1) can be simplified by using the approximation $\sin y \approx y$, and it then becomes a simple, linear equation with constant coefficients. In this instance, the frequency of oscillation corresponds to the natural frequency. In this laboratory, we are interested in considering oscillations of the simple pendulum that may not be small.[1]

---

[1]Large amplitude oscillations of the simple pendulum are either ignored or given only

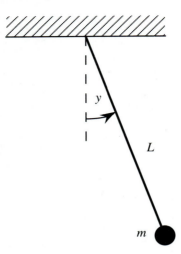

FIGURE 9.1
Simple pendulum suspended from a fixed support. The support, which has length L is assumed to be massless. y denotes the angular displacement from the vertical (equilibrium) position.

9.3   A SPECIAL CASE—THE INVERTED PENDULUM

We consider the initial conditions with $y(0) = 0$ and $y'(0) = \omega_0$. First, multiply both sides of Eq. 9.1 by y' and then integrate by hand (*Mathematica* will not do this integration in the form we need) from 0 to t, obtaining

$$y'^2/2 - \omega_0^2 - 2\omega_n^2 \cos y + 2\omega_n^2 = 0. \tag{9.2}$$

Making the substitution $\cos y = 1 - \sin^2 y/2$, we then rearrange this result into the following form:

$$\frac{y'}{\sqrt{1 - 4(\omega_n^2/\omega_0^2)\sin^2 y/2}} = \omega_0. \tag{9.3}$$

Suppose now that the initial velocity $\omega_0 = 2\omega_n$. In this case, Eq. (9.3) reduces to:

$$\frac{y'}{\sec y/2} = \omega_0. \tag{9.4}$$

First, we integrate the left hand side of this equation using *Mathematica*:

```
In[1]:= Integrate[Sec[y/2], {y, 0, y}]
```

the briefest of treatments in engineering mathematics books. Since the simple pendulum is arguably the most commonly encountered nonlinear oscillator, a tool like *Mathematica*, which makes working with the underlying special functions relatively easy, is wonderfully appropriate for the job at hand.

```
                  y          y              y          y
Out[1]= 2 (-Log[Cos[-]  -  Sin[-]] + Log[Cos[-]  +  Sin[-]])
                  4          4              4          4
```

The right hand side can be integrated by inspection and with these two results, we ask *Mathematica* to solve for y:

```
In[2]:= Solve[% == w0 t, y]

          Solve::ifun:
              Warning: Inverse functions are being used by Solve, so
                 some solutions may not be found.

Out[2]= {}
```

Unfortunately *Mathematica* was unable to do anything with the solution in this form. However, we can use the trigonometric identity $\tan(\alpha + \pi/4) = (\cos\alpha + \sin\alpha)/(\cos\alpha - \sin\alpha)$ and the equation to be solved is cast into the following form and solved with `Solve[]`:

```
In[3]:= 2 Log[Tan[Pi/4 + y/4]]  == w0 t

                   Pi   y
Out[3]= 2 Log[Tan[-- + -]]  == t w0
                   4    4

In[4]:= Solve[%,y]

          Solve::ifun:
              Warning: Inverse functions are being used by Solve, so
                 some solutions may not be found.

                                      t w0
Out[4]= {{y -> -Pi + 4 ArcTan[Sqrt[E    ]]}}
```

Thus when $\omega_0 = 2\omega_n$, the simple pendulum possesses a nonperiodic solution which can be expressed in terms of elementary functions:[2]

$$y = 4\tan^{-1}[\sqrt{\exp(\omega_0 t)}]. \tag{9.5}$$

In this case, $y \to \pi$ as $t \to \infty$, so that the pendulum asymptotically approaches (but never reaches) the unstable equilibrium position $y = \pi$. Note that this special value of ω_0 will give the pendulum exactly the kinetic energy required to invert the bob. (See Exercise 2.)

---

[2]This is not a well-known result!

9.4   PERIODIC OSCILLATIONS OF THE PENDULUM

We now suppose that $\omega_0 < 2\omega_n$. This initial velocity range guarantees that the pendulum will not flip over. Let $k = \omega_0/2\omega_n$. We make the change of dependent variable $\cos y/2 = \sqrt{1 - k^2 \sin^2 \phi}$ and substitute this into Eq. (9.3) to obtain

$$\int_0^\phi \frac{d\phi}{\sqrt{1 - k^2 \sin^2 \phi}} = \frac{\omega_0 t}{2k} \tag{9.6}$$

The left-hand side of this equation is an elliptic integral of the first kind. It can be inverted with the *amplitude* function,[3] so that

$$\phi = \text{am}\,(\omega_0 t/2k | k^2). \tag{9.7}$$

We now solve for y:

$$y = 2\sin^{-1}[k\,\text{sn}\,(\omega_0 t/2k | k^2)], \tag{9.8}$$

where $\text{sn}\,(t|k^2) = \sin[\text{am}\,(t|k^2)]$ represents the *Jacobian Sine* function.

This result is straightforward to implement in *Mathematica* by invoking the `JacobiSN[]` function:

```
In[5]:= y = 2 ArcSin[k JacobiSN[w0 t / (2 k), k^2]]

                     t w0    2
Out[5]= 2 ArcSin[k JacobiSN[----, k ]]
                     2 k
```

For example, to plot the solution to the simple pendulum when $\omega_0 = 1$ and $k = 1/2$, we use the `Plot[]` function:

```
In[6]:= Plot[y /. {k -> 1/2, w0 -> 1} , {t, 0, 4 Pi}]

Out[6]= -Graphics-
```

Jacobian elliptic functions are periodic with period $4K$ where $K(k^2)$ is the complete elliptic integral of the first kind. This function is available in *Mathematica* as the `EllipticK[]` function. From Eq. (9.8), we find that the pendulum period is $T_0 = 8kK/\omega_0$. In our example, we find that the numerical value of the period is

---

[3]The customary form for this function is $\text{am}\,(t|k^2)$ and the parameter k is called the *modulus* of the elliptic function.

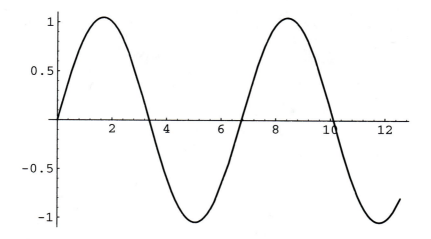

FIGURE 9.2
Exact solution to the simple pendulum equation for $\omega_0 = 1$ and $k = 1/2$.

```
In[7]:= 4  N[EllipticK[1/4]]

Out[7]= 6.743
```

which agrees with the result in Fig. 9.2.

EXERCISES

9.1. Use *Mathematica* and verify that the expression Out[5] satisfies Eq. (9.1).

9.2. Show that $\omega_0 = 2\omega_n$ corresponds exactly to the kinetic energy need to invert the bob from its resting equilibrium position.

9.3. Suppose the initial angular velocity is $\omega_0 > 2\omega_n$. Is it still possible to describe the motion of the pendulum (which cannot be periodic!) in terms of elliptic functions?

9.4. Determine an expression that describes the projected motion of the pendulum bob onto a plane perpendicular to the gravitational field.

9.5. Determine an expression that describes the projected motion of the pendulum bob onto a plane parallel to the gravitational field and perpendicular to the plane of the bob.

9.6. Solve the pendulum equation numerically and compare your result to that shown in Fig. 9.2.[4]

9.7. If Eq. 9.1 is modified to add a linear friction term, conjecture a form that the solution might take. Use *Mathematica* to substitute this guess back into the

[4]You may peek ahead to Chapter 11.

differential equation. Does it work? Compare it to a numerical solution.[5] How good was the guess?

[5]Ditto.

10.1 LABORATORY GOALS

a. To use the `DSolve[]` function to determine solutions to systems of ordinary differential equations.

b. To use matrix methods to determine the solutions to homogeneous and non-homogeneous systems.

10.2 HOMOGENEOUS LINEAR SYSTEMS

We treat here systems of first-order linear ordinary differential equations with constant coefficients. For example, consider the system:

$$x_1' = 4x_1 + 2x_2, \tag{10.1}$$

$$x_2' = 3x_1 + 3x_2. \tag{10.2}$$

There are several ways to attack this system in *Mathematica*. First, we write this system as a list containing two symbolic equations, to which we give the name `example`:

```
In[1]:= example = {x1'[t] == 4 x1[t] + 2 x2[t],
                   x2'[t] == 3 x1[t] + 3 x2[t]}

Out[1]= {x1'[t] == 4 x1[t] + 2 x2[t], x2'[t] == 3 x1[t] + 3 x2[t]}
```

Now we call `DSolve[]` to generate the general solution:

```
In[2]:= DSolve[example, {x1[t], x2[t]}, t]

                  t              5 t                  5 t
                 E  (2 C[1] + 3 E    C[1] - 2 C[2] + 2 E    C[2])
Out[2]= {{x1[t] -> ----------------------------------------------------,
                                         5


        x2[t] ->

                  t            5 t                5 t
                 E  (-3 C[1] + 3 E    C[1] + 3 C[2] + 2 E    C[2])
                 ------------------------------------------------------}}
                                         5
```

Initial conditions can also be prescribed. Suppose that $x_1(0) = 1$ and $x_2(0) = -1$. We modify the *Mathematica* list `example` by appending the initial conditions to it. We do this by calling the `Append[]` function, which appends the second argument to the list passed as the first argument, and then the `Flatten[]` function to remove the extra curly braces:[1]

```
In[3]:= example = Flatten[Append[example,
                            {x1[0] == 1, x2[0] == -1}]]

Out[3]= {x1'[t] == 4 x1[t] + 2 x2[t], x2'[t] == 3 x1[t] + 3 x2[t],

         x1[0] == 1, x2[0] == -1}
```

We again use `DSolve[]`, but this time the call will produce the particular solution:

```
In[4]:= DSolve[example, {x1[t], x2[t]}, t]

                  t       5 t             t       5 t
                 E  (4 + E   )           E  (-6 + E   )
Out[4]= {{x1[t] -> -------------, x2[t] -> --------------}}
                        5                       5
```

---

[1] Try the `Append[]` call without `Flatten[]`. Not only are there too many curly braces, they wind up in the wrong place. The `Flatten[]` function is a handy tool for doing list housekeeping.

An alternate solution method involves the matrix exponential form of the solution. For constant coefficient homogeneous systems of the form $X' = AX$, the solution can be written as $X = \exp(At)C$ where A is the coefficient matrix and C is a vector containing the initial conditions. In the example given in Eqs. (10.2) and (10.2), the coefficient matrix A is represented as:

```
In[5]:= A = {{4, 2}, {3, 3}}

Out[5]= {{4, 2}, {3, 3}}
```

The matrix exponential is determined with the `MatrixExp[]` function:

```
In[6]:= MatrixExp[A t]

                t             5 t         t            5 t
              E  (2 + 3 E    )     2 E  (-1 + E   )
Out[6]= {{---------------, ----------------},
                5                    5

                t            5 t        t            5 t
            3 E  (-1 + E   )     E  (3 + 2 E   )
         {----------------, ---------------}}
                5                    5
```

Now we multiply this by a vector composed of the two initial conditions:

```
In[7]:= % . {1, -1}

                t            5 t       t             5 t
            -2 E  (-1 + E   )     E  (2 + 3 E   )
Out[7]= {------------------ + ----------------,
                5                    5

               t            5 t       t            5 t
           3 E  (-1 + E   )     E  (3 + 2 E   )
         ---------------- - ----------------}
                5                    5

In[8]:= Simplify[%]

              t        5 t       t            5 t
            E  (4 + E   )     E  (-6 + E   )
Out[8]= {--------------, ---------------}
                5                    5
```

This result (except for the form of the list) is identical to that obtained using the `DSolve[]` function. Note that use of the `MatrixExp[]` does not involve the vexing problem of determining the canonical form of the matrix. The underlying linear algebraic manipulations of eigenvalues and eigenvectors is performed automatically by *Mathematica*. Either method is straightforward to apply. The matrix approach does permit easy evaluation of the eigenvalues in the event that stability questions arise. The `DSolve[]` approach makes it easier to go back and compute numerical solutions by modifying the argument list and calling `NDSolve[]` instead (see Chapter 11).

10.3   NONHOMOGENEOUS LINEAR SYSTEMS

To illustrate the solution of nonhomogeneous systems, we modify the system used in the previous section by adding a nonhomogeneous term to each equations:

$$x_1' = 4x_1 + 2x_2 + \sin t, \tag{10.3}$$

$$x_2' = 3x_1 + 3x_2 - \cos t. \tag{10.4}$$

and utilize the same initial conditions, viz. $x_1(0) = 1$ and $x_2(0) = -1$. We reuse the symbol `example` and specifically add to it the two initial conditions as symbolic equations:

```
In[9]:= example = {x1'[t] == 4 x1[t] + 2 x2[t] + Sin[t],
           x2'[t] == 3 x1[t] + 3 x2[t] - Cos[t],
           x1[0] == 1, x2[0] == -1}

Out[9]= {x1'[t] == Sin[t] + 4 x1[t] + 2 x2[t],

         x2'[t] == -Cos[t] + 3 x1[t] + 3 x2[t], x1[0] == 1,

         x2[0] == -1}
```

As before, `DSolve[]` generates the particular solution:

```
In[10]:= DSolve[example, {x1[t], x2[t]}, t]

                       t        6 t
                 222 E    + 28 E      - 65 Cos[t] - 20 Sin[t]
Out[10]= {{x1[t] -> -------------------------------------------,
                                       185

                     t        6 t
               -333 E    + 28 E      + 120 Cos[t] - 20 Sin[t]
         x2[t] -> -------------------------------------------}}
                                   185
```

The method of variation of parameters can also be used to determine the solution in this case. If a nonhomogeneous system is written as $X' = AX + G$, then the general solution is given by $X = \Phi C + \Phi \int \Phi^{-1} G \, dt$ where Φ is a fundamental matrix of the system. Since $\exp(At)$ is a fundamental matrix, we see the way clear for applying this formula to obtain the general solution to our nonhomogeneous problem. First we compute the fundamental matrix with the `MatrixExp[]` function:

```
In[11]:= Phi = MatrixExp[A t]

                t          5 t         t          5 t
               E  (2 + 3 E   )    2 E   (-1 + E   )
Out[11]= {{---------------, ----------------},
                  5                 5


               t          5 t         t          5 t
             3 E  (-1 + E   )    E  (3 + 2 E   )
             {---------------, ---------------}}
                    5                 5
```

Now we can apply the variation of parameters formula using the functions `Inverse[]` and `Integrate[]`.[2]

```
In[12]:= gsol = Phi . {C[1], C[2]} + Phi .
                Integrate[Inverse[Phi] . {Sin[t], -Cos[t]}, t]

              t          5 t             t          5 t
             E  (2 + 3 E   ) C[1]    2 E   (-1 + E   ) C[2]
Out[12]= {------------------- + ---------------------- +
                  5                      5


                                              3
                                  3 (37 + ----) Cos[t]
                                          5 t
              t          5 t             E                4 Sin[t]
           2 E   (-1 + E   ) (--------------------- - --------)
                                        t                6 t
                                   185 E             37 E
          ------------------------------------------------------- +
                                 5
```

---

[2]Note that `Integrate[]` performs the appropriate integration on each component of the list passed to it as the first argument.

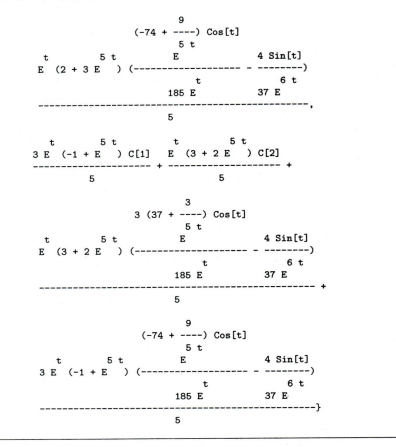

In building this expression, we utilized a list to represent the nonhomogeneous term and we also used the . operator to perform the matrix–vector multiplications.

We now apply the initial conditions, using the substitution operator /. to set t to zero:

```
In[13]:= {(gsol[[1]] /. t -> 0) == 1,
          (gsol[[2]] /. t -> 0) == -1}

              13                 24
Out[13]= {-(--) + C[1] == 1, -- + C[2] == -1}
              37                 37
```

Now we solve this set of equations for the constants with a call to **Solve[]**:

```
In[14]:= Solve[%, {C[1], C[2]}]

                  50              61
Out[14]= {{C[1] -> --, C[2] -> -(--)}}
                  37              37
```

Finally, we substitute this back into the solution, with calls to `Flatten[]` and `Simplify[]` to clean up the result:

```
In[15]:= Simplify[Flatten[gsol /. %]]

               t       6 t
          222 E  + 28 E    - 65 Cos[t] - 20 Sin[t]
Out[15]= {---------------------------------------,
                            185

                 t       6 t
           -333 E  + 28 E    + 120 Cos[t] - 20 Sin[t]
          ----------------------------------------}
                            185
```

This, apart from the form of the list, is the same as that obtained with `DSolve[]`. In the nonhomogeneous case, using `DSolve[]` involves decidedly less manipulation of intermediate results. On the other hand, `DSolve[]` can be painfully slow, especially if there are unassigned constants in the problem. Both approaches have their place.

10.4 CHEMICAL MIXING

Consider the chemical mixing problem depicted in Fig. 10.1. Tank A and Tank B are connected by a series of pipes. Initially, Tank A contains 20 liters of water and 1000 grams of salt, while Tank B contains 40 liters of water and no salt. At the start of the mixing operation ($t = 0$), fresh water is pumped into Tank A at the rate of 3 liters per minute. Salt water is exchanged between the tanks at the indicated rates. We wish to determine the amount of salt in both tanks for $t > 0$.

Note from Fig. 10.1 that amount of solution flowing into and out of each tank is the same. Therefore, the quantity of salt solution in each tank never changes (although the concentration does). Let x_1 represent the mass of salt in Tank A and x_2 represent the mass in Tank B. The pure water inlet adds no salt to Tank A. Since 6 l/min of solution are leaving Tank A and Tank A has a volume of 20 l, the salt mass in Tank A is being decreased by 6/20 times the instantaneous amount of salt in Tank A, namely x_1. Tank A is also gaining

Pure Water:
3 l/min

Mix: 3 l/min

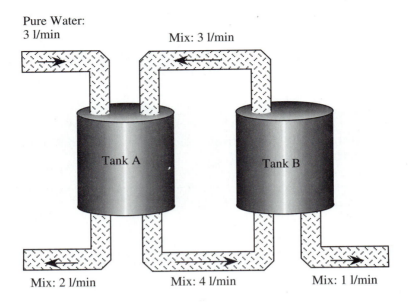

Mix: 2 l/min   Mix: 4 l/min   Mix: 1 l/min

FIGURE 10.1
Each tank starts with a different concentration and amount of salt water.

salt from Tank B and the rate of $3/40$ times the instantaneous amount of salt in Tank B, namely x_2. The total rate of change of salt in Tank A is therefore $x_1' = -(6/20)x_1 + (3/40)x_2$. A similar argument can be used to establish the rate of change of salt in Tank B (see Exercise 2). The system of differential equations which governs this problem is :

$$x_1' = -\frac{6}{20}x_1 + \frac{3}{40}x_2, \qquad (10.5)$$

$$x_2' = \frac{4}{20}x_1 - \frac{4}{40}x_2. \qquad (10.6)$$

along with the initial conditions $x_1(0) = 1000$ and $x_2(0) = 0$. This system is entered into *Mathematica* as follows:

```
In[16]:= tanks = {x1'[t] == (-6/20) x1[t] + (3/40) x2[t],
               x2'[t] == (4/20) x1[t] + (-4/40) x2[t],
               x1[0] == 20, x2[0] == 0}

                   -3 x1[t]   3 x2[t]            x1[t]   x2[t]
Out[16]= {x1'[t] == -------- + -------, x2'[t] == ----- - -----,
                      10        40                  5      10

         x1[0] == 1000, x2[0] == 0}
```

As before, `DSolve[]` generates the particular solution:

```
In[17]:= sol = DSolve[tanks, {x1[t], x2[t]}, t]

Out[17]=
                          ((-4 - Sqrt[10]) t)/20
                        E
Out[17]= {{x1[t] -> 1000 (---------------------- +
                                    2

         ((-4 - Sqrt[10]) t)/20    ((-4 + Sqrt[10]) t)/20
        E                         E
        ---------------------- + ---------------------- -
              Sqrt[10]                    2

         ((-4 + Sqrt[10]) t)/20
        E
        ----------------------),
              Sqrt[10]

                      2    ((-4 - Sqrt[10]) t)/20
        x2[t] -> 1000 (-(Sqrt[-] E                      ) +
                      5

            2    ((-4 + Sqrt[10]) t)/20
        Sqrt[-] E                      )}}
            5
```

We plot the two solutions together with the following call to `Plot[]`:

```
In[18]:= Plot[{x1[t] /. sol, x2[t] /. sol}, {t, 0, 40}]

Out[18]= -Graphics-
```

Intuititon tells us that the salt in Tank B ought to rise as the solution in Tank A is mixed with that in Tank B. We would also expect to see both salt amounts eventually go to zero, owing to the influx of fresh water into the system. The resulting illustration of both solutions is shown in Fig. 10.2, and our conjectures are confirmed. The amount of salt in Tank A continuously decreases, but the salt in Tank B rises rapidly at first, achieving a maximum value of about 400 grams at about 7 seconds after mixing begins. After that the amount of salt in Tank B also decreases continuously. To confirm our suspicion we evaluate both solutions in the limit as $t \to \infty$ with calls to the `Limit[]` function and `N[]`:[3]

---

[3]The `N[]` function is really needed here. Without it, *Mathematica* returns the limit un-

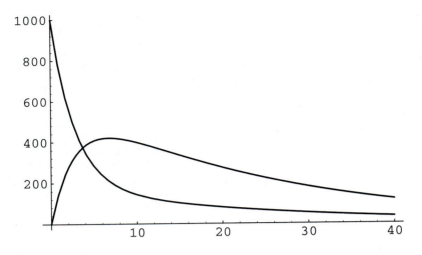

FIGURE 10.2
Solutions to the tank mixing problem. Both solutions approach 0 as $t \to \infty$.

```
In[19]:= Limit[N[{x1[t], x2[t]} /. sol], t -> Infinity]

Out[19]= {{0, 0}}
```

The steady state masses in both tanks is zero.

We note here that although there are some special systems with non-constant coefficients which can be solved symbolically, it is usually easier to proceed immediately to a numerical solution method. This is discussed in Chapter 11.

EXERCISES

10.1. Determine the general solution to the following system:

$$x_1'' + x_2' + 3x_1 = \sin t, \tag{10.7}$$

$$x_1' + x_2' - x_2 = t. \tag{10.8}$$

10.2. Complete the derivation of the differential system [Eq. (10.6)] that governs the mixing tank problem.

10.3. Determine the precise time at which both salt masses are equal in the mixing problem. What is the mass in each tank at this time?

evaluated. Try it for yourself. The problem occurs because of the complexity of the expression. The call to N[] simplifies the expression in a nice way. Note that *Mathematica* will evaluate this simpler expression correctly without using N[]: Limit[Exp[-t], t -> Infinity].

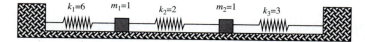

FIGURE 10.3
System of springs and masses used in Exercise 4.

10.4. Consider the system of springs and masses shown in Fig. 10.3. Assume that both masses start from their equilibrium positions. The first mass (m_1) has an initial speed of $1/2$ while the second mass (m_2) is motionless. Derive a system of first-order equations for this compound spring-mass problem and determine the mass positions as functions of time. Plot the results for $0 \le t \le 10$.

10.5. Suppose both masses are at rest and that a driving force $F(t) = \sin \omega t$ is applied to the first mass. For what value of ω will the two masses collide? You may treat the masses as points and assume that the springs are infinitely compressible.

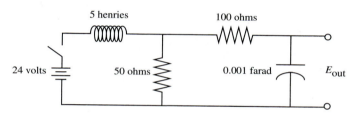

FIGURE 10.4
Electric circuit used in Exercise 6.

10.6. An electric circuit as shown in Fig. 10.4 initially has no current flowing through it and there is no charge on the capacitor. At $t = 0$, the switch is closed, and a constant 24 volts is applied to the system. Determine the output voltage E_{out}.

CHAPTER
11

NUMERICAL SOLUTIONS OF ODES

11.1 LABORATORY GOALS

a. To determine the numerical solution of second order ordinary differential equations.
b. To determine the solutions to systems of first order differential equations.
c. To use the results of the `NDSolve[]` and `ParametricPlot[]` functions to generate phase plane solution portraits.

11.2 SECOND-ORDER EQUATIONS

Many important problems involving second-order initial value problems are non-linear and cannot be solved in closed-form. Numerical methods often present the best way of getting at the solutions to these problems.

Mathematica can solve differential equations numerically, while sparing the user from the need to select and implement a particular algorithm or library call. For example consider the motion of a simple pendulum with unit natural frequency:[1]

$$y'' + \sin y = 0. \qquad (11.1)$$

If we try to solve this differential equation in *Mathematica*, we obtain the following result:

---

[1]The simple pendulum is discussed in detail in Chapter 9.

104

```
In[1]:= pend = y''[t] + Sin[y[t]] == 0

Out[1]= Sin[y[t]] + y''[t] == 0

In[2]:= DSolve[pend, y[t], t]

        DSolve::dnim:
            Built-in procedures cannot solve this differential
                equation.

Out[2]= DSolve[Sin[y[t]] + y''[t] == 0, y[t], t]
```

The `NDSolve[]` function, which has the same syntax as `DSolve[]`, will compute a numerical solution.[2] Suppose that $y(0) = 0$ and $y'(0) = 1$. The numerical solution is determined with:

```
In[3]:= NDSolve[{pend, y[0] == 0, y'[0] == 1},
            y[t], {t, 0, 4Pi}]

Out[3]= {{y[t] -> InterpolatingFunction[{0., 12.5664}, <>][t]}}
```

The solution is given in the form of a call to `InterpolatingFunction[]`, shown in `Out[3]`, shown in abbreviated form.[3] It is usually not necessary to examine the details of a particular interpolating function. To see a sketch of the result, the `Plot[]` function can be used:

```
In[4]:= Plot[y[t] /. %, {t, 0, 4 Pi}]

Out[4]= -Graphics-
```

The result of this call to `Plot[]` is shown in Fig. 11.1.

11.3 MANIPULATING MULTIPLE SOLUTIONS

Suppose we want to compare the motion of the simple pendulum for a variety of initial angular positions. We can combine the `NDSolve[]` function with the `Table[]` function for this purpose:

---

[2] `NDSolve[]` uses an adaptive algorithm for computing solutions. There are a number of special parameters that can be set to enable `NDSolve[]` to attack especially delicate numerical computations. The interested reader should consult the *Mathematica* book.

[3] The symbol `<>` indicates that the shortened form of the output form has been used.

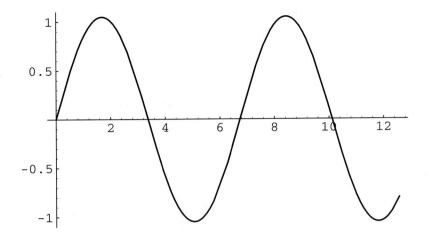

FIGURE 11.1
Numerical solution to the simple pendulum problem obtained by *Mathematica*. Compare to
Fig. 9.2.

```
In[5]:= Table[NDSolve[{pend, y[0] == y0, y'[0] == 0},
            y[t], {t, 0, 2Pi}],
            {y0, 0.2, 3.2, 0.5}]

Out[5]= {{{y[t] -> InterpolatingFunction[{0., 6.28319}, <>][t]}},

          {{y[t] -> InterpolatingFunction[{0., 6.28319}, <>][t]}},

          {{y[t] -> InterpolatingFunction[{0., 6.28319}, <>][t]}},

          {{y[t] -> InterpolatingFunction[{0., 6.28319}, <>][t]}},

          {{y[t] -> InterpolatingFunction[{0., 6.28319}, <>][t]}},

          {{y[t] -> InterpolatingFunction[{0., 6.28319}, <>][t]}},

          {{y[t] -> InterpolatingFunction[{0., 6.28319}, <>][t]}}}
```

In this example we started with an initial angle of 0.2 radians and incremented
that quantity by 0.5 radians until the value of 3.2 (a little bigger than π radians)
was achieved. Next we build a table of just the interpolating functions:

```
In[6]:= Table[(y[t] /. %[[j]]), {j,1,7}]

Out[6]= {{InterpolatingFunction[{0., 6.28319}, <>][t]},
```

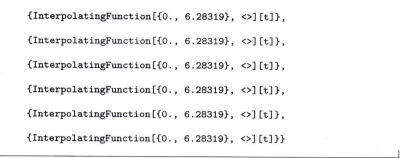

```
{InterpolatingFunction[{0., 6.28319}, <>][t]},

{InterpolatingFunction[{0., 6.28319}, <>][t]},

{InterpolatingFunction[{0., 6.28319}, <>][t]},

{InterpolatingFunction[{0., 6.28319}, <>][t]},

{InterpolatingFunction[{0., 6.28319}, <>][t]},

{InterpolatingFunction[{0., 6.28319}, <>][t]}}
```

This list can be plotted with the `Plot[]` function, but the list must be enclosed

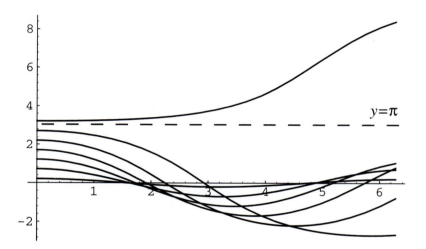

FIGURE 11.2
Numerical solution to the simple pendulum problem for seven values of the starting angle.

within the `Evaluate[]` function in order to be properly handled by *Mathematica*:

```
In[7]:= Plot[Evaluate[%], {t, 0, 2 Pi}]

Out[7]= -Graphics-
```

Figure 11.2 shows the result of this multiple solution evaluation. Note that for the solution with the largest initial angular displacement, $y(0) = 3.2$, the solution *increases* with increasing t. In this case, the pendulum has been started from the *other* side of its unstable equilibrium position, indicated by the dashed line in

Fig. 11.2. If that calculation is run out sufficiently far, you will be able to see periodic solutions, but around a different equilibrium position. Also note that the periods of the other solutions change with increasing amplitude. This is a characteristic behavior of nonlinear vibrations.

11.4 SYSTEMS OF ODES

Mathematica can also handle the numerical solution of systems of ordinary differential equations. Consider the Van der Pol equation:

$$y'' + \epsilon y'(y^2 - 1) + y = 0. \tag{11.2}$$

This equation models the behavior of certain types of nonlinear oscillators which contain positive feedback. First, we re-write this equation as a system of two first-order differential equations:[4]

$$y' = x, \tag{11.3}$$

and

$$x' = -y - \epsilon x'(y^2 - 1). \tag{11.4}$$

Consider first the solution for $y(0) = 1/2$, $x(0) = 0$, with $\epsilon = 0.1$:

```
In[8]:= VDP1 = {y'[t] == x[t], x'[t] == - y[t] -
          0.1 (y[t]^2 - 1) x[t], y[0] == 1/2, x[0] == 0}

                                                        2
Out[8]= {y'[t] == x[t], x'[t] == -y[t] - 0.1 x[t] (-1 + y[t] ),

                   1
          y[0] == -, x[0] == 0}
                   2

In[9]:= sol1 = NDSolve[VDP1, {x[t], y[t]}, {t, 0, 20}]

Out[9]= {{x[t] -> InterpolatingFunction[{0., 20.}, <>][t],

          y[t] -> InterpolatingFunction[{0., 20.}, <>][t]}}
```

We then plot both components of the solution with the **Plot[]** function:

```
In[10]:= Plot[{x[t] /. sol1, y[t] /. sol1}, {t,0, 20}]

Out[10]= -Graphics-
```

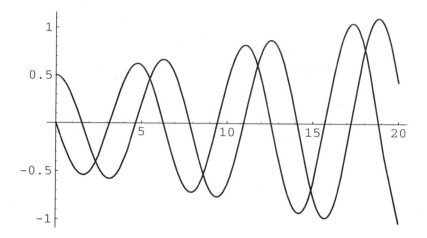

FIGURE 11.3
Numerical solution to the Van der Pol equation with $y(0) = 0.5$, $y'(0) = 0$, and $\epsilon = 0.1$.

The result is shown in Fig. 11.3. Note that solution $y(t)$, though oscillatory, grows with time. The behavior of solutions to the Van der Pol equation can also be studied in the phase plane. Phase-plane portraits can be studied using the `ParametricPlot[]` function. First, we separate the two solution components:

```
In[11]:= f1 = x[t] /. sol1[[1]]

Out[11]= InterpolatingFunction[{0., 20.}, <>][t]

In[12]:= g1 = y[t] /. sol1[[1]]

Out[12]= InterpolatingFunction[{0., 20.}, <>][t]
```

We then generate the phase-plane portrait using these two results and the `ParametricPlot[]` function. A list consisting of two parametric equations is passed as the first argument, a list denoting the domain of the parameter is passed as the second:

```
In[13]:= ParametricPlot[{f1, g1}, {t, 0, 20}]

Out[13]= -Graphics-
```

[4]We could have used `NDSolve[]` directly on the Van der Pol equation. Writing it as a system facilitates the construction of a phase-plane portrait.

The phase-plane portrait is shown in Fig. 11.4. Note that $x = 0$ and $y = 0$ is

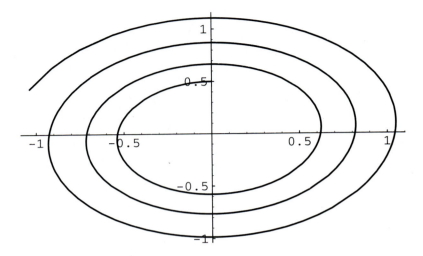

FIGURE 11.4
Phase-plane portrait of the solution to the Van der Pol equation with $y(0) = 0.5$, $y'(0) = 0$, and $\epsilon = 0.1$. The solution curve spirals outward from the origin, indicating that $(0,0)$ is an *unstable* equilibrium point.

a stationary point of the Van der Pol equation. The stability of this point can be graphically determined from the phase-plane portrait. Note that the solution curve spirals away from the origin, indicating that the origin is an *unstable* equilibrium point.

EXERCISES

11.1. Determine the solution to the simple pendulum equation when $y(0) = 0$ for values above and below and at $y'(0) = 2$. Compare these results with those obtained in Chapter 9.

11.2. The Duffing equation is given by $y'' + \beta y + (y + \epsilon y^3) = 0$. Compare the solutions to the Duffing equation when $\beta = 1$, $y(0) = 0.1$, $y'(0) = 0$, and for several values in the range $-1 \leq \epsilon \leq 1$.[5]

11.3. Consider the motion of a heavily-damped pendulum with sinusoidal forcing, governed by the equation $y'' + y' + \sin y = \cos \omega t$. Experiment with different values of ω and examine the response of the pendulum. Does it possess a resonant frequency? Generate some phase-plane portraits.[6]

---

[5]Duffing's equation models the motion of a damped, nonlinear spring. If $0 < \epsilon$ the spring is stiffer than the companion linear spring. For $\epsilon < 0$, the spring is softer. If you're up for a challenge, try solving Duffing's equation with $\beta = 0$ using elliptic functions.

[6]Chaos anyone?

11.4. Examine the solution to the Lorenz equations, given by

$$x' = -3(x - y),\qquad\qquad(11.5)$$

$$y' = -xz + 26.5x - y,\qquad\qquad(11.6)$$

$$z' = xy - z,\qquad\qquad(11.7)$$

$$(11.8)$$

with $x(0) = z(0) = 0$, and $y(0) = 1$. Use the interval $0 \leq t \leq 20$, and the `ParametricPlot3D[]` function. This function takes a list of *three* parametric equations for its first argument. The figure you get is a picture of the famous Lorenz attractor. [Hint: Call `NDSolve[]` with `MaxSteps -> 3000`].

12

VARIABLE COEFFICIENT ODES

12.1 LABORATORY GOALS

a. To determine solutions to the Cauchy-Euler equation.

b. To determine solutions to other special second-order ODEs.

c. To determine eigenvalues and eigenfunctions of Sturm-Liouville problems.

12.2 CAUCHY-EULER EQUATIONS

A second-order ODE with non-constant coefficients that sometimes arises in boundary value problems is the Cauchy-Euler or *equidimensional* equation:

$$x^2 y'' + bxy' + cy = 0. \tag{12.1}$$

Solutions to this equation can take on three different forms, depending upon the relative magnitude and sign of b and c. For example, consider the differential equation

$$x^2 y'' + xy' + y = 0, \quad y(1) = 1, \ y(10) = 2. \tag{12.2}$$

We can use the **DSolve[]** function directly on this problem:

```
In[1]:= DSolve[{x^2 y''[x] + x y'[x] +  y[x] == 0,
               y[1] == 1, y[10] == 2}, y[x], x]

Out[1]= {{y[x] -> Csc[Log[10]] (Sin[Log[10] - Log[x]] +

         2 Sin[Log[x]])}}
```

Note that the auxiliary equation (obtained by assuming $y = x^r$) is $r^2 + 1 = 0$, so that the roots are complex conjugates. We plot this result with the `Plot[]` function:

```
In[2]:= Plot[y[x] /. %, {x, 1, 10}]

Out[2]= -Graphics-
```

In Fig. 12.1 we see that indeed the solution satisfies the boundary conditions at each end.

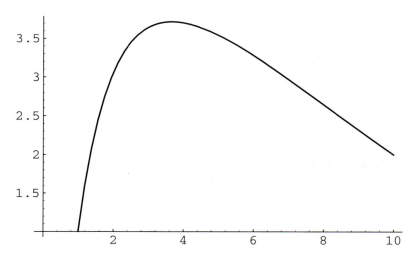

FIGURE 12.1
Solution to Eq. 12.2.

As another example, we solve

$$x^2 y'' - x y' + y = 0, \quad y(1) = 1, y(5) = -1. \tag{12.3}$$

This equation has the characteristic equation $(r - 1)^2$, which yields repeated roots and a different solution form given here:

```
In[3]:= DSolve[{x^2 y''[x] - x y'[x] + y[x] == 0,
               y[1] == 1, y[5] == -1}, y[x], x]

                      6 Log[x]
Out[3]= {{y[x] -> x (1 - --------)}}
                      5 Log[5]

In[4]:= Plot[y[x] /. %, {x, 1, 5}]

Out[4]= -Graphics-
```

The result shown in Fig. 12.2 satisfies the boundary conditions at each end.

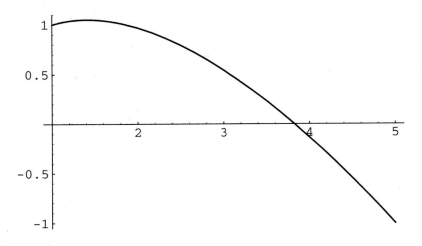

FIGURE 12.2
Solution to Eq. 12.3.

Mathematica can also solve Cauchy-Euler equations of higher order (see Exercise 2).

12.3   OTHER SPECIAL EQUATIONS

Many other second-order differential equations turn up in engineering mathematics. *Mathematica* also recognizes a good number of these, and it can present the general solutions in many cases.[1]

---

[1]Particular solutions are another matter. Sometimes, the boundary conditions to be imposed are something like $\lim_{x \to \infty} y(x) = 0$ or $y(x)$ is bounded as $x \to 0$. *Mathematica* is not yet able to handle conditions like this, so some degree of human intervention is required in order to obtain a particular solution.

Consider first Airy's equation:

$$y'' - ty = 0, \tag{12.4}$$

This ODE occurs in certain wave propagation problems in which the square of the refractive index is a linear function. Here is what `DSolve[]` does with it:

```
In[5]:= DSolve[y''[x] - x y[x] == 0, y[x], x]

Out[5]= {{y[x] -> AiryBi[x] C[1] + AiryAi[x] C[2]}}
```

The general solution is given by *Mathematica* in terms of the Airy functions `AiryAi[]` and `AiryBi[]`. (The standard notation for these functions is $Ai(x)$ and $Bi(x)$.) *Mathematica* understands the numerical and analytical properties of these functions, and this ability will be demonstrated in the next section.

Next we consider Bessel's equation:

$$x^2 y'' + xy' + (x^2 - \nu^2)y = 0. \tag{12.5}$$

Suppose first that $\nu = 2$. Here is what `DSolve[]` finds:

```
In[6]:= bessel = x^2 y''[x] + x y'[x] + (x^2 - 4)y[x] == 0

             2                    2
Out[6]= (-4 + x ) y[x] + x y'[x] + x  y''[x] == 0

In[7]:= DSolve[bessel, y[x], x]

Out[7]= {{y[x] -> BesselY[2, x] C[1] + BesselJ[2, x] C[2]}}
```

The two linearly-independent solutions are expressed by the functions `BesselY[]` and `BesselJ[]`. The usual mathematical notation is $Y_\nu(x)$ and $J_\nu(x)$.

The next equation we consider is Legendre's equation:

$$(1 - x^2)y'' - 2xy' + n(n+1)y = 0, \tag{12.6}$$

where n is an integer. In this example, let $n = 1$. Here is what `DSolve[]` does in this case:

```
In[8]:= leg = (1 - x^2) y''[x] -2 x y'[x] + 2 y[x] == 0

                                  2
Out[8]= 2 y[x] - 2 x y'[x] + (1 - x ) y''[x] == 0
```

```
In[9]:= DSolve[leg, y[x], x]

Out[9]= {{y[x] -> (Sqrt[-1 + x] x Sqrt[1 + x] C[1] +

            (Log[-1 + x] + Log[1 + x])/2
          E                                       x C[2]

            1    1    Log[-1 + x]    Log[1 + x]
          (- - ---- + ----------- - ---------- -
            x   C[1]       2             2

            Log[-1 + C[1]]    Log[1 + C[1]]                2
            -------------- + -------------)) / Sqrt[-1 + x ]}}
                  2                2
```

The standard notations for the linearly independent solutions to Legendre's equation are $P_n(x)$ and $Q_n(x)$. $P_n(x)$ are called Legendre polynomials, and $Q_n(x)$ are called the associated Legendre functions. *Mathematica* has these as the functions **LegendreP[]**. Note, though, that this form is not used in the presentation of the solution by **DSolve[]**.

Another well-known equation from mathematical physics is Hermite's equation:

$$y'' - 2xy + 2ny = 0, \tag{12.7}$$

where n is an integer. This equation arises in the solution of the quantum harmonic oscillator. Suppose for example that $n = 2$. Then

```
In[10]:= hermite = y''[x] - 2x y'[x] + 2 y[x] == 0

Out[10]= 2 y[x] - 2 x y'[x] + y''[x] == 0

In[11]:= DSolve[hermite, y[x], x]

                                          2
                           2            C[1]
                          x           E      x C[2]
Out[11]= {{y[x] -> x C[1] - E    C[2] + ------------ +
                                            C[1]

         Sqrt[Pi] x C[2] Erfi[x] - Sqrt[Pi] x C[2] Erfi[C[1]]}}
```

The *Mathematica* function **Erfi[]** is the imaginary error function.[2] One of the forms solutions to this equation takes is the Hermite polynomial. In *Mathematica*

___

[2]The function **Erfi[]** is not listed in the *Mathematica* book! You can, however, query *Mathematica* about its definition with the ?? operator:

```
??Erfi

Erfi[z] gives the imaginary error function erfi(z) == -i
```

these are given by the function `HermiteH[]`. These are not part of the solution presented by `DSolve[]`.

12.4   APPLICATIONS

Consider the modified Airy's equation:

$$y'' - (x - \lambda)y = 0, \tag{12.8}$$

together with boundary conditions $y(0) = y(1) = 0$. This type of differential equation is called a Sturm-Liouville equation. The constant λ is an eigenvalue and we seek values of this constant such that the modified Airy equation has nontrivial solutions.

```
In[12]:= DSolve[y''[x] - (x - lam) y[x] == 0, y[x], x]

Out[12]:= {{y[x] -> AiryBi[-lam + x] C[1] + AiryAi[-lam + x] C[2]}}
```

If we had provided the two boundary conditions to `DSolve[]` it would have determined that both constants were zero. In other words, `DSolve[]` would only return the trivial solution.

To find nontrivial solutions, we apply the boundary conditions at both ends. This yields a pair of simultaneous equations for the two constants. Since these equations form a homogeneous system, the coefficient matrix must be singular. To construct this matrix, first extract the general solution for further manipulation, assigning it to the variable `airy`:

```
In[13]:= airy = y[x] /. Flatten[%]

Out[13]:= AiryBi[-lam + x] C[1] + AiryAi[-lam + x] C[2]
```

Now we construct the coefficient matrix by selecting the coefficients of `C[1]` and `C[2]` and evaluating those coefficients at the appropriate boundary point:[3]

```
erf(i z).

Attributes[Erfi] = Listable, Protected
```

---

[3]Study the construction of `In[14]` carefully. Convince yourself that the indices really do get the right terms.

```
In[14]:= cm = {{airy[[1, 1]], airy[[2, 1]]} /. x ->0,
               {airy[[1, 1]], airy[[2, 1]]} /. x ->1}

Out[14]= {{AiryBi[-lam], AiryAi[-lam]},

         {AiryBi[1 - lam], AiryAi[1 - lam]}}
```

Values of λ that make this matrix singular will permit the existence of nontrivial solutions Eq. (12.8). We will need to find them numerically with the `FindRoot[]` function. Before doing that, however, we must estimate the location of the first root. We do this graphically by plotting the determinant of our coefficient matrix:

```
In[15]:= Plot[Det[cm], {lam, 0, 20}]

Out[15]= -Graphics-
```

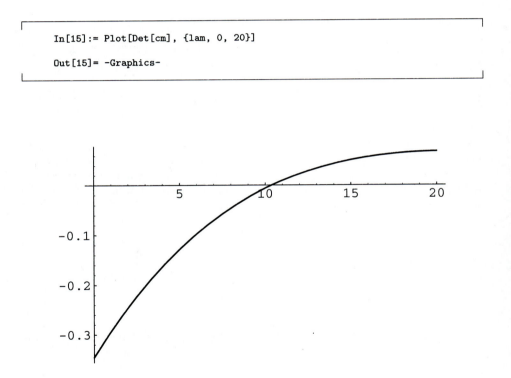

FIGURE 12.3
The determinant of the coefficient matrix plotted as a function of λ.

As shown in Fig. 12.3, the first zero occurs just beyond $\lambda = 10$. We will use 10 as guess at the root when invoking `FindRoot[]`:

```
In[16]:= FindRoot[Det[cm] == 0, {lam, 10}]

Out[16]= {lam -> 10.3685}
```

We now substitute this back into our expression for the solution and solve for C[2] in terms of C[1] at the boundary $x = 0$:[4]

```
In[17]:= airy1 = airy /. %

Out[17]= AiryBi[-10.3685 + x] C[1] + AiryAi[-10.3685 + x] C[2]

In[18]:= Solve[(% /. x -> 0) == 0, C[2]]

Out[18]= {{C[2] -> -0.574981 C[1]}}
```

Now we substitute this back into our expression for the solution and obtain:

```
In[19]:= airy1 = airy1 /. Flatten[%]

Out[20]= -0.574981 AiryAi[-10.3685 + x] C[1] +

             AiryBi[-10.3685 + x] C[1]
```

Recall that eigenfunctions of homogeneous boundary-value problems are unique up to a multiplicative constant. So, in order to plot the result, we set the arbitrary constant C[1] to unity:

```
In[21]:= Plot[airy1 /. C[1] -> 1, {x, 0, 1}]

Out[21]= -Graphics-
```

The eigenfunction is sketched in Fig. 12.4.

EXERCISES

12.1. Determine the general solution to $x^2 y'' - xy' + y = x^2$.

12.2. Determine the general solution to $x^3 y''' - 3x^2 y'' + 7xy' - 8y = 0$.

---

[4]Note that the same result would be obtained at the other boundary.

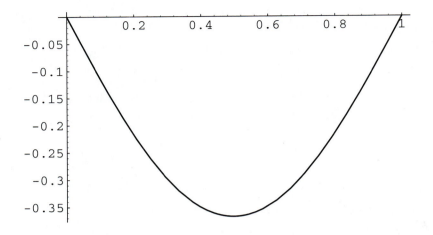

FIGURE 12.4
Solution to Eq. 12.8 for the eigenvalue $\lambda = 10.3685$.

12.3. Determine the general solution to Laguerre's equation:

$$xy'' + (\alpha + 1 - x)y' + ny = 0, \tag{12.9}$$

where n is an integer. [Hint: Pick explicit values for α and n.]

12.4. Determine the general solution to Chebyshev's equation:

$$(1 - x^2)y'' + -xy' + n^2y = 0, \tag{12.10}$$

where n is an integer.

12.5. Determine the general solution to the parametric Bessel's equation of order three:

$$x^2y'' + xy' + (\lambda^2 x^2 - 9)y = 0. \tag{12.11}$$

Suppose that $y(0)$ is bounded and $y(2) = 0$. Determine the smallest positive eigenvalue and its corresponding eigenfunction.

12.6. Consider the Cauchy-Euler equation

$$x^2y'' + xy' - \lambda^2 y = 0 \tag{12.12}$$

with $y(1) = y(2) = 0$. Determine the lowest eigenvalue and plot the corresponding eigenfunction.

12.7. Verify that second eigenfunction of the Airy equation describe in Section 12.3 is orthogonal to the first eigenfunction. [Hints: Use `NIntegrate[]` and consider what the weighting function should be.]

12.8. Suppose a long pipe containing steam is wrapped with a layer of insulation as suggested in Fig. 12.5. The pipe radius is $a = 3$ cm, and the insulation is 2.5 cm thick, so that the outer radius of the insulated pipe is $b = 5.5$ cm. Assuming no

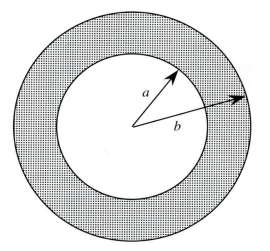

FIGURE 12.5
Cross-section of pipe insulation.

angular variations in the insulation jacket, the temperature in the insulation is described by the one-dimensional Laplace equation in polar coordinates:

$$\frac{d^2u}{dr^2} + \frac{1}{r}\frac{du}{dr} = 0,$$

with $u(a)$ and $u(b)$ prescribed.

(a) If the steam temperature is 110 degrees Centigrade, and the insulated pipe is in a duct whose nominal ambient temperature is 25 degrees Centigrade, determine the temperature distribution inside the insulation.

(b) What is the average temperature of the insulation?

CHAPTER
13

FOURIER SERIES

13.1 LABORATORY GOALS

a. To determine Fourier trigonometric series coefficients symbolically and numerically.

b. To plot and compare Fourier series and the functions they approximate.

13.2 FOURIER SINE SERIES

Consider the function $f(x) = 1$, $1/3 < x < 2/3$, and 0 otherwise in the interval $[0, 1]$ with $f(x + 1) = f(x)$.

This periodic function $f(x)$ can be defined in *Mathematica* as

```
In[1]:= f[x_] := If[ (Mod[x, 1] > 1/3) && (Mod[x, 1] < 2/3), 1, 0]
```

The `Mod[]` function returns the remainder after dividing x by 1, thus causing the `If[]` function to always return a value of 1 when x is in the middle third of any unit interval.[1] The graph of this function in the interval $[0, 3]$ is produced with the *Mathematica* command

[1]The operator `&&` performs a logical **and** of the expressions on either side. The result is either **True** of **False**, values interpreted by the `If[]` function in a natural way. The `&&` operator behaves just like the similarly-named operator in the C programming language.

122

```
In[2]:= Plot[f[x], {x,   0, 3}]

Out[2]= -Graphics-
```

and shown in Fig. 13.1.

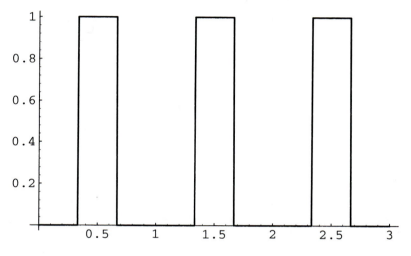

FIGURE 13.1
The square-wave function. The vertical lines are artifacts from the graphics process, not part of the function.

We seek expressions for the Fourier sine and cosine coefficients of $f(x)$. First we determine expressions for the Fourier sine terms. These are given by the following:

$$b_n = \frac{2}{L} \int_0^L f(x) \sin\left(\frac{n\pi x}{L}\right) \, dx, \tag{13.1}$$

In our example, $L = 1$. An expression for the Fourier coefficients can be built up within *Mathematica* in the following way:

```
In[3]:= b[n_] := b[n] = 2 Integrate[Sin[n Pi x], {x, 1/3, 2/3}]
```

The use of the form b[n_] := b[n] forces *Mathematica* to "remember" the value of b[n] it calculates for each value of n, making subsequent computations which repeatedly use b[n] much more efficient.[2]

---

[2]There is a subtle difference between the function definitions in In[1] and In[3]. In

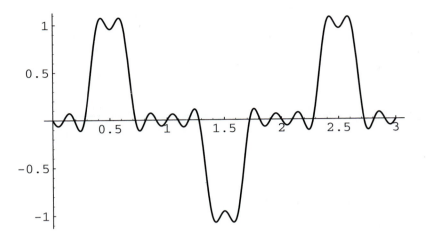

FIGURE 13.2
Tenth Partial Sum of the Fourier sine Series for $f(x)$.

We can now have *Mathematica* determine as many coefficients as we require. In this case, we shall use the **Table[]** function to list the first ten Fourier sine coefficients for $f(x)$:

```
In[4]:= Table[b[n], {n, 1, 10}]

          2       -4       2       2       -4
Out[4]= {--, 0, ----, 0, ----, 0, ----, 0, ----, 0}
         Pi      3 Pi     5 Pi    7 Pi     9 Pi
```

Note that all coefficients with even subscripts are zero (why?).

The partial sums of the Fourier sine series for $f(x)$ can be constructed with the **Sum[]** function:

```
In[5]:= F[x_, n_] := Sum[ b[j] Sin[j Pi x], {j,1,n}]
```

In[1], the symbol x is a dummy, replaced by whatever argument is passed when the function is invoked. Not so in In[3]: the symbol n is a dummy, but not the symbol x. If we wanted x to be a dummy, we'd have to use the following declaration:

```
b[n_, x_] := 2 Integrate[Sin[n Pi x], x, 1/3, 2/3]
```

The manner of declaration can be important when passing function like this as arguments to other functions. For a more detailed discussion of this issue, see *Programming in Mathematica*.

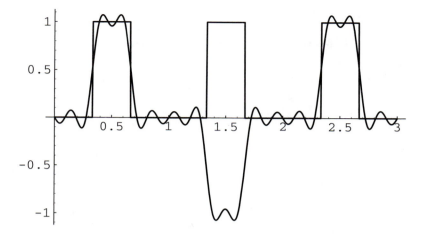

FIGURE 13.3
Composite Figure created with **Show[]**. The graph of the square wave $f(x)$ is shown together with the graph of the tenth partial sum of the Fourier sine series for $f(x)$ on the interval $[0, 3]$.

Sum[] takes as arguments an expression and a list indicating an index variable with its range. The partial sum of the first ten terms of the Fourier sine series look like this when sketched:

```
In[6]:= Plot[F[x, 9], {x,0,3}]

Out[6]= -Graphics-
```

This result is shown in Fig. 13.2. The function and its Fourier sine series can be viewed together with the **Show[]** command:

```
In[7]:= Show[%2, %6]

Out[7]= -Graphics-
```

with the result shown in Fig. 13.3.

Convergence of the partial sums to $f(x)$ within the interval $[0, 1]$ is evident in this figure. Note the disparity between the partial sum and $f(x)$ within $[1, 2]$. This occurs because the Fourier sine series is an odd periodic function. Agreement with $f(x)$ is guaranteed only within $[0, 1]$, the interval in which the coefficients are calculated. The Fourier series also shows evidence of Gibb's phenomenon, in the vicinity of the corners of the square wave.[3]

13.3 FOURIER COSINE SERIES

The Fourier cosine series for $f(x)$ discussed in the preceding section is also straightforward to compute. These coefficients are given as

$$a_0 = \frac{1}{L} \int_0^L f(x)\, dx \tag{13.2}$$

and

$$a_n = \frac{2}{L} \int_0^L f(x) \cos\left(\frac{n\pi x}{L}\right)\, dx, \tag{13.3}$$

where, in our example, $L = 1$.

These coefficients can be represented in *Mathematica* as follows:

```
In[8]:= a[0] = Integrate[ 1, {x, 1/3, 2/3}]

         1
Out[8]= -
         3

In[9]:= a[n_] := a[n] = 2 Integrate[ Cos[n Pi x], {x, 1/3, 2/3}]
```

As before, we construct a table of the first eleven terms of the Fourier cosine coefficients:

```
In[10]:= Table[a[n], {n,0,10}]

          1        Sqrt[3]        Sqrt[3]          -Sqrt[3]
Out[10]= {-, 0, -(-------), 0, -------, 0, 0, 0, --------, 0,
          3         Pi            2 Pi              4 Pi

Sqrt[3]
-------}
 5 Pi
```

Note that all the odd-numbered coefficients are zero (why?).[4]

Partial sums are set up and plotted just as they were before with `Plot[]` and `Sum[]`:

---

[3] Gibb's phenomenon states that the partial sums of a Fourier series will always overshoot in the vicinity of a discontinuity of the function, a consequence of the non-uniform convergence of the series.

[4] Also note that $a_6 = 0$. Can you think of a symmetry argument that would account for this? Would you expect any other even coefficients to be zero?

```
In[11]:= G[x_, n_] := Sum[a[j] Cos[j Pi x], {j, 0, n}]

In[12]:= Plot[G[x, 10], {x, 0, 3}]

Out[12]= -Graphics-
```

as shown in Fig. 13.4.   This figure and the illustration of $f(x)$ can also be

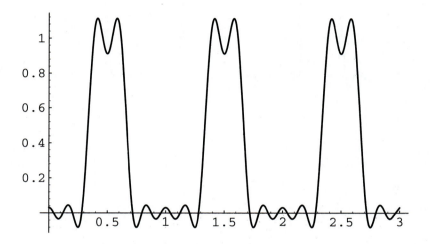

FIGURE 13.4
Eleventh Partial Sum of the Fourier cosine series for $f(x)$.

overlain with the **Show**[] command:

```
In[13]:= Show[%2, %12]

Out[14]= -Graphics-
```

with the result shown in Fig. 13.5.   The partial sum and the function $f(x)$ are in much better agreement on $[1, 2]$ because the Fourier cosine series (and its partial sums) are even, as is $f(x)$.

13.4   THE FOURIERTRANSFORM **PACKAGE**

Mathematica is distributed with a package containing a variety of handy functions for manipulating Fourier Series. This package is loaded with the following

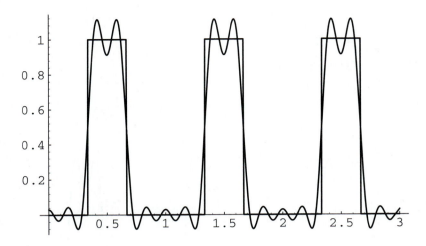

FIGURE 13.5
Composite Figure created with **Show[]**. The graph of the square wave $f(x)$ is shown together with the graph of the eleventh partial sum of the Fourier cosine series for $f(x)$ on the interval $[0, 3]$.

command:

```
In[15]:= <<Calculus'Fouriertransform'
```

The functions available in this package are useful for computing symbolic or numerical values of Fourier coefficients and for generating Fourier series. Before we use some of these functions in the next section, a word of caution is in order. Depending upon the analytical nature of the function involved, using one of the **FourierTransform** package functions may produce no result or, even worse, an inaccurate one. Note that in the previous two sections we never used the explicit form of **f[x]** in our integrations; instead we integrated over a restricted interval in which $f(x) \neq 0$. The *form* of **f[x]** does not lend itself to a clean symbolic integration. Moreover, the use of a numerical integration (the **NIntegrate[]** function) is also fraught with difficulty. The discontinuities in $f(x)$, together with the oscillatory factor **Sin[n Pi x]** can result in unacceptable performance of the integration routines unless certain numerical integration options are altered for the calculation.[5]

[5] Try the following command:
NIntegrate[f[x] Sin[n Pi x], {x, 0, 1}]

Nevertheless, if the integrand can be expressed "cleanly," that is, as a continuous function, then the package functions are the best choice and ought to be used. We will illustrate their use in the next section.

13.5   FOURIER SERIES

Consider the function

$$h(x) = (1 - x)(x + 1)(x - 2), \quad -1 \le x \le 1, \tag{13.4}$$

with $h(x+2) = h(x)$ so that $h(x)$ has period 2. This function is represented and plotted in *Mathematica* as follows:

```
In[16]:= h[x_] := (1 - x) (x + 1) (x - 2)

In[17]:= Plot[h[x], {x, -1, 1}]

Out[17]= -Graphics-
```

Note that this function is *asymmetric* with respect to the origin and the *y*-axis as shown in Fig. 13.6. Because it is neither even nor odd, a full Fourier series must be used to represent it.

Although we could have *Mathematica* work with the explicit integration formulas, we instead use the `FourierTrigSeries` function to evaluate the coefficients and assemble the series for us. For example, define H as the *tenth* partial sum of the Fourier series of $h(x)$. Then in *Mathematica*,

```
In[18]:= H = FourierTrigSeries[h[x], {x, -1, 1}, 10]

                             2           2
                  4      6 - 6 Pi   6 + 2 Pi
Out[18]= -(-) + (--------- - ---------) Cos[Pi x] +
                  3         4           4
                          Pi          Pi


              2            2
   -(3 - 12 Pi )    3 + 4 Pi
   (------------- + ---------) Cos[2 Pi x] +
          4             4
        8 Pi          8 Pi


            2          2
   2 - 18 Pi    2 + 6 Pi
```

Numerous warning messages will appear. These will also appear if the functions provided in the `FourierTransform` package are used. These can most easily be avoided by using the simplest possible form of the integrand, as we did in the main body of the previous sections.

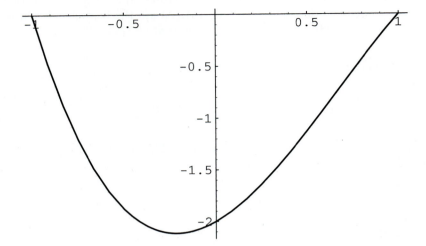

FIGURE 13.6
Tenth Partial Sum of the Fourier sine Series for $f(x)$.

```
(----------  -  ---------) Cos[3 Pi x] +
        4            4
      27 Pi        27 Pi


             2              2
  -(3 - 48 Pi )    3 + 16 Pi
  (------------- + ----------) Cos[4 Pi x] +
         4              4
       128 Pi        128 Pi


           2            2
   6 - 150 Pi    6 + 50 Pi
  (----------- - ----------) Cos[5 Pi x] +
        4             4
     625 Pi        625 Pi


             2            2
   -(1 - 36 Pi )   1 + 12 Pi
  (------------- + ----------) Cos[6 Pi x] +
         4              4
       216 Pi        216 Pi


           2             2
   6 - 294 Pi    6 + 98 Pi
  (----------- - ----------) Cos[7 Pi x] +
        4             4
     2401 Pi       2401 Pi


              2              2
   -(3 - 192 Pi )    3 + 64 Pi
```

```
(-------------- + ----------) Cos[8 Pi x] +
       4              4
   2048 Pi        2048 Pi


            2              2
   2 - 162 Pi    2 + 54 Pi
 (----------- - ----------) Cos[9 Pi x] +
       4              4
   2187 Pi        2187 Pi


              2                2
   -(3 - 300 Pi )   3 + 100 Pi
 (-------------- + -----------) Cos[10 Pi x] +
        4              4
    5000 Pi        5000 Pi

 12 Sin[Pi x]    3 Sin[2 Pi x]    4 Sin[3 Pi x]
 ------------ - ------------- + ------------- -
      3               3                3
     Pi             2 Pi             9 Pi

 3 Sin[4 Pi x]    12 Sin[5 Pi x]    Sin[6 Pi x]
 ------------- + -------------- - ----------- +
       3                3               3
     16 Pi           125 Pi          18 Pi

 12 Sin[7 Pi x]    3 Sin[8 Pi x]    4 Sin[9 Pi x]
 -------------- - ------------- + ------------- -
       3                3                3
     343 Pi           128 Pi           243 Pi

 3 Sin[10 Pi x]
 --------------
        3
     250 Pi
```

which is a formidable result! A feel for the relative sizes of the coefficients can be obtained by forcing numerical evaluations of all the coefficients with the N[] function:

```
In[19]:= N[H]

Out[19]= -1.33333 - 0.810569 Cos[3.14159 x] +

   0.202642 Cos[6.28319 x] - 0.0900633 Cos[9.42478 x] +

   0.0506606 Cos[12.5664 x] - 0.0324228 Cos[15.708 x] +

   0.0225158 Cos[18.8496 x] - 0.0165422 Cos[21.9911 x] +

   0.0126651 Cos[25.1327 x] - 0.010007 Cos[28.2743 x] +

   0.00810569 Cos[31.4159 x] + 0.387018 Sin[3.14159 x] -
```

```
0.0483773 Sin[6.28319 x] + 0.014334 Sin[9.42478 x] -

0.00604716 Sin[12.5664 x] + 0.00309615 Sin[15.708 x] -

0.00179175 Sin[18.8496 x] + 0.00112833 Sin[21.9911 x] -

0.000755895 Sin[25.1327 x] + 0.000530889 Sin[28.2743 x] -

0.000387018 Sin[31.4159 x]
```

which can be plotted with the following call to `Plot[]`:

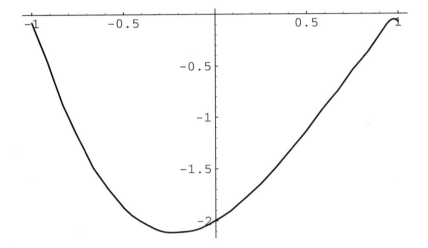

FIGURE 13.7
Tenth Partial Sum of the Fourier Series for $h(x)$.

```
In[20] := Plot[%, {x, -1, 1}]

Out[20]= -Graphics-
```

and the result shown in Fig. 13.7. Finally, $h(x)$ and its ten-term Fourier partial sum can be displayed together using the `Show[]` function. The regions in which the fit between the two is worst is highlighted in Fig. 13.8.

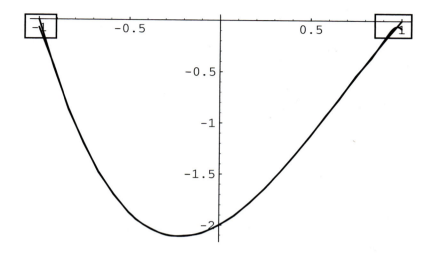

FIGURE 13.8
The tenth Fourier partial sum of $h(x)$ and $h(x)$ are plotted together in this graph. Approximation error caused by truncation of the trigonometric series is most noticeable at the endpoints of the interval.

```
In[21]:= Show[%17, %20]

Out[21]= -Graphics-
```

EXERCISES

13.1. Compute the Fourier sine series coefficients for $f(x) = 4x(1 - x)$, $x \in [0, 1]$. How fast do these coefficients decrease?

13.2. Compute the Fourier cosine series coefficients for the previous problem. Compare the magnitudes. Discuss your results.

13.3. Compute the Fourier series coefficients for $g(x) = e^x$, $x \in [-\pi, \pi]$. How many terms in the series are needed to "reasonably" reproduce the behavior of $g(x)$. Support your answer with sketches of $g(x)$ and the partial sums of the Fourier Series.

13.4. Compute the Fourier cosine series coefficients for $h(x) = H$, $-1/H < x < 1/H$, and $h(x) = 0$ everywhere else in $[0, 1]$. Discuss what happens to the coefficients as $H \to 0$. Provide sketches to illustrate the behavior of the partial sums.

13.5. Compute the Fourier sine and cosine series coefficients for the periodic Dirac delta function. Let the period be π.

13.6. A periodic sawtooth driving force $F(t)$, as shown in Fig. 13.9, is applied to a damped spring-mass system with mass $m = 1/2$ kg, and damping coefficient

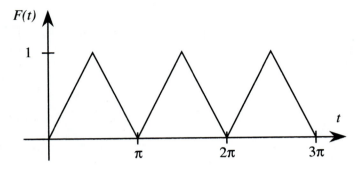

FIGURE 13.9
Sawtooth driving force.

$\beta = 1$ N-sec/m. Assuming the mass starts form it's equilibrium position at rest, determine the motion of the mass when the spring constant is
(a) 7 N/m.
(b) 8 N/m.
(c) 9 N/m.
Describe any qualitative differences you observe in the solutions. [Hint: Expand $F(t)$ in a Fourier series, and retain at least 8 terms.]

CHAPTER
14

THE HEAT
EQUATION

14.1   LABORATORY GOALS

a. To compute approximate solutions to the one-dimensional heat equation.

b. To visualize solutions in space and time with the `Plot3D[]` function.

14.2   ONE-DIMENSIONAL SOLUTION

As a consequence of the balance of energy and Fourier's Law of heat conduction,[1] the flow of heat in a thin, laterally-insulated homogeneous rod is modeled by the one-dimensional heat equation:

$$u_t = ku_{xx}, \tag{14.1}$$

together with an initial condition $u(x,0) = f(x)$ and homogeneous boundary conditions. In Eq. (14.1), the subscripts denote partial differentiation with respect to the indicated variable. Thus $u_t = \partial u / \partial t$.

Supposing the temperatures at either end are to be held at zero degrees so that $u(0,t) = u(L,t) = 0$, the separation-of-variables solution for this problem is

$$u(x,t) = \sum_{n=1}^{\infty} b_n \sin(n\pi x/L) \exp(-kn^2\pi^2 t/L^2), \tag{14.2}$$

---

[1]For a derivation, see e.g. Ray C. Wiley, and Louis C. Barrett, *Advanced Engineering Mathematics*, McGraw-Hill, New York, 1982, pp. 500–502.

135

with

$$b_n = (2/L) \int_0^L f(x) \sin(n\pi x/L) \, dx. \tag{14.3}$$

We will use *Mathematica* to determine the Fourier coefficients b_n and to examine

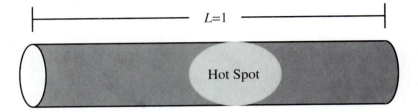

FIGURE 14.1
Uniform rod with asymmetric initial temperature.

the partial sums of Eq. (14.2).

14.3   ASYMMETRIC INITIAL TEMPERATURE

Let us examine the behavior of the heat equation solution given by Eq. (14.2) when the rod is heated so that a small region of high temperature occurs near the middle of the bar as suggested in Fig. 14.1. One way to model this "hot spot" is with the function

$$f(x) = 4x^3(1-x)^2, \tag{14.4}$$

which gives the bar an asymmetric temperature distribution. This can be set up in *Mathematica* as

```
In[1]:= f[x_] :=  4 x ^3 ( 1 - x)^2
```

A sketch of $f(x)$ can be generated by `Plot[]`

```
In[2]:= Plot[f[x], {x,0,1}]

Out[2]= -Graphics-
```

with the result shown in Fig. 14.2. The Fourier sine coefficients can be computed with the *Mathematica* expression

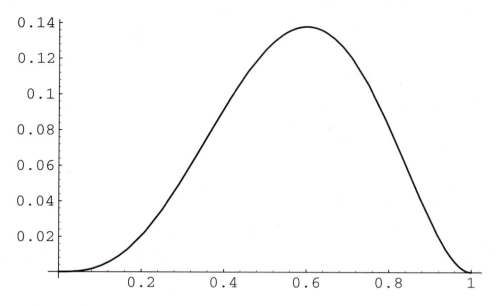

FIGURE 14.2
Initial condition $f(x)$ for example heat equation.

```
In[3]:= b[n_] := b[n] = Integrate[2 f[x] Sin[n Pi x], {x, 0, 1}]
```

Note the appearance of the extra term **b[n]** =. This will have the effect of forcing *Mathematica* to "remember" a value of **b[n]** once it has been computed. If a relatively small number of these values are remembered, but would otherwise have been repeatedly calculated, then substantial speed-ups will be seen in subsequent computations.[2]

Since we will be using ten-term partial sums later in this chapter, we can use the **Table[]** function to generate those values of **b[n]** now:

```
In[4]:= Table[b[n], {n, 1, 10}]

                     2                          2
          -384    8 (-72 + 2 Pi )    -12    2 (-9 + Pi )
Out[4]= {---- - ----------------,   --- + ------------,
           5           5              5          5
          Pi          Pi            Pi         Pi
```

[2]This trick was introduced in Chapter 13.

$$\frac{-128}{81\ Pi^5} - \frac{8\ (-24 + 6\ Pi^2)}{81\ Pi^5}, \quad \frac{-3}{8\ Pi^5} + \frac{-9 + 4\ Pi^2}{16\ Pi^5},$$

$$\frac{-384}{3125\ Pi^5} - \frac{8\ (-72 + 50\ Pi^2)}{3125\ Pi^5}, \quad \frac{-4}{81\ Pi^5} + \frac{2\ (-3 + 3\ Pi^2)}{81\ Pi^5},$$

$$\frac{-384}{16807\ Pi^5} - \frac{8\ (-72 + 98\ Pi^2)}{16807\ Pi^5}, \quad \frac{-3}{256\ Pi^5} + \frac{-9 + 16\ Pi^2}{512\ Pi^5},$$

$$\frac{-128}{19683\ Pi^5} - \frac{8\ (-24 + 54\ Pi^2)}{19683\ Pi^5}, \quad \frac{-12}{3125\ Pi^5} + \frac{2\ (-9 + 25\ Pi^2)}{3125\ Pi^5}\}$$

Assuming that $k = 1$, the partial sums can be expressed in *Mathematica* as

```
In[5]:= F[x_,t_,n_] := Sum[b[j] Sin[j Pi x]
                           Exp[- j^2 Pi^2 t], {j,1,n}]
```

Note that the index variable j is *local* to the Sum[] function. To see, for example, the temperature distribution at $t = 0.1$, a plot of the partial sums can be generated with

```
In[6]:= Plot[F[x, 0.1, 10], {x, 0, 1}]

Out[6]= -Graphics-
```

with the result shown in Fig. 14.3. The peak temperature has fallen considerably from its initial value and the shape of the temperature distribution appears very nearly sinusoidal. To better see the evolution of heat distribution in the bar, a time-lapse surface can be generated with the Plot3D[] function.

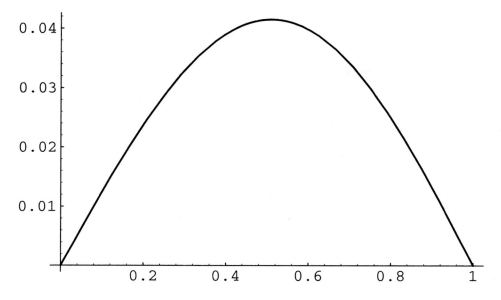

FIGURE 14.3
Solution to example heat equation for $t = 0.1$.

14.4   DISPLAYING HEAT FLOW DYNAMICS

The time-lapse surface can be constructed with the following *Mathematica* command:

```
In[7]:= Plot3D[F[x,t,10], {x,0,1}, {t,0,0.1}]

Out[7]= -SurfaceGraphics-
```

Plot3D[] takes a function of two variables as its first argument, followed by a pair of lists. Each list gives the range for that respective variable. In this example the call to Plot3D[] generates a surface over the x-t plane, with $0 \le x \le 1$ and $0 \le t \le 0.1$. The surface obtained with this command is shown in Fig. 14.4.   *Mathematica* attempts to draw the "best possible" surface according to a reasonable set of aesthetic and technical criteria. However, the default decisions *Mathematica* makes occasionally are not adequate.

To improve the appearance of this change surface, we can change the viewpoint from which the surface is sketched. The points calculated with the Plot3D[] command can be re-used by combining those points with the View-Point option within the Show[] command.[3]

---

[3]The default ViewPoint is {1.3, -2.4, 2}. The ViewPoint option also works with

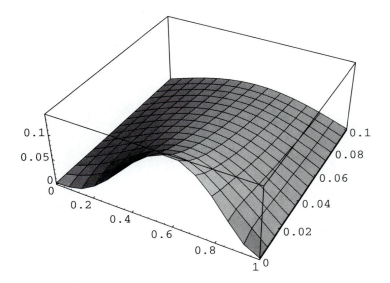

FIGURE 14.4
Solution to example heat equation.

For example, this call to `Show[]` with indicated setting of `ViewPoint` gives a better look at the surface for small values of time:

```
In[8]:= Show[%, Viewpoint -> {0, -4, 1.6}]

Out[8]= -SurfaceGraphics-
```

The result is shown in Fig. 14.5.[4]   This perspective gives a better feel for the asymmetry of the initial temperature and how that temperature evolves in time.

14.5   DISCUSSION

The time-lapse surface shown in Fig. 14.5 reveals some interesting details about the behavior of solutions to the heat equation. Notice how the shape of the initial temperature distribution initially changes. As t increases, the temperature decreases rapidly, and a definite sinusoidal shape emerges almost immediately.

`Plot3D[]` and many other surface-rendering functions.

[4]The *Mathematica* front-end for the Macintosh, MicroSoft Windows, the NeXT workstation, and some Unix workstations provide a tool for interactively determining new viewpoints. Users of workstations without front-ends usually have to experiment with a few viewpoints in order to find just the right one.

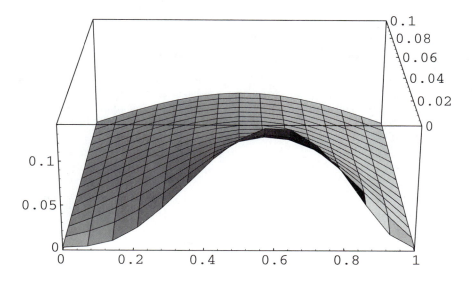

FIGURE 14.5
Solution to example heat equation; Plot produced with `Viewpoint -> {0, -4, 1.6}`.

The time-dependent terms in Eq. 14.2 decay exponentially. However, the higher order terms ($n = 2, 3, \ldots$) decay much faster than the first term ($n = 1$). That term has a pure sinusoidal shape in this example and it comes to dominate the dynamic behavior of the heat flow.

   This suggests that when trying to model heat flow in other problems, if t is sufficiently big, then only the first term in the Fourier series need be kept. Many terms need be kept only when t is very small.

EXERCISES

14.1. Suppose the initial temperature were described by $f(x) = 4x^3(1 - x)^3$. Use *Mathematica* to show that every other coefficient vanishes. Why? How might the partial sums be set up in *Mathematica* in order to exploit this fact?

14.2. Solve the sample problem if both ends of the bar are insulated (so that $u_x = 0$ at each end).

14.3. Solve the sample problem if the initial condition is

$$f(x) = \exp[-128(x - 1/4)^2] + \exp[-128(x - 3/4)^2]$$

subject to both ends being held at zero degrees.

14.4. Consider two identical rods but with different initial temperature distributions. For the first bar, the initial temperature is precisely equal to the first mode of its Fourier Sine series with unit amplitude. For the second bar, the initial temperature is equal to the second mode with unit amplitude. Suppose both bars start with an equal amount of heat. Which bar cools faster? Think of a good *physical* reason to explain your result.

14.5. What determines when t is big or small? In the example $t = 0.1$ was big. [Hint: Examine an assumption that was made.]

14.6. Consider a bar of length $L = 2$ whose left end is held at constant temperature zero degrees and whose right end is free to radiate heat into the ambient medium. The appropriate boundary condition is $-u_x(2, t) = \kappa(u(2, t) - u_0)$, where κ is a constant and u_0 is the temperature of the ambient medium. Supposing that $\kappa = 1$ and $u_0 = 0$, determine the solution to the heat equation if the initial temperature is given by Eq. (14.4).

CHAPTER
15

THE VIBRATING BAR

15.1 LABORATORY GOALS

a. Compute solutions to a fourth-order ordinary differential equation.

b. Determine eigenvalues and eigenfunctions for different boundary conditions.

15.2 VIBRATING BAR

In this chapter, we consider the shapes undertaken by a thin uniform bar which is set in motion through some sort of initial impulse. If we let $u(x,t)$ represent the vertical displacement of the bar from its horizontal, equilibrium position, and neglect all forces but the restoring elastic force, the partial differential equation for the displacement is given by

$$\frac{\partial^4 u}{\partial x^4} = \frac{-1}{c^2}\frac{\partial^2 u}{\partial t^2}, \tag{15.1}$$

where c^2 is a constant which depends upon the material properties of the bar.

Since Eq. (15.1) is fourth-order, *four* boundary conditions are required.[1] The boundary conditions typically take one of the forms shown in Table 15.1:

---

[1]Note that two initial conditions are also required if the full dynamic behavior of the bar is to be examined. Since we are concerned only with determining the mode shapes and frequencies, we can limit ourselves to considering just the interaction among the solution and the boundary conditions.

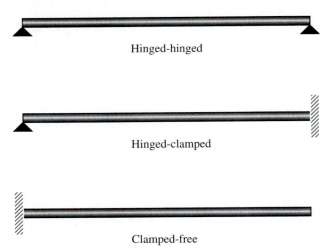

FIGURE 15.1
Three examples illustrating different kinds of boundary conditions for a vibrating bar.

TABLE 15.1
Boundary conditions used with the vibrating bar.

Boundary	Formulation
clamped	$u = u_x = 0$
hinged	$u = u_{xx} = 0$
free	$u_{xx} = u_{xxx} = 0$

Consider the three particular sets of boundary conditions listed below:

$$u(0,t) = u_{xx}(0,t) = 0, u(L,t) = u_{xx}(L,t) = 0, \tag{15.2}$$

$$u(0,t) = u_{xx}(0,t) = 0, u(L,t) = u_x(L,t) = 0, \tag{15.3}$$

$$u(0,t) = u_x(0,t) = 0, u_{xx}(L,t) = u_{xxx}(L,t) = 0, \tag{15.4}$$

The first set corresponds to a bar which is hinged at both ends as suggested in Fig. 15.1. The second set describes a bar which is hinged at one end and clamped at the other, as indicated in the middle illustration. Finally, the third set of boundary conditions describes a cantilevered bar, i.e. one that is clamped at on end and free at the other, as shown in the bottom bar in Fig. 15.1.

15.3   SEPARATION OF VARIABLES

In order to determine the properties of solutions to Eq. 15.1, we assume that $u(x,t) = y(x)g(t)$. Applying the standard separation of variables method, we obtain two ordinary differential equations:

$$y'''' - \lambda^4 y = 0, \tag{15.5}$$

and

$$g'' + \lambda^4 c^2 = 0, \tag{15.6}$$

where λ^4 is the separation constant whose values must be determined. We note here that solutions to Eq. 15.6 have the form $g(t) = d_1 \cos(\lambda^2 ct) + d_2 \sin(\lambda^2 ct)$. Thus, the vibration frequencies of the various modes are proportional to λ^2.

First, we use *Mathematica* to determine the general solution to Eq. 15.5. This is done with the `DSolve[]` function:

```
In[1]:= DSolve[y''''[x] - lam^4 y[x] == 0, y[x], x]

               C[1]       -I lam x              I lam x
Out[1]= {{y[x] -> ------ + E         C[2] + E           C[3] +
               lam x
              E

          lam x
         E       C[4]}}
```

Note that the fourth derivative is indicated by using the ' operator four times in `In[1]`. The four arbitrary constants are denoted by the symbols `C[1]`, `C[2]`, `C[3]`, and `C[4]`. Note that `DSolve[]` returns complex exponentials instead of trigonometric functions. We will make the conversion to trig functions in a subsequent step.

We assign the value of the general solution to the function `g[x]`:

```
In[2]:= g[x_] = %[[1, 1, 2]]

          C[1]      -I lam x           I lam x          lam x
Out[2]= ------ + E         C[2] + E          C[3] + E       C[4]
          lam x
         E
```

We shall use this function in subsequent steps in order to determine non-trivial solutions for different combinations of boundary conditions.

15.4   THE HINGED-HINGED BAR

We consider the hinged-hinged bar with boundary conditions given by Eq. 15.2. First, we establish a list of the four arbitrary constants:

```
In[3]:= coeffs = {C[1], C[2], C[3], C[4]}

Out[3]= {C[1], C[2], C[3], C[4]}
```

Now, we construct a list of equations corresponding to the four boundary conditions. This list is assigned to the symbol BC1:

```
In[4]:= BC1 = {g[0] == 0, g[L] == 0,
               (D[g[x], {x, 2}] /. x -> 0) == 0,
               (D[g[x], {x, 2}] /. x -> L) == 0}

Out[4]= {C[1] + C[2] + C[3] + C[4] == 0,

         C[1]       -I L lam         I L lam        L lam
         ------ + E          C[2] + E         C[3] + E     C[4] ==
         L lam
        E

                2          2          2          2
         0, lam  C[1] - lam  C[2] - lam  C[3] + lam  C[4] == 0,

            2
         lam  C[1]    -I L lam    2          I L lam    2
         --------- - E         lam  C[2] - E         lam  C[3] +
           L lam
          E

            L lam    2
          E       lam  C[4] == 0}
```

In constructing this list, we used the D[] function to directly compute second derivatives. When computing higher order derivatives, the second argument to D[] is a list containing the independent variable and the order of the desired derivative. Keeping in mind that we are seeking *non-trivial* solutions to this system of equations, we determine those values of λ that make this system of equations singular. To do this, we first build the coefficient matrix. This is done with the Table[] and Coefficient[] functions:

```
In[5]:= Table[Coefficient[BC1[[i, 1]], coeffs[[j]]],
             {i, 1, 4}, {j, 1, 4}]

                        -(L lam)    -I L lam    I L lam    L lam
Out[5]= {{1, 1, 1, 1}, {E        , E        , E        , E     },

            2      2      2      2
         {lam , -lam , -lam , lam },
```

```
       2
  lam        -I L lam    2        I L lam    2
{------, -(E          lam ), -(E          lam ),
  L lam
 E


  L lam     2
 E      lam }}
```

What we have done is manipulate *Mathematica*'s representation of a system of equations as a list of lists and systematically isolated and extracted to desired terms. At any rate, we now have the coefficient matrix. Now we take its determinant with the **Det[]** function:

```
In[6]:= Det[%]

              (-1 - I) L lam    4    2 I L lam    4    2 L lam    4
Out[6]= 4 E                 (lam   - E        lam  - E       lam  +

        (2 + 2 I) L lam    4
       E               lam  )
```

Before proceeding further, we load the **Trigonometry** package:

```
In[7]:= <<Algebra'Trigonometry'
```

Now we use the **ComplexToTrig[]** function to eliminate the complex exponentials:

```
In[8]:= Simplify[ComplexToTrig[%%]]

                 2 L lam    4
         8 I (-1 + E       ) lam  Sin[L lam]
Out[8]= -------------------------------------
                      L lam
                     E
```

This expression is the final result of the determinant computation.

We seek those values of λ that make the determinant vanish. First, we use the **Solve[]** function to see what *Mathematica* can find:

```
In[9]:= Solve[% == 0, lam]

        Solve::ifun:
            Warning: Inverse functions are being used by Solve, so
                some solutions may not be found.

                            I Pi
Out[9]= {{lam -> 0}, {lam -> ----}}
                             L
```

The warning message which appears above suggest caution in interpreting results found by *Mathematica*. In fact, the two solutions returned are of no use to us. The first, $\lambda = 0$ will yield only trivial solutions, while the second is complex-valued—but we need *real* eigenvalues.[2]

It is worth noting here that we have run into a real limitation of *Mathematica*, and indeed, any computer algebra system. The determinant equation possess infinitely many solutions, some real and some complex. We need to examine the equation by hand, at least for a while, in order to ascertain the nature of the roots we seek. In this case, in is clear from inspecting Out[8] that this expression will be zero when $\sin(\lambda L)$ is zero. This implies that $\lambda = n\pi/L$ with $n = 1, 2, \ldots$. Since we are interested in obtaining the fundamental mode, we select $\lambda = \pi/L$ and substitute this back into the system of equations and then use the Solve[] function to determine solutions:

```
In[10]:= Solve[BC1 /. lam -> Pi / L, coeffs]

Out[10]= {{C[1] -> 0, C[2] -> -C[3], C[4] -> 0}}
```

We substitute this result back into the expression for our eigenfunction, converting the complex exponentials to trigonometric form and simplifying the result with the Simplify[] function:

```
In[11]:= Simplify[ComplexToTrig[g[x] /. %]]

Out[11]= {2 I C[3] Sin[lam x]}
```

Finally, we substitute the lowest eigenvalue in as well:

---

[2]Why?

```
In[12]:= % /. lam -> Pi / L

                    Pi x
Out[12]= {2 I C[3] Sin[----]}
                     L
```

We remove the coefficient (which is arbitrary at this point):[3]

```
In[13]:= %[[1, 3]]

              Pi x
Out[13]= Sin[----]
               L
```

and obtain the fundamental mode of the hinged-hinged bar: $y = \sin(\pi x/L)$. This result is plotted with the following call to `Plot[]`, setting $L = 1$, and the result is shown in Fig. 15.2.

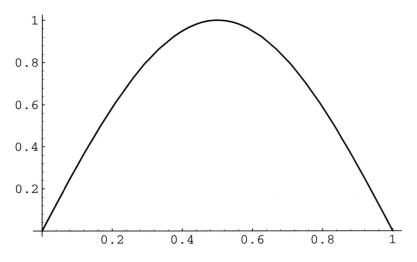

FIGURE 15.2
Fundamental mode of the hinged-hinged bar.

[3]It looks like there are *four* elements in the list of `Out[12]`. Actually, 2 I is considered by *Mathematica* as a single term.

```
In[14]:= Plot[% /. L -> 1, {x, 0, 1}]

Out[14]= -Graphics-
```

Note that the eigenvalues and eigenfunctions for the hinged-hinged bar are identical to those of the vibrating string. However, while the characteristic frequencies of the string are proportional to the eigenvalues, those of the bar are proportional to the square of the eigenvalues. Thus, the spectrum of bar harmonics, i.e. higher-order modes, is much different than that for string harmonics.

15.5   THE HINGED-CLAMPED BAR

We turn now to the solution of the boundary value problem of the hinged-clamped bar. The boundary conditions to be satisfied are given in Eq. 15.3 and are set up in *Mathematica* as:

```
In[15]:= BC2 = {g[0] == 0, g[L] == 0,
             (D[g[x], {x, 2}] /. x -> 0) == 0,
             (D[g[x], {x, 1}] /. x -> L) == 0}

Out[15]= {C[1] + C[2] + C[3] + C[4] == 0,

          C[1]        -I L lam          I L lam          L lam
          ------ + E           C[2] + E          C[3] + E        C[4] ==
          L lam
         E

                 2           2           2           2
         0, lam   C[1] - lam   C[2] - lam   C[3] + lam   C[4] == 0,

           lam C[1]          -I L lam
         -(--------) - I E            lam C[2] +
            L lam
           E

              I L lam             L lam
          I E         lam C[3] + E       lam C[4] == 0}
```

As we did in the previous section, we use the list manipulating ability of *Mathematica* to extract the coefficients of the four equations to obtain the coefficient matrix:

```
In[16]:= Table[Coefficient[BC2[[i, 1]], coeffs[[j]]],
             {i, 1, 4}, {j, 1, 4}]
```

```
                  -(L lam)    -I L lam    I L lam    L lam
Out[16]= {{1, 1, 1, 1}, {E          , E          , E         , E      },

              2     2     2     2
          {lam , -lam , -lam , lam },

               lam          -I L lam          I L lam        L lam
          {-(------), -I E          lam, I E          lam, E        lam}}
             L lam
           E
```

Next, we convert the exponential forms to trigonometric forms and examine the simplified determinant:

```
In[17]:= Simplify[Det[ComplexToTrig[%]]]

                 3                 2 L lam
Out[17]= (-4 I lam  (-Cos[L lam] + E        Cos[L lam] -

                         2 L lam           L lam
             Sin[L lam] - E        Sin[L lam])) / E
```

Those real roots of this expression will determine the eigenvalues for the hinged-clamped bar. In order to better see where these roots lie, we need only examine the numerator of this expression. We multiply the numerator by i and then simplify it so that we have only a real-valued expression with which to contend:

```
In[18]:= Simplify[I Numerator[%]]

             3                 2 L lam
Out[18]= 4 lam  (-Cos[L lam] + E        Cos[L lam] - Sin[L lam] -

              2 L lam
             E        Sin[L lam])
```

The `Numerator[]` function conveniently returns the numerator of an expression.

Finally, we extract the third term from this last result (since the `4 lam^3` will only introduce a trivial root) and assign it to the variable `eigeneq`:

```
In[19]:= eigeneq = %[[3]]

                        2 L lam
Out[19]= -Cos[L lam] + E        Cos[L lam] - Sin[L lam] -
```

```
        2 L lam
       E         Sin[L lam]
```

Our first attack is to see what roots *Mathematica* can extract directly from this:

```
In[20]:= Solve[eigeneq == 0, lam]

        Solve::ifun:
            Warning: Inverse functions are being used by Solve, so
                some solutions may not be found.

Out[20]= {}
```

The empty list of Out[20] together with the warning message indicates that *Mathematica* found no roots.   Since the equation must have real roots, we try

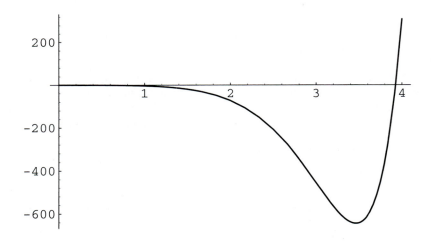

FIGURE 15.3
The first zero of this curve corresponds to the fundamental eigenvalue of the the hinged-clamped bar.

a graphical solution to see where they might be. In order to do this, we need to specify a value for *L*, and so we set it equal to 1 and plot the result:

```
In[21]:= Plot[eigeneq /. L -> 1, {lam, 0, 4}]

Out[21]= -Graphics-
```

As shown in Fig. 15.3, the first root appears for $3 < \lambda < 4$. This give us enough information to use the `FindRoot[]` function to estimate the eigenvalue:

```
In[22]:= FindRoot[(eigeneq /. L -> 1) == 0, {lam, 3.5}]

Out[22]= {lam -> 3.9266}
```

and we see that $\lambda = 3.9266$. We substitute this value of λ back into the boundary conditions and attempt to solve for non-trivial values of the coefficients:

```
In[23]:= Solve[BC2 /. %, coeffs]

Out[23]= {{C[1] -> 0, C[2] -> 0, C[3] -> 0, C[4] -> 0}}
```

Unfortunately, *Mathematica* reports only the trivial solution. What happened? Since we used the `FindRoot[]` function to determine the eigenvalue, the result was only approximate—not exact. Therefore, when we substituted this value back into the boundary conditions, the resulting system was still non-singular, and so *Mathematica* returned the trivial solution.

In order to work around this difficulty, we will have to partially manipulate the boundary conditions by hand. First, we substitute $L = 1$ and $\lambda = 3.9266$ into BC2:

```
In[24]:= BC2 /. L -> 1 /. %%

Out[24]= {C[1] + C[2] + C[3] + C[4] == 0,

          0.0197105 C[1] + (-0.707381 + 0.706832 I) C[2] +

          (-0.707381 - 0.706832 I) C[3] + 50.7343 C[4] == 0,

          15.4182 C[1] - 15.4182 C[2] - 15.4182 C[3] +

          15.4182 C[4] == 0, -0.0773954 C[1] +

          (2.77545 + 2.77761 I) C[2] +

          (2.77545 - 2.77761 I) C[3] + 199.213 C[4] == 0}
```

Next, we solve the first and third equation of this system for `C[1]` and `C[2]`:

```
In[25]:= Solve[{%24[[1]], %24[[3]]}, {C[1], C[2]}]

Out[25]= {{C[1] -> -0.5 (C[3] + C[4]) -

                  0.0324292 (-15.4182 C[3] + 15.4182 C[4]),

            C[2] -> -0.5 (C[3] + C[4]) +

                  0.0324292 (-15.4182 C[3] + 15.4182 C[4])}}
```

Now, we substitute this result into the second and fourth equations of BC2:

```
In[26]:= reduceset = {%24[[2]] /. %, %24[[4]] /. %}

Out[26]= {{(-0.707381 - 0.706832 I) C[3] + 50.7343 C[4] +

                  0.0197105 (-0.5 (C[3] + C[4]) -

                      0.0324292 (-15.4182 C[3] + 15.4182 C[4])) +

                  (-0.707381 + 0.706832 I)

                  (-0.5 (C[3] + C[4]) +

                      0.0324292 (-15.4182 C[3] + 15.4182 C[4])) == 0},

            {(2.77545 - 2.77761 I) C[3] + 199.213 C[4] -

                  0.0773954 (-0.5 (C[3] + C[4]) -

                      0.0324292 (-15.4182 C[3] + 15.4182 C[4])) +

                  (2.77545 + 2.77761 I)

                  (-0.5 (C[3] + C[4]) +

                      0.0324292 (-15.4182 C[3] + 15.4182 C[4])) == 0}}
```

Now we solve the first equation for one of the remaining variables. In this case we solve for C[3]:

```
In[27]:= Solve[reduceset[[1]], C[3]]

Out[27]:= {{C[3] -> (0. - 35.8746 I) C[4]}}
```

We can now eliminate C[3] from our expressions for C[1] and C[2]:

```
In[28]:= %25 /. %27

Out[28]= {{{C[1] -> (-1. + 0. I) C[4],

            C[2] -> (0. + 35.8746 I) C[4]}}}
```

Finally, having expressed all our constants in terms of C[4], we can eliminate all but one constant from the eigenfunction:

```
In[29]:= g[x] /. %22 /. %27 /. %28

              (-1. + 0. I) C[4]                           -3.9266 I x
Out[29]= {{{------------------- + (0. + 35.8746 I) E              C[4] -
                  3.9266 x
                 E

                               3.9266 I x           3.9266 x
                (0. + 35.8746 I) E          C[4] + E          C[4]}}}
```

We strip away the brackets:

```
In[30]:= fundmode = %[[1,1,1]]

            (-1. + 0. I) C[4]                      -3.9266 I x
Out[30]= ------------------- + (0. + 35.8746 I) E          C[4] -
                3.9266 x
               E

                             3.9266 I x           3.9266 x
              (0. + 35.8746 I) E          C[4] + E          C[4]
```

Now we factor out the C[4] and simplify:

```
In[31]:= fundmode = Simplify[ComplexToTrig[Apart[%, C[4]]]]

            -1. C[4]          3.9266 x
Out[31]= --------- + 1. E          C[4] + 71.7491 C[4] Sin[3.9266 x]
            3.9266 x
           E
```

In order to see the shape of this mode, we set C[4] to any value (in this case, 1) and use the Plot[] function to sketch it over the interval $0 \leq x \leq 1$:

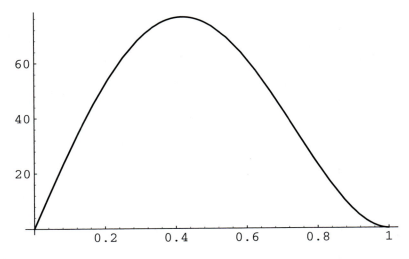

FIGURE 15.4
Fundamental mode of the hinged-clamped bar.

```
In[32]:= Plot[fundmode /. C[4] -> 1 , {x,0,1}]

Out[32]= -Graphics-
```

The result of this command is shown in Fig. 15.4. The behavior of the clamped boundary is easily seen at the right end of the interval.

15.6 EXAMINING MANY EIGENVALUES

We turn now to the problem of obtaining many eigenvalues. In many cases, some careful manipulation of the expression for the eigenvalues is required. For example, suppose we wish to determine the first five eigenvalues for the hinged-clamped bar. Recall from Fig. 15.3 that the magnitude of the expression plotted grew exponentially with λ. This can make a graphical analysis impossible, since scaling requirements may render some zeroes impossible to see. To work around this difficulty, we scale the expression for the eigenvalues, eigeneq, by a factor of $\exp(2L\lambda)$, which ensures that its magnitude remains bounded. We then plot the result:

```
In[33]:= eigeneq = eigeneq / Exp[2 L lam]

                         2 L lam
Out[33]= (-Cos[L lam] + E        Cos[L lam] - Sin[L lam] -
```

```
         2 L lam                    2 L lam
    E              Sin[L lam]) / E

In[34]:= Plot[eigeneq /. L -> 1, {lam, 0, 20}]

Out[34]= -Graphics-
```

We can now easily see the approximate location of all the eigenvalues for $\lambda < 20$,

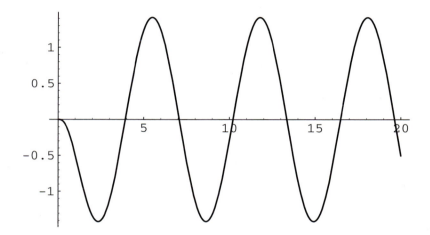

FIGURE 15.5
Zeroes of this curve correspond to the eigenvalues of the hinged-clamped bar.

as shown in Fig. 15.5. To determine accurate estimates for all these eigenvalues, we will use the Do[] function to build a procedure to iteratively use FindRoot[] to build a list of the eigenvalues. First, we initialize two quantities: root is our initial guess and eiglist2 will be our list of eigenvalues:

```
In[35]:= root = 3.5; eiglist2 = {}

Out[35]= {}
```

Now, we build the procedure. FindRoot[] is called to find the first root, and the result, stored in the variable result is appended to the list with the AppendTo[] function. We then update the estimate of the location of the next eigenvalue by adding 4 to the value just found. (This insight was obtained by studying the graphical solution.) The `Do[]` function executes the procedure five times, at the end of which `eiglist2` contains the first five eigenvalues:[4]

```
In[36]:= Do[{result = FindRoot[(eigeneq /. L -> 1) == 0,
                                {lam, root}];
              AppendTo[eiglist2, result[[1, 2]]];
              root = 4 + lam /. result}, {i, 1, 5}]
```

We also build a list of the eigenvalues for the hinged-hinged bar. Recall that $\lambda = n\pi$. This list is easily built with the `Table[]` function:

```
In[37]:= eiglist1 = Table[n Pi, {n, 1, 5}]

Out[37]= {Pi, 2 Pi, 3 Pi, 4 Pi, 5 Pi}
```

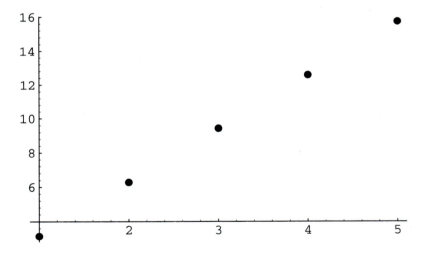

FIGURE 15.6
First five eigenvalues of the hinged-hinged bar.

These eigenvalues can be plotted with the `ListPlot[]` function. The `Plot-Style` option is used to change the size of the plotted points, as can be seen in Fig. 15.6.

---

[4]Notice the use of the ; operator in the `Do[]` body. This prevents the output from these particular commands from being listed to the screen.

```
In[38]:= ListPlot[eiglist1, PlotStyle -> PointSize[0.02]]

Out[38]= -Graphics-
```

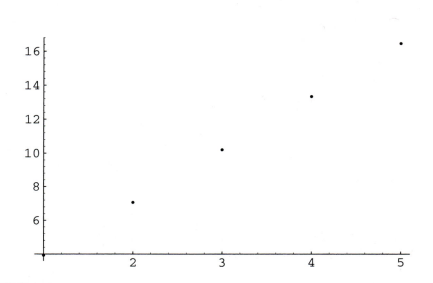

FIGURE 15.7
First five eigenvalues of the clamped-clamped bar.

A similar command is used to plot the eigenvalues of the hinged-clamped bar and this plot is shown in Fig. 15.7:

```
In[39]:= ListPlot[eiglist2]

Out[39]= -Graphics-
```

Finally, we can use the **Show**[] function to overlay the two plots. We use two plotting options, **Frame** and **GridLines**, to enhance the visibility of our result, shown in Fig. 15.8:

```
In[40]:= Show[%, %%, Frame -> True, GridLines -> Automatic]

Out[40]= -Graphics-
```

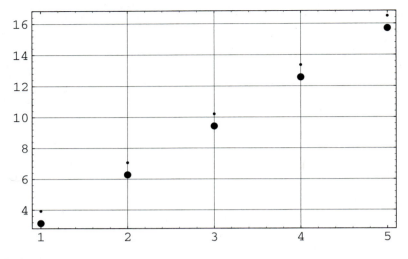

FIGURE 15.8
First five eigenvalues of both the hinged-hinged and clamped-clamped bars.

Note that the eigenvalues of the hinged-clamped bar appear to be shifted up by a uniform amount over the equivalent eigenvalues of the hinged-hinged bar. As we observed earlier, since the vibration frequencies are proportional to the square of the eigenvalues, we can see that the harmonic structure—the distribution of vibration frequencies—is substantially different in these two cases. This is one way in which to see that changing just one boundary condition in this type of problem can drastically alter the quantitative and qualitative nature of solutions.

EXERCISES

15.1. Determine the fundamental mode for the cantilevered bar (assume that $L = 1$). Compare the fundamental frequency to that of the other two bars. Which is highest? Which is lowest?

15.2. Determine the fundamental mode for a clamped-clamped bar (assume that $L = 1$.)

15.3. What would the length of a cantilevered bar have to be in order to have the same fundamental frequency of the hinged-hinged bar discussed in the text?

15.4. Determine the shape of the second mode of the cantilevered bar.

CHAPTER
16

THE VIBRATING ANNULUS

16.1 LABORATORY GOALS

a. To determine the characteristic frequencies of a vibrating annular membrane.

b. To employ the `BesselJ[]` and `BesselY[]` functions for the computation of Bessel functions of different orders.

c. To use the `CylindricalPlot3D[]` function to plot modal surfaces of a vibrating annulus.

16.2 DESCRIPTION OF THE ANNULUS

Consider the annular membrane whose cross section is shown in Fig. 16.1.

Assuming that the membrane is of uniform composition and under uniform tension, the partial differential equation which governs the small-amplitude vibrations of this membrane is, in cylindrical coordinates,

$$(1/c^2)u_{tt} = u_{rr} + (1/r)u_r + (1/r^2)u_{\theta\theta}, \tag{16.1}$$

where $u(r, \theta, t)$ represents the height of the membrane above or below its equilibrium position and c represents the speed of vibrations in the membrane. The boundary conditions are given by

$$u(a, \theta, t) = u(b, \theta, t) = 0, \tag{16.2}$$

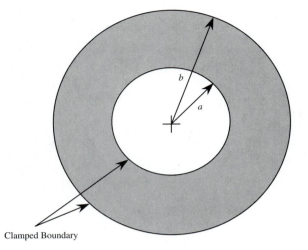

FIGURE 16.1
Annulus with clamped edges.

which indicated that the membrane is clamped along its inner and outer edge. The initial condition is given as $u(r,\theta,0) = f(r,\theta)$. Suppose the inner radius $a = 2$ and the outer radius $b = 4$. In addition, if we take the wave speed $c = 1$,[1] what statements can we make about the eigenfrequencies and eigenmodes of this membrane as it vibrates?

16.3 SEPARATION OF VARIABLES SOLUTION

By assuming solutions of the form $u(r,\theta,t) = \phi(r,\theta)G(t)$, Eq. 16.1 is reduced to the following pair of equations:

$$\phi_{rr} + (1/r)\phi_r + (1/r^2)\phi_{\theta\theta} + \lambda\phi = 0, \tag{16.3}$$

and

$$G''(t) + \lambda G(t) = 0. \tag{16.4}$$

The boundary conditions also become $\phi(a,\theta) = \phi(b,\theta) = 0$.

A further assumption is made concerning the form of ϕ: that $\phi(r,\theta) = R(r)\Theta(\theta)$. When this result is substituted into Eq. 16.3, we obtain two more ordinary differential equations:

$$r^2 R''(r) + r R'(r) + (\lambda r^2 + \mu)R(r) = 0, \tag{16.5}$$

which is a parametric Bessel's equation, and

$$\Theta''(\theta) + \mu\Theta(\theta) = 0. \tag{16.6}$$

---

[1]The problem can always be rescaled to make this so.

This assumption results in the explicit boundary conditions $R(a) = R(b) = 0$ and the implicit condition that Θ possess 2π-periodicity. The latter condition on Θ demands that

$$\mu = m^2, \quad m = 0, 1, 2, \ldots \tag{16.7}$$

. The solution to the radial portion of the problem is

$$R(r) = c_1 J_m(\sqrt{\lambda_{mn}} r) + c_2 Y_m(\sqrt{\lambda_{mn}} r), \tag{16.8}$$

where J_m and Y_m are the Bessel functions of the first and second kind respectively of order m. (Note that we now double-index λ.) Imposition of the boundary conditions at $a = 2$ and $b = 4$ results in the following pair of equations:

$$c_1 J_m(2\sqrt{\lambda_{mn}}) + c_2 Y_m(2\sqrt{\lambda_{mn}}) = 0, \tag{16.9}$$

and

$$c_1 J_m(4\sqrt{\lambda_{mn}}) + c_2 Y_m(4\sqrt{\lambda_{mn}}) = 0. \tag{16.10}$$

In order to have non-trivial solutions for c_1 and c_2, it is necessary and sufficient that

$$J_m(2\sqrt{\lambda_{mn}})Y_m(4\sqrt{\lambda_{mn}}) - J_m(4\sqrt{\lambda_{mn}})Y_m(2\sqrt{\lambda_{mn}}) = 0. \tag{16.11}$$

The roots of Eq. 16.11 will correspond to the eigenvalues.

16.4 DETERMINATION OF THE EIGENVALUES

In order to find values for the four lowest eigenvalues, we first use *Mathematica* to provide a graphical solution to Eq. 16.11. The function to be plotted is first determined by passing the coefficient matrix to `Det`:

```
In[1]:= a = Det[{{BesselJ[n, 2 lam], BesselY[n, 2 lam]},
            {BesselJ[n, 4 lam], BesselY[n, 4 lam]}}]

Out[1]= -(BesselJ[n, 4 lam] BesselY[n, 2 lam]) +
            BesselJ[n, 2 lam] BesselY[n, 4 lam]
```

The arguments of `BesselJ[]` and `BesselY[]` are identical. The first is the order, and the second is the independent variable.

In order to be sure that the *first* four eigenvalues are found, it is not enough to look for the first four zeroes of Eq. 16.11 when $m = 0$. We also need to check the zeroes when $m = 1, 2, 3$ as well. This is done with the following call to `Plot[]`:

```
In[2] := Plot[{a /. n -> 0, a /. n -> 1,
           a /. n -> 2, a /. n -> 3}, {lam, 0.1, 4}]

Out[2]= -Graphics-
```

`Plot[]` is passed a list built up by successively substituting incremented values of the index. [2]

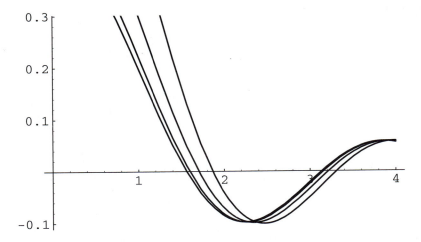

FIGURE 16.2
Graphical solution of Eq. 16.11 for values of $m = 0, 1, 2, 3$ and $0 < \sqrt{\lambda_{mn}} < 4$.

In Fig. 16.2, the first four roots correspond to the order of the increasing index m. Since all roots are less than 2, we can use the `FindRoot[]` function to generate numerical approximation to these roots. In this example, we use the `Table[]` function to generate the four roots:

```
In[3]:= eigs = Table[FindRoot[a /. n -> i, {lam, 2}], {i, 0, 3}]

Out[3]= {{lam -> 1.56152}, {lam -> 1.59829}, {lam -> 1.70346},
         {lam -> 1.86444}}
```

These results correspond to the four smallest values of $\sqrt{\lambda_{mn}}$. The eigenfrequencies can then be determined from the relation $f_{mn} = \sqrt{\lambda_{mn}}/(2\pi c)$.

[2]Note that since Y_m is undefined at the origin, the plotting domain begins at 0.1.

16.5   SKETCHING THE EIGENMODES

In order to determine the appearance of the fourth eigenmode, we must first return to Eq. 16.8 and eliminate one of the arbitrary constants. This can be done, of course, since the values of $\sqrt{\lambda_{mn}}$ found above are precisely those that make the system represented by Eqs. 16.9 and 16.10 have nontrivial solutions. In particular, for the fourth eigenvalue ($m = 3$ and $n = 1$),

$$c_1/c_2 = -Y_3(\sqrt{4\lambda_{31}})/J_3(\sqrt{4\lambda_{31}}), \tag{16.12}$$

which is represented in *Mathematica* with

```
In[4]:= b = - BesselY[3, 4 lam /. eigs[[4]]] /
           BesselJ[3, 4 lam /. eigs[[4]]]

Out[4]= 0.674072
```

The mode function ϕ is then given by

$$\phi = \cos(3\theta)[(c_1/c_2)J_3(\sqrt{\lambda_{31}}r) + Y_3(\sqrt{\lambda_{31}}r)]. \tag{16.13}$$

This is set up in *Mathematica* with the following:

```
In[5]:= phi = Cos[3 th] (b BesselJ[3, r lam /. eigs[[4]]] +
               BesselY[3, r lam /. eigs[[4]]])

Out[5]= (0.674072 BesselJ[3, 1.86444 r] + BesselY[3, 1.86444 r])
        Cos[3 th]
```

In order to visualize this result, we need to load the package `ParametricPlot3D`:

```
In[6]:= <<Graphics`ParametricPlot3D`
```

The `CylindricalPlot3D[]` function presents a very nice rendition of ϕ.[3] It is called with the same type of arguments as `Plot3D`:

```
In[7]:= CylindricalPlot3D[2 phi, {r, 2, 4}, {th, 0, 2 Pi},
             PlotPoints -> 25]

Out[7]= -Graphics3D-
```

---

[3]Note that we have scaled the amplitude of ϕ by a factor of 2. This improves the visibility of the surface features. We have also asked for more resolutions with the `PlotPoints` option.

Note that the surface features can clearly be seen in Fig. 16.3. By changing

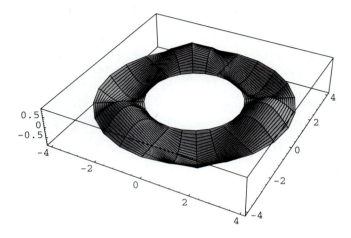

FIGURE 16.3
Perspective view of the fourth eigenmode of the annulus.

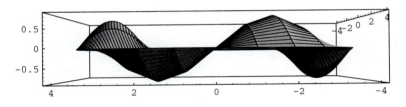

FIGURE 16.4
Side view of the fourth eigenmode of the annulus.

the viewpoint, we can also verify that the clamped boundary conditions have indeed been satisfied:

```
In[8]:= Show[%, ViewPoint->{0.030, 2.960, -0.030}]

Out[8]= -Graphics3D-
```

This result is displayed in Fig. 16.4, in which it is readily seen that clamped boundary conditions along the inner and outer radii have been satisfied.

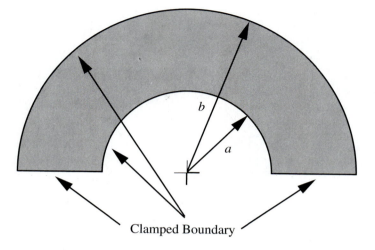

FIGURE 16.5
Half annulus for Exercise 2; $a = 2$ and $b = 4$.

EXERCISES

16.1. Determine the first four vibration frequencies if the inner boundary condition is changed to $u_r(a, \theta) = 0$. (This is called a free boundary.) Sketch each mode. Discuss differences between this result and the one presented in the text.

16.2. Determine the first four vibration frequencies for the half-annulus shown in Fig. 16.5. Sketch the fourth mode.

16.3. Consider a second annulus with inner radius $a = 4$. What would the outer radius have to be in order to ensure that the fundamental frequency of this annulus matches the one discussed in the text?

16.4. Compare the eigenfrequencies of the annular membrane to those of a rectangular membrane of similar dimensions. In what ways are the structure of the two spectra similar?

CHAPTER
17

APPROXIMATING
EIGENVALUES

17.1 LABORATORY GOALS

a. To use difference equations to estimate eigenvalues of a boundary value problem.

b. To use the `Table[]` and `If[]` functions to construct a tridiagonal matrix of arbitrary size.

17.2 MOTIVATION

As seen in Chapters 15 and 16, the eigenvalues of a boundary value problem are extremely useful to the engineer seeking to understand the behavior of complicated systems. The examples presented so far assume that an analytical representation of the eigenfunctions can be found. The search for eigenvalues is then reduced to finding the roots of certain complicated transcendental equations. In many cases, the boundary-value problem may not yield a solution in terms of known functions. In such an instance, an approximation method for estimating eigenvalues, especially the lowest few, is needed. One such method involves the use of difference equations.

17.3 USING DIFFERENCE EQUATIONS

Consider the Sturm-Liouville boundary value problem

$$y'' + \lambda y = 0, \tag{17.1}$$

with $y(0) = y(1) = 0$. The eigenvalues for this problem are well known: $\lambda_n = n^2\pi^2, n = 1, 2, \ldots$, and the eigenfunctions are $y_n(x) = c_n \sin\sqrt{\lambda_n}x$. To illustrate the method of difference equations, we first note that the second derivative term is equal to the following limit:

$$y'' = \lim_{h \to 0} \frac{y(x-h) - 2y(x) + y(x+h)}{h^2}. \tag{17.2}$$

If h is small enough, then the second derivative can be approximated by the difference quotient on the right-hand side of Eq. (17.2).

Suppose now we let $h = 1/2$. Divide the interval $0 \leq x \leq 1$ into two halves, and let $x_0 = 0$, $x_1 = 1/2$, and $x_2 = 0$, and if we let $y(x_j) = y_j$, we can write Eq. (17.1) as:

$$\frac{y_0 - 2y_1 + y_2}{1/4} + \lambda y_1 = 0. \tag{17.3}$$

Using the fact that $y_0 = y(0) = 0$ and $y_2 = y(x_2) = 0$, the equation reduces to

$$(8 - \lambda)y_1 = 0. \tag{17.4}$$

This method predicts that the lowest eigenvalue is $\lambda = 8$, while the true value is π^2. To increase the accuracy of the method, we choose a smaller step size. This time, choose $h = 1/3$, so that we are using the difference approximation on a mesh of 4 points. This time, we are led to a pair of equations:

$$\frac{y_0 - 2y_1 + y_2}{1/9} + \lambda y_1 = 0, \tag{17.5}$$

$$\frac{y_1 - 2y_2 + y_3}{1/9} + \lambda y_2 = 0. \tag{17.6}$$

Using our boundary conditions, this reduces to

$$\frac{-2y_1 + y_2}{1/9} + \lambda y_1 = 0, \tag{17.7}$$

$$\frac{y_1 - 2y_2}{1/9} + \lambda y_2 = 0. \tag{17.8}$$

This can be written in matrix form as

$$\begin{bmatrix} -2 + \lambda/9 & 1 \\ 1 & -2 + \lambda/9 \end{bmatrix} \begin{bmatrix} y_1 \\ y_2 \end{bmatrix} = \begin{bmatrix} 0 \\ 0 \end{bmatrix} \tag{17.9}$$

In order for this system to have non-trivial solutions, the coefficient matrix must be singular. This provides a way of determining the eigenvalues. We enter the coefficients as a 2x2 matrix in *Mathematica*:

```
In[1]:= a = {{-2 + lam / 9, 1}, {1, -2 + lam / 9}}

            lam                    lam
Out[1]= {{-2 + ---, 1}, {1, -2 + ---}}
             9                      9
```

We set the determinant, taken with the `Det[]` function, equal to zero and use `Solve[]` to find the admissible values of λ:

```
In[2]:= Solve[Det[a] == 0, lam]

Out[2]= {{lam -> 9}, {lam -> 27}}
```

The smaller root is an improved approximation to the first eigenvalue, while the larger root is a first approximation to the second eigenvalue.

If we extend this process to a mesh of five points, so that $h = 1/4$, we obtain the following coefficient matrix:

$$a = \begin{bmatrix} -2 + \lambda/16 & 1 & 0 \\ 1 & -2 + \lambda/16 & 1 \\ 0 & 1 & -2 + \lambda/16 \end{bmatrix}. \tag{17.10}$$

We enter the following *Mathematica* expression:

```
In[3]:= a = {{-2 + lam / 16, 1, 0}, {1, -2 + lam / 16, 1},
             {0, 1, -2 + lam / 16}}

               lam                    lam                    lam
Out[3]= {{-2 + ---, 1, 0}, {1, -2 + ---, 1}, {0, 1, -2 + ---}}
               16                     16                     16
```

and then use `Det[]` and `Solve[]` to determine the approximate eigenvalues:

```
In[4]:= Solve[Det[a] == 0, lam]

                                    64 - 32 Sqrt[2]
Out[4]= {{lam -> 32}, {lam -> ---------------},
                                          2

                64 + 32 Sqrt[2]
      {lam -> ---------------}}
                      2
```

We can get a clearer picture of the results by converting then to decimal form using `N[]`:

```
In[5]:= N[%]

Out[5]= {{lam -> 32.}, {lam -> 9.37258}, {lam -> 54.6274}}
```

The Sort[] function will put this list in ascending order:

```
In[6]:= Sort[%]

Out[6]= {{lam -> 9.37258}, {lam -> 32.}, {lam -> 54.6274}}
```

We can see three eigenvalue approximations in this result. Our estimate for the lowest has improved even more, our estimate for the second has improved, although it is still not very good, while the third result gives a first estimate for the third eigenvalue.

17.4 GENERATING THE COEFFICIENT MATRIX

We can continue this procedure indefinitely, obtaining better and better estimates for the eigenvalues, but the entry of the elements of the coefficient matrix can become unwieldly. We note the special structure of the coefficient matrix for $h = 1/n$, so that there are $n + 1$ mesh points: coefficient matrix:

$$a = \begin{bmatrix} -2 + \lambda/n^2 & 1 & 0 & 0 & \cdots \\ 1 & -2 + \lambda/n^2 & 1 & 0 & \cdots \\ \vdots & \vdots & \ddots & \vdots & \vdots \\ \cdots & 1 & -2 + \lambda/n^2 & 1 & 0 \\ \cdots & 0 & 0 & 1 & -2 + \lambda/n^2 \end{bmatrix}. \qquad (17.11)$$

The coefficient matrix has a *tridiagonal* structure. The diagonals immediately above and below the main diagonal have non-zero entries, while the rest of the matrix has zero entries. We can use the Table[] function together with three If[] statements to build tridiagonal coefficient matrices of any given size. The following function defines a[n] to be an $n \times n$ tridiagonal coefficient matrix:

```
In[7]:= Clear[a]

In[8]:= a[n_] := Table[If[i == j, -2 + lam / (n + 1)^2,
                       If[i == j + 1, 1,
                          If[i == j - 1, 1, 0]]],
                    {i, 1, n}, {j, 1, n}]
```

Note that we first needed to use the Clear[] function to erase the information already stored about that symbol from the previous section. Consider the 5x5 coefficient matrix, which is printed out in standard form with the following command:

```
In[9]:= a[5]//MatrixForm
```

$$
\begin{pmatrix}
-2 + \dfrac{lam}{36} & 1 & 0 & 0 & 0 \\[2ex]
1 & -2 + \dfrac{lam}{36} & 1 & 0 & 0 \\[2ex]
0 & 1 & -2 + \dfrac{lam}{36} & 1 & 0 \\[2ex]
0 & 0 & 1 & -2 + \dfrac{lam}{36} & 1 \\[2ex]
0 & 0 & 0 & 1 & -2 + \dfrac{lam}{36}
\end{pmatrix}
$$

We are now in a position to apply this method to coefficient matrices of arbitrary size. For example, the following command builds a 6x6 coefficient matrix, sets the determinant to zero, uses NSolve[] to find the roots,[1] and sorts the result using Sort[] in ascending order:

```
In[10]:= Sort[NSolve[Det[a[6]] == 0, lam]]

Out[10]= {{lam -> 9.70505}, {lam -> 36.898}, {lam -> 76.1929},

          {lam -> 119.807}, {lam -> 159.102}, {lam -> 186.295}}
```

This procedure can be used to determine eigenvalues to arbitrary degrees of precision. For example, we can examine just the first eigenvalue of the 15x15 coefficient matrix by appending [[1]] to our expression:

```
In[11]:= Sort[NSolve[Det[a[15]] == 0, lam]][[1]]

Out[11]= {lam -> 9.83794}
```

---

[1]Once the matrix is 5x5 or larger, the polynomial obtained by taking the determinant is at least fifth degree. The Solve[] function may not return accurate results in this case. For example, for the 6x6 case, Solve[] yields eigenvalues with very small imaginary parts. The eigenvalues of a Sturm-Liouville boundary value problem are always real.

The relative error of this estimate is less than 0.4%.

17.5 APPLICATION TO VIBRATING STRING

We now apply the method described here for computing the fundamental frequency of a vibrating string with variable mass. In particular, suppose the thickness of a string increases linearly with its length, as suggested in Fig. 17.1. In this

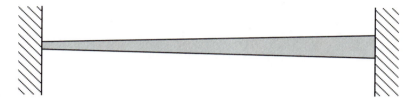

FIGURE 17.1
Vibrating string of variable thickness. Both ends are fixed to solid supports.

case the linear density of the string is assumed to have the form $\rho(x) = \rho_0(1+\alpha x)$, where ρ_0 and α are constants. If the string is under a uniform tension T, the governing wave equation for small amplitude transverse oscillations of the string is

$$u_{tt} = \frac{T}{\rho(x)} u_{xx}. \tag{17.12}$$

We will consider the case in which both ends of the string are fixed to non-moving supports, so that $u(0,t) = u(L,t) = 0$. We assume that $u(x,t) = \phi(x)G(t)$, and apply the method of separation of variables to obtain the following pair of ordinary differential equations:

$$\phi'' + \frac{\rho(x)\lambda}{T}\phi = 0, \tag{17.13}$$

and

$$G'' + \lambda G = 0. \tag{17.14}$$

From the second equation, we see that $G(t) = c_1 \sin(\sqrt{\lambda}t) + c_2 \cos(\sqrt{\lambda}t)$ and so the vibration frequencies are given by $f = \sqrt{\lambda}/(2\pi)$.

Let us suppose that $L = 1$, $T = 1$, $\rho_0 = 1$, and $\alpha = 0.2$. The boundary value problem is then written as

$$\phi'' + (1 + 0.2x)\lambda\phi = 0, \tag{17.15}$$

together with the boundary conditions $\phi(0) = \phi(1) = 0$. If we divide the interval into $n+2$ steps, then $h = 1/(n+1)$, and the difference equations can be written as

$$\phi_{k-1} - 2\phi_k + \phi_{k+1} + \left(1 + 0.2\frac{k}{n+1}\right)\lambda\phi_k = 0, \tag{17.16}$$

for $k = 1, 2, \ldots, n$. These difference equations lead to a tridiagonal coefficient matrix whose determinant must vanish. As before, the values for λ which make this matrix singular will be the approximate eigenvalues.

First, we use the **Table[]** function to define a coefficient matrix of arbitrary size. We use the same approach as in the previous section by modifying the function we had defined for **a[n]** to define a new function **b[n]**:

```
In[12] := b[n_] := Table[If[i == j,
                   -2 + ((1 + 0.2 i / (n + 1))lam /
                             (n + 1)^2),
                 If[i == j + 1, 1 ,
                     If[i == j - 1, 1, 0]]],
               {i, 1, n}, {j, 1, n}]
```

Since we are interested only in the first eigenvalue, we first try **n = 6**:

```
In[13] := Sort[NSolve[Det[b[6]] == 0, lam]][[1]]

Out[13]= {lam -> 8.81941}
```

Is this value of λ reasonable? If the string had a constant linear density $\rho = 1$, then $\lambda = \pi^2 \approx 9.8696$. If the string had a constant linear density $\rho = 1.2$, then $\lambda = \pi^2/1.2 \approx 8.2247$. Since our string has a density that varies between these values, it is reasonable to expect that the eigenvalue should have a value between these two extremes, which is precisely what we find. A more accurate estimate is obtained from a 15x15 coefficient matrix:

```
In[14] := Sort[NSolve[Det[b[15]] == 0, lam]][[1]]

Out[14]= {lam -> 8.94034}
```

We conclude that the fundamental frequency is approximately

```
In[15] := N[Sqrt[lam] / (2 Pi)] /. %

Out[15]= 0.47588
```

EXERCISES

17.1. Determine estimates for the two lowest eigenvalues for the boundary value problem

$$y'' + \lambda y = 0, y(0) = 0, y(1) = 0 \qquad (17.17)$$

for all coefficient matrix sizes from 2x2 through 25x25. Determine the relative error in the approximations and plot this as a function of n. Can you conjecture a rate at which the approximations converge to the true answer? What implications does this have for the practicality of this method? Can you formulate a rule-of-thumb regarding the size of the coefficient matrix required for a given relative error?

17.2. Use the method of difference equations to estimate the first two eigenvalues of the following boundary-value problem:

$$y'' + \lambda y = 0, y(0) = 0, y'(\pi) = 0. \qquad (17.18)$$

Compare your results to the exact eigenvalues. How big must the coefficient matrix be in order to obtain an estimate of the lowest eigenvalue that is accurate to 1%? 0.1%?

17.3. Use the method of difference equations to estimate the first three eigenvalues of the following boundary value problem:

$$y'' + \lambda y = 0, y(0) = 0, y'(1) - y(1) = 0. \qquad (17.19)$$

Compare these results with numerical estimates obtained from the transcendental equation for the eigenvalues. How big must the coefficient matrix be in order to obtain an estimate of the lowest eigenvalue that is accurate to 1%? 0.1%?

FIGURE 17.2
Vibrating rope system. The left half is made of wire and the right half is made of hemp.

17.4. Suppose a wire rope of density 1 kg/m is tied to a hemp rope of density 0.2 kg/m and configured as suggested in Fig. 17.2. If the combination rope is subject to a uniform tension of 100 N, determine the fundamental frequency of the combination rope for small amplitude transverse oscillations.

17.5. The method of difference equations can also be used for higher order equations. See if you can implement this method to determine the eigenvalues for the vibrating bar. In particular, estimate the smallest eigenvalue for

$$y'''' - \lambda^4 y = 0, \qquad (17.20)$$

subject to $y(0) = y''(0) = 0$ and $y(1) = y''(1) = 0$. Compare to the exact result. [Hint: The coefficient matrix will be *pentadiagonal* in this case.]

CHAPTER
18

VECTOR
DIFFERENTIATION

18.1 LABORATORY GOALS

a. To determine the gradient of a scalar function.

b. To determine the divergence and curl of a vector function.

c. To establish vector identities using *Mathematica*.

18.2 THE GRADIENT, DIVERGENCE, AND CURL

Before proceeding further, the `VectorAnalysis` package should be loaded:

```
In[1]:= <<Calculus'VectorAnalysis'
```

The packages just loaded contains three functions which can be used to perform many common vector differentiation operations. The `Grad[]` function can be used to evaluate the gradient of a scalar function of three variables. For example, let $f(x, y, z) = 2xz + z^2 e^y$. Then ∇f is determined as follows:

```
In[2]:= f = 2 x z + z^2 Exp[y]

            y  2
Out[2]= 2 x z + E  z

In[3]:= gradf = Grad[f]

          y  2           y
Out[3]= {2 z, E  z , 2 x + 2 E  z}
```

The components can be picked out as needed. Directional derivatives can now be obtained. For example, suppose we require the rate of change of f in the direction of $2\mathbf{i} + 3\mathbf{j} - \mathbf{k}$ at the point $(2, 1, 1)$. First, define the vector in *Mathematica* and then normalize it:[1]

```
In[4]:= v = {2, 3, -1}

Out[4]= {2, 3, -1}

In[5]:= v = v / Sqrt[v . v]

            2        3            1
Out[5]= {Sqrt[-], --------, -(--------)}
            7      Sqrt[14]    Sqrt[14]
```

Now take the dot product of the gradient with the unit vector using the . operator, and evaluate the result at the point $(2, 1, 1)$:

```
In[6]:= (gradf . v) /. {x -> 2, y -> 1, z -> 1}

              8        3 E      4 + 2 E
Out[6]= Sqrt[-] + -------- - --------
              7    Sqrt[14]   Sqrt[14]

In[7]:= Simplify[%]

            E
Out[7]= --------
         Sqrt[14]
```

And so the result is $e/\sqrt{14}$.

---

[1] That is, we scale it so that it is a unit vector.

The `Div[]` function can be used to find the divergence of a vector function of three variables.[2] For example, let $\mathbf{g} = y\mathbf{i} + 2xz\mathbf{j} + ze^x\mathbf{k}$. The divergence of $\mathbf{g}$ is found as:

```
In[8]:= g = {y, 2 x z, z Exp[x]}

                x
Out[8]= {y, 2 x z, E  z}

In[9]:= Div[g]

          x
Out[9]= E
```

The `Curl[]` function can be used to determine the curl of any three-component vector. For example, applied to $\mathbf{g}$, we obtain:

```
In[10]:= Curl[g]

                  x
Out[10]= {-2 x, -(E  z), -1 + 2 z}
```

Even with functions not explicitly defined, these functions can be used. For example, the familiar identity $\nabla \times \nabla\phi(x, y, z) = 0$ can be verified as follows:

```
In[11]:= Grad[phi[x, y, z]]

               (1,0,0)              (0,1,0)
Out[11]= {phi        [x, y, z], phi        [x, y, z],

               (0,0,1)
          phi        [x, y, z]}

In[12]:= Curl[%]

Out[12]= {0, 0, 0}
```

In `Out[11]`, parenthesized superscripts denote the order of partial differentiation with respect to the first, second, or third variable. In standard mathematical notation, `Out[11]` would be written as

$$\frac{\partial\phi}{\partial x}\mathbf{i} + \frac{\partial\phi}{\partial y}\mathbf{j} + \frac{\partial\phi}{\partial z}\mathbf{k}.$$

---

[2]The `Div[]` function will not work on two-component vectors. If you need a two-dimensional divergence, just set the third component to zero.

18.3 OTHER VECTOR DIFFERENTIATION OPERATORS

In addition to those discussed in the previous section, *Mathematica* also can apply the Laplacian operator and biharmonic operator. For example, to compute the Laplacian of f, $\nabla^2 f$, we use the `Laplacian[]` function:

```
In[13]:= Laplacian[f]

              y    y  2
Out[13]= 2 E    + E   z
```

Let $h = e^x \cos y$. Then $\nabla^2 h$ is found to be

```
In[14]:= h = Exp[x] Cos[y]

            x
Out[14]= E   Cos[y]

In[15]:= Laplacian[h]

Out[15]= 0
```

Recall that $h(x, y)$ is the real part of the analytic function e^z, and so is harmonic, i.e. the Laplacian vanishes.

The biharmonic operator is defined to be the Laplacian of the Laplacian. It is applied with the `Biharmonic[]` function.

```
In[16]:= Biharmonic[f]

              y    y  2
Out[16]= 4 E    + E   z

In[17]:= Laplacian[Laplacian[f]]

              y    y  2
Out[17]= 4 E    + E   z
```

18.4 ESTABLISHING VECTOR IDENTITIES

These operators can be used to establish many useful vector identities that would be extremely tedious to verify by hand. For example, the claim is made that if **F** and **G** are any two differentiable vector fields,

$$\nabla(\mathbf{F} \cdot \mathbf{G}) = (\mathbf{F} \cdot \nabla)\mathbf{G} + (\mathbf{G} \cdot \nabla)\mathbf{F} + \mathbf{F} \times (\nabla \times \mathbf{G}) + \mathbf{G} \times (\nabla \times \mathbf{F}). \qquad (18.1)$$

Before proceeding, we note that $(\mathbf{F} \cdot \nabla)\mathbf{G} = \mathbf{F} \cdot (\nabla\mathbf{G})$ where $\nabla\mathbf{G}$ is represented as a 3×3 matrix.[3] Since we have used the symbols `f` and `g`, we clear them and define our two vectors:[4]

```
In[18]:= Clear[f, g]

In[19]:= F = {F1[x, y, z], F2[x, y, z], F3[x, y, z]}

Out[19]= {F1[x, y, z], F2[x, y, z], F3[x, y, z]}

In[20]:= G = {G1[x, y, z], G2[x, y, z], G3[x, y, z]}

Out[20]= {G1[x, y, z], G2[x, y, z], G3[x, y, z]}

In[21]:= Grad[F]

                (1,0,0)              (0,1,0)
Out[21]= {{F1       [x, y, z], F1       [x, y, z],

              (0,0,1)              (1,0,0)
          F1       [x, y, z]}, {F2       [x, y, z],

              (0,1,0)              (0,0,1)
          F2       [x, y, z], F2       [x, y, z]},

              (1,0,0)              (0,1,0)
         {F3       [x, y, z], F3       [x, y, z],

              (0,0,1)
          F3       [x, y, z]}}
```

This result illustrates the result of taking the gradient of a vector. First, we compute the left-hand side of the identity:

---

[3]Or a tensor of rank two.

[4]When we call `Clear[]`, *Mathematica* forgets all it knows about symbols passed to it as arguments. Had we not done this, *Mathematica* would give us warning messages about possible spelling errors when defining F and G.

```
In[22]:= lhs = Grad[F . G]
```

```
                          (1,0,0)
Out[22]= {G1[x, y, z] F1        [x, y, z] +

                          (1,0,0)
      G2[x, y, z] F2        [x, y, z] +

        .
        .
        .

                          (0,0,1)
      F2[x, y, z] G2        [x, y, z] +

                          (0,0,1)
      F3[x, y, z] G3        [x, y, z]}
```

Note that we have omitted all but the first and last pair of lines in the output expression. Now we determine the right-hand side. The `CrossProduct[]` is called to evaluate cross products. Note that we terminate the expression with the semicolon operator ; in order to suppress the output:

```
In[23]:= rhs = (Grad[G] . F) + (Grad[F] . G) +
         CrossProduct[F, Curl[G]] +
         CrossProduct[G, Curl[F]];
```

Now, we subtract one side from the other and simplify:

```
In[24]:= Simplify[rhs - lhs]

Out[24]= {0, 0, 0}
```

This establishes the result.

EXERCISES

18.1. Compute ∇f and verify that $\nabla \times \nabla f = 0$:
   (a) $f = \cos(x + y + z)$
   (b) $f = 2e^x \log(yz)$
   (c) $f = \sqrt{\sin(x + \cos y)}$

18.2. Compute $\nabla \cdot \mathbf{F}$ and $\nabla \times \mathbf{F}$, and verify that $\nabla \cdot (\nabla \times \mathbf{F}) = \mathbf{0}$.
   (a) $\mathbf{F} = x\mathbf{i} + y\mathbf{j} + 3z\mathbf{k}$

(b) $\mathbf{F} = \sinh x\mathbf{i} + \cosh z\mathbf{j} + y^2\mathbf{j}$ [Hint: Use the *Mathematica* functions `Cosh[]` and `Sinh[]`.]

(c) $\mathbf{F} = J_0(x)\mathbf{i} + J_1(y)\mathbf{j} + J_2(z)\mathbf{k}$ where J_n is the Bessel function of the first kind of order n.

18.3. Let f and g be scalar fields. Prove that

$$\nabla \cdot (\nabla f \times \nabla g) = 0$$

18.4. Let $\mathbf{F}$ and $\mathbf{G}$ be vector fields. Prove that

$$\nabla \times (\mathbf{F} \times \mathbf{G}) = (\mathbf{G} \cdot \nabla \mathbf{F}) - (\mathbf{F} \cdot \nabla \mathbf{G}) + (\nabla \cdot \mathbf{G})\mathbf{F} - (\nabla \cdot \mathbf{F})\mathbf{G}.$$

18.5. Verify that

$$f = \tan^{-1}\left(\frac{2y}{x^2 + y^2 - 1}\right)$$

is a solution to Laplace's equation $\nabla^2 f = 0$.

18.6. Suppose the temperature along the surface of a metal plate is given by $T(x, y) = 90 - x^2 - 3y^2$. An insect, located at $(x, y) = (0, 1)$, travels along a path which lowers its temperature as quickly as possible. Along what direction will the insect set out?

CHAPTER
19

COORDINATE
SYSTEMS

19.1 LABORATORY GOALS

a. To use *Mathematica* to convert among various coordinate systems.
b. To perform vector algebra in cylindrical and spherical coordinates.
c. To perform vector differentiation in cylindrical and spherical coordinates.

19.2 SETTING THE COORDINATE SYSTEM

Before proceeding further, the **VectorAnalysis** package should be loaded:

```
In[1]:= <<Calculus'VectorAnalysis'
```

The current coordinate system can be checked by evaluating the **Coordinate-System** variable:

```
In[2]:= CoordinateSystem

Out[2]= Cartesian
```

By default, the coordinate system is cartesian. The default names of the individual coordinate system are given by invoking the `Coordinates[]` function with no arguments:

```
In[3]:= Coordinates[]

Out[3]= {x, y, z}
```

The default coordinate system can be changed with the `SetCoordinates[]` function. Here we change the default system to cylindrical coordinates by passing the `Cylindrical` keyword as the argument:

```
In[4]:= SetCoordinates[Cylindrical]

Out[4]= Cylindrical[r, theta, z]
```

The ranges of the coordinates can be obtained with the `Coordinate Ranges[]` function:

```
In[5]:= CoordinateRanges[]

Out[5]= {Inequality[0, LessEqual, r, Less, Infinity],

         Inequality[-Pi, Less, theta, LessEqual, Pi],

         -Infinity < z < Infinity}
```

The next two calls change the coordinate system to spherical coordinates and list the coordinate ranges for the spherical coordinate system. Note our use of the `Spherical` keyword:

```
In[6]:= SetCoordinates[Spherical]

Out[6]= Spherical[r, theta, phi]

In[7]:= CoordinateRanges[]

Out[7]= {Inequality[0, LessEqual, r, Less, Infinity],

             0 <= theta <= Pi, Inequality[-Pi, Less, phi, LessEqual,

         Pi]}
```

Mathematica can also handle many other three-dimensional coordinate systems.[1] A complete list is provided in Table 19.1.

TABLE 19.1
Coordinate systems available in *Mathematica*.

Bipolar	EllipticCylindrical
Bispherical	OblateSpheroidal
Cartesian	ParabolicCylindrical
ConfocalEllipsoidal	Paraboloidal
ConfocalParaboloidal	ProlateSpheroidal
Conical	Spherical
Cylindrical	Toroidal

19.3 CHANGING COORDINATES

Mathematica also provides a function for mapping coordinates between systems. For example, consider the spherical coordinate $(\rho, \theta, \phi) = (5, \pi/2, \pi)$. This point is located five units from the origin, and the polar angle is $\pi/2$ so that point lies in the xy-plane. Finally, the azimuthal angle is π, and so the point must lie on the x-axis. The result is therefore $(x, y, z) = (-5, 0, 0)$. The CoordinatesTo-Cartesian[] function does this conversion from the default coordinate system:

```
In[8]:= CoordinatesToCartesian[{5, Pi/2, Pi}]

Out[8]= {-5, 0, 0}
```

A companion function, CoordinatesFromCartesian[] converts a given cartesian coordinate into the default coordinate system.

```
In[9]:= CoordinatesFromCartesian[{3, 3, 4}]

                         8       Pi
Out[9]= {Sqrt[34], ArcCos[Sqrt[--]], --}
                        17       4
```

This function also handles symbolic entries. Thus, to obtain the formulas for computing the spherical coordinates in terms of x, y, and z, we give the following command:

---

[1]Two-dimensional coordinate systems are easily handled by using the appropriate cylindrical version in three dimensions and setting the z-coordinate to zero.

```
In[10]:= CoordinatesFromCartesian[{x, y, z}]

                  2    2    2                        z
Out[10]= {Sqrt[x  + y  + z ], ArcCos[------------------],
                                         2    2    2
                                      Sqrt[x  + y  + z ]

         ArcTan[x, y]}
```

By specifying a coordinate system as an additional argument, either of these two functions can change to or from cartesian coordinates from other systems. For example, this calculation gives the conversion from cylindrical coordinates to spherical coordinates:

```
In[11]:= CoordinatesFromCartesian[
            CoordinatesToCartesian[{r, theta, z}, Cylindrical]]

                  2    2           2    2            2
Out[11]= {Sqrt[z  + r  Cos[theta]  + r  Sin[theta] ],

                                     z
         ArcCos[---------------------------------------------],
                      2    2           2    2            2
                Sqrt[z  + r  Cos[theta]  + r  Sin[theta] ]

         ArcTan[r Cos[theta], r Sin[theta]]}
```

19.4 VECTOR MULTIPLICATION IN OTHER SYSTEMS

The DotProduct[] and CrossProduct[] functions[2] will operate correctly in other coordinate systems. For example, let us set the default system to cylindrical coordinates:

```
In[12]:= SetCoordinates[Cylindrical]

Out[12]= Cylindrical[r, theta, z]
```

Let us compute the dot product of the two vectors $\mathbf{r}_1$ and $\mathbf{r}_2$:

---

[2]These were introduced in Chapter 2.

```
In[13]:= r1 = {2, 0, 2}

Out[13]= {2, 0, 2}

In[14]:= r2 = {1, Pi, 1}

Out[14]= {1, Pi, 1}

In[15]:= DotProduct[r1, r2]

Out[15]= 0
```

Evidently the `DotProduct[]` function is not doing the computation in cartesian coordinates! In cartesian coordinates, these two vectors would be written as $\mathbf{r}_1 = (2, 0, 2)$ and $\mathbf{r}_2 = (-1, 0, 1)$. These two vectors are obviously orthogonal.

Cross products in cylindrical coordinates are computed correctly also. For example, in cylindrical coordinates, the unit vectors $\mathbf{i}$ and $\mathbf{j}$ are expressed as $(1, 0, 0)$ and $(1, \pi/2, 0)$ respectively. Computing their cross product yields:

```
In[16]:= CrossProduct[{1, 0, 0}, {1, Pi/2, 0}]

Out[16]= {0, 0, 1}
```

which corresponds to $\mathbf{k}$, the correct result.

Another coordinate system can be used with either of these functions without resetting the default coordinate system. For example, in spherical coordinates, $\mathbf{i} = (1, \pi/2, 0)$, while $\mathbf{j} = (1, \pi/2, \pi/2)$. The function `CrossProduct[]` is invoked with the keyword `Spherical` as the last argument:

```
In[17]:= CrossProduct[{1, Pi/2, 0}, {1, Pi/2, Pi/2}, Spherical]

Out[17]= {1, 0, 0}
```

This last result corresponds to the vector $\mathbf{k}$.

19.5   VECTOR DIFFERENTIATION IN OTHER SYSTEMS

The gradient, divergence, and curl are all straightforward to determine in alternate coordinate systems. For example, let $u = r^2 z^4 \sin 2\theta$ and $\mathbf{v} = z^2 \mathbf{e}_r + 2\mathbf{e}_\theta + r\mathbf{e}_z$ where $\mathbf{e}_r$, $\mathbf{e}_\theta$, and $\mathbf{e}_z$ are the unit vectors in cylindrical coordinates.

```
In[18]:= u = r^3 z^4 Sin[2 theta]

           3  4
Out[18]= r   z  Sin[2 theta]

In[19]:= Grad[u]

              2  4                  2  4
Out[19]= {3 r   z  Sin[2 theta], 2 r   z  Cos[2 theta],

             3  3
          4 r   z  Sin[2 theta]}
```

Thus, $\nabla u = 3r^2 z^4 \sin 2\theta \mathbf{e}_r + 2r^2 z^4 \cos 2\theta \mathbf{e}_\theta + 4r^3 z^3 \sin 2\theta \mathbf{e}_z$. Also,

```
In[20]:= v = {z^2, 2, r}

            2
Out[20]= {z , 2, r}

In[21]:= Div[v]

            2
           z
Out[21]= --
           r

In[22]:= Curl[v]

                       2
Out[22]= {0, -1 + 2 z, -}
                       r
```

And so $\nabla \cdot \mathbf{v} = z^2/r$ and $\nabla \times \mathbf{v} = (-1 + 2z)\mathbf{e}_\theta + 2\mathbf{e}_z/r$.

19.6 PLOTTING IN OTHER COORDINATES

Mathematica has a pair of functions useful for visualizing surfaces in cylindrical and spherical coordinates. These are in the **ParametricPlot3D** package, which is loaded as follows:

```
In[23]:= <<Graphics`ParametricPlot3D`
```

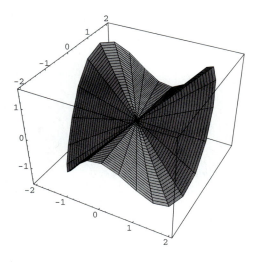

FIGURE 19.1
Surface generated by $z = r \cos\theta \sin 2\theta$ with the `CylindricalPlot3D[]` function.

For example, consider the function $f(r,\theta) = r \cos\theta \sin 2\theta$ in cylindrical coordinates. A sketch of this function as a surface over the disk $r \leq 2$ is obtained with the `CylindricalPlot3D[]` functions:

```
In[24]:= CylindricalPlot3D[r Cos[theta] Sin[2 theta],
         {r, 0, 2}, {theta, 0, 2Pi}, PlotPoints -> 30]

Out[24]= -Graphics3D-
```

The result is displayed in Fig. 19.1. Note the use of the `PlotPoints` option to increase the apparent smoothness of the rendered surface.

Similar capabilities are available in spherical coordinates. For example, consider the surface generated by the function $f(\theta,\phi) = 1 + \sin 2\phi$ in the region $0 \leq \theta \leq \pi/2$ and $0 \leq \phi \leq \pi$. The surface is generated by the `Spherical-Plot3D[]` function:

```
In[25]:= SphericalPlot3D[1 + Sin[2 phi],
         {theta, 0, Pi/2}, {phi, 0, Pi}]

Out[25]= -Graphics3D-
```

Figure 19.2 illustrates the result of this call to `SphericalPlot3D[]`. Can you interpret what is happening to the surface?

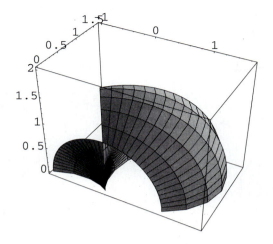

FIGURE 19.2
Surface generated by $r = 1 + \sin 2\phi$ with the `SphericalPlot3D[]` function.

EXERCISES

19.1. Show that $u = c_1 r^n \cos n\theta + c_2 r^n \sin n\theta$ is a solution to Laplace's equation in cylindrical coordinates.

19.2. Evaluate ∇u, $\nabla^2 u$, $\nabla \cdot \mathbf{v}$, and $\nabla \times \mathbf{v}$ (in spherical coordinates) if $u = r \cos \phi$ and $\mathbf{v} = r\mathbf{e}_\theta - r^3 \mathbf{e}_\phi$.

19.3. Let $u = r^\alpha$. For what value(s) of α is u a solution to Laplace's equation $\nabla^2 u = 0$ (in spherical coordinates)?

19.4. Let $u = r^\alpha$. For what value(s) of α is u a solution to the biharmonic equation $\nabla^4 u = 0$ (in spherical coordinates)?

19.5. Generate a plot of the cylindrical annulus bounded by $1 \le r \le 2$, $0 \le \theta \le 2\pi$, and $-1 \le z \le 1$. [Hint: Build the faces one at a time and use the `Show[]` command to display them together.]

CHAPTER
20

VECTOR FUNCTIONS OF A SINGLE VARIABLE

20.1 LABORATORY GOALS

a. Determine the derivatives of vector-valued functions of a single variable.
b. Manipulate these derivatives to obtain the curvature and torsion of space curves.
c. Develop proficiency with the `ParametricPlot3D[]` function.
d. Compute the length of a curve from its parametric representation.

20.2 THREE-DIMENSIONAL PARTICLE MOTION

Consider the vector $\mathbf{r} = x(t)\mathbf{i} + y(t)\mathbf{j} + z(t)\mathbf{k}$. We will assume that the position functions x, y, and z are all sufficiently differentiable. This vector corresponds to the motion of a particle in three-dimensional space, with the position vector of the particle represented by $\mathbf{r}$. The velocity and acceleration of this particle are computed by taking the derivative of $\mathbf{r}$ with respect to t: $\mathbf{v} = d\mathbf{r}/dt$ and $\mathbf{a} = d\mathbf{v}/dt$. To illustrate the use of *Mathematica* to do these kind of manipulations, suppose that $\mathbf{r} = \cos(t)\mathbf{i} + \sin(t)\mathbf{j} + (t/4)\mathbf{k}$. In *Mathematica*, this would be represented as:

```
In[1]:= r1 = {Cos[t], Sin[t], t/4}

                   t
Out[1]= {Cos[t], Sin[t], -}
                   4
```

First, we sketch the curve traced out by **r** over the interval $0 \le t \le 2\pi$ with the `ParametricPlot3D[]` function:

```
In[2]:= ParametricPlot3D[r1, {t, 0, 2 Pi}]

        ParametricPlot3D::ppcom:
          Function r1 cannot be compiled; plotting will proceed
          with the uncompiled function.

Out[2]= -Graphics3D-
```

(Note that the warning message may be safely ignored.)   We recognize in Fig.

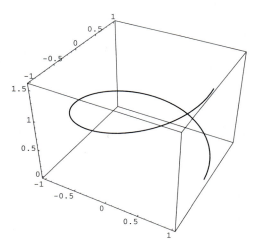

FIGURE 20.1
Helix traced out by $\mathbf{r} = \cos(t)\mathbf{i} + \sin(t)\mathbf{j} + (t/4)\mathbf{k}$ for $t \in [0, 2\pi]$.

20.1 that **r** traces out a helix. The velocity of this particle can be obtained simply by taking the derivative of **r** with respect to time with the `D[]` function:

```
In[3]:= v1 = D[r1,t]
```

```
                            1
    Out[3]= {-Sin[t], Cos[t], -}
                            4
```

and the acceleration is given by

```
    In[4]:= a1 = D[v1, t]

    Out[4]= {-Cos[t], -Sin[t], 0}
```

The speed of our particle can be computed by noting that $|\mathbf{v}| = \sqrt{\mathbf{v} \cdot \mathbf{v}}$. In *Mathematica*, we use the . operator to take dot products between vectors, and so

```
    In[5]:= speed1 = Sqrt[v1 . v1]

                  1          2         2
    Out[5]= Sqrt[-- + Cos[t]  + Sin[t] ]
                 16
```

and this result can be simplified with the **Simplify[]** function:

```
    In[6]:= speed1 = Simplify[speed1]

            Sqrt[17]
    Out[6]= --------
               4
```

To determine when the velocity and acceleration vectors are orthogonal, we can examine the dot product between them:

```
    In[7]:= v1 . a1

    Out[7]= 0
```

and thus the two vectors are always perpendicular. Finally, to determine the length of the helix traced out in Fig. 20.1, we apply the arc length formula $s = \int_a^b |\mathbf{v}| dt$ and we obtain

```
In[8]:= s1 = Integrate[speed1, {t, 0, 2 Pi}]

        Sqrt[17] Pi
Out[9]= -----------
             2
```

20.3 THE TNB COORDINATE SYSTEM

We now examine ways in which *Mathematica* can be used to examine the geometric properties of curves in 3-dimensional space. Before proceeding further, we need to load the **CrossProduct** package:[1]

```
In[10]:= <<LinearAlgebra`CrossProduct`
```

In many applications it is useful to employ the **TNB** coordinate system, which is built upon three mutually orthogonal unit vectors which follow the path of a particle in space. The unit tangent vector, **T**, is defined as

$$\mathbf{T} = \mathbf{v}/|\mathbf{v}|. \tag{20.1}$$

This vector always points in the direction of particle travel. The unit normal vector **N** is defined as

$$\mathbf{N} = d\mathbf{T}/dt/|d\mathbf{T}/dt|, \tag{20.2}$$

and this vector always points inward and perpendicular to the path of travel. The third vector, **B**, called the binormal vector is defined as

$$\mathbf{B} = \mathbf{T} \times \mathbf{N}. \tag{20.3}$$

These three unit vectors can be constructed in *Mathematica* for any space curve which is sufficiently differentiable. Referring to the helix described in the previous section, we first construct **T**:

```
In[11]:= t1 = v1 / speed1

          -4 Sin[t]   4 Cos[t]      1
Out[11]= {---------, --------, --------}
          Sqrt[17]   Sqrt[17]  Sqrt[17]
```

---

[1]This package loads a function called **Cross[]** which does essentially the same thing as the **CrossProduct[]** function. **Cross[]** is limited to cartesian coordinates.

In order to keep the *Mathematica* expressions manageable, we construct $d\mathbf{T}/dt$:

```
    In[12]:= dt1 = D[t1, t]

             -4 Cos[t]   -4 Sin[t]
    Out[12]= {---------, ---------, 0}
              Sqrt[17]    Sqrt[17]
```

and then build the unit normal $\mathbf{N}$:

```
    In[13]:= n1 = dt1 / Simplify[Sqrt[dt1 . dt1]]

    Out[13]= {-Cos[t], -Sin[t], 0}
```

We can quickly verify that these two vectors are orthogonal by taking the dot product between them:

```
    In[14]:= t1 . n1

    Out[14]= 0
```

Next, we construct the binormal $\mathbf{B}$. To do this, we will use the `Cross[]` function which was loaded as a separate package earlier:

```
    In[15]:= b1 = Simplify[Cross[t1, n1]]

              Sin[t]      Cos[t]       4
    Out[15]= {--------, -(--------), --------}
              Sqrt[17]    Sqrt[17]   Sqrt[17]
```

These three vectors are now available for additional computations.

20.4   CURVATURE AND TORSION

A basic result from advanced calculus is that the curvature κ of a space curve is given by

$$\kappa = \frac{|\mathbf{v} \times \mathbf{a}|}{|\mathbf{v}|^3} \qquad (20.4)$$

Using the results already obtained for the helix described in the previous section, we can compute its curvature as follows:

```
In[16]:= kappa1 = Simplify[Sqrt[Cross[v1, a1] . Cross[v1, a1]] /
            (speed1^3)]

            16
Out[16]= --
            17
```

which shows the curvature of this helix is constant. Since the radius of curvature is simply the reciprocal of the curvature, i.e. $\rho = 1/\kappa$,

```
In[17]:= roc1 = 1 / kappa1

            17
Out[17]= --
            16
```

Next, we consider computing the torsion τ of space curves. If the component functions are sufficiently differentiable, the torsion can be computed with the following formula:

$$\tau = \frac{\begin{vmatrix} \dot{x} & \dot{y} & \dot{z} \\ \ddot{x} & \ddot{y} & \ddot{z} \\ \dddot{x} & \dddot{y} & \dddot{z} \end{vmatrix}}{|\mathbf{v} \times \mathbf{a}|^2}, \tag{20.5}$$

where x, y, and z are the three coordinate components of $\mathbf{r}$ and the dots denote time derivatives.

Equation (20.5) is surprisingly straightforward to implement in *Mathematica*. The first and second rows of the determinant are just the components of $\mathbf{v}$ and $\mathbf{a}$, while the third row is $d\mathbf{a}/dt$. We build this row first:

```
In[18]:= i1 = D[a1, t]

Out[18]= {Sin[t], -Cos[t], 0}
```

and then construct the expression for the torsion using Det[]:

```
In[19]:= torsion = Simplify[Det[{v1, a1, i1}] /
            Sqrt[Cross[v1, a1] . Cross[v1, a1]]]

                1
Out[19]= --------
            Sqrt[17]
```

and we see that the torsion for our helix is a constant.

EXERCISES

20.1. Suppose a particle moves with the position components described below. Determine the tangential and normal acceleration components and the radius of curvature for each case:

(a) $x = t^2$, $y = t$, $z = t + 1$
(b) $x = \cos t$, $y = \sin t$, $z = \sqrt{t}$
(c) $x = e^t$, $y = \cos t$, $z = t$.

20.2. Determine the arc length for each of the curves in Exercise 1 over the interval $0 < t < 2\pi$.

20.3. Compute the torsion for each of the curves in Exercise 1. In each instance, determine those values of t for which the torsion is maximized and minimized.

21

VECTOR
INTEGRATION

21.1 LABORATORY GOALS

a. To use evaluate surface and volume integrals.

b. To apply the divergence theorem and Stoke's theorem to evaluation of surface and volume integrals.

21.2 THE DIVERGENCE THEOREM

Before proceeding further, we require the `VectorAnalysis` package:

```
In[1]:= <<Calculus'VectorAnalysis'
```

Let $\mathcal{V}$ be a closed region in three-dimensional space with piece-wise smooth boundary $\mathcal{S}$. Let $\mathbf{v} = x(y+1)z^3\mathbf{j}$ be a continuously differentiable vector field defined in a region $\mathcal{R}$ of three-dimensional space. If $\mathbf{n}$ denotes the unit normal on $\mathcal{S}$, then the divergence theorem says that

$$\int_{\mathcal{V}} \nabla \cdot \mathbf{v} \, dV = \int_{\mathcal{S}} \mathbf{n} \cdot v \, dA. \tag{21.1}$$

We illustrate the divergence theorem with the following example. Let $\mathcal{V}$ be the triangular prism shown in Fig. 21.1. Its faces are given by the planes $x = 0$, $x = 2$, $y = 0$, $z = 0$, and $y + z = 1$. First we determine $\nabla \cdot \mathbf{v}$:

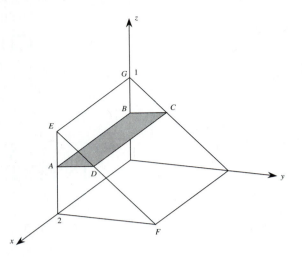

FIGURE 21.1
Triangular prism in the first octant.

```
In[2]:= v = {0, x(y+1)z^3, 0}

                    3
Out[2]= {0, x (1 + y) z , 0}

In[3]:= divv = Div[v]

             3
Out[3]= x z
```

To compute the volume integral on the left-hand side of Eq. (21.1), we let $dV = dx\,dy\,dz$ in such a way that the shaded plane $ABCD$ sweeps out the prism by beginning at the segment EG and ending at the xy-plane. In this case, $0 \le x \le 2$, $0 \le y \le 1 - z$, and $0 \le z \le 1$. We can now evaluate this as an iterated integral:

```
In[4]:= Integrate[
           Integrate[
             Integrate[divv, {x, 0, 2}],
                      {y, 0, 1 - z}],
                      {z, 0, 1}]

            1
Out[4]= --
           10
```

The right-hand side of Eq. (21.1) is evaluated in five pieces. Note that on the face where $x = 0$, $\mathbf{n} = -\mathbf{i}$, and by inspection $\mathbf{n} \cdot \mathbf{v} = 0$. The same result holds for the face at $x = 2$ since $\mathbf{n} = \mathbf{i}$ there. In addition, on the face $z = 0$, $\mathbf{n} = -\mathbf{k}$, and $\mathbf{n} \cdot \mathbf{v} = 0$ there as well. On the face $y = 0$, the unit normal is $-\mathbf{j}$. In this instance, the surface integral is straightforward to evaluate:

```
In[5]:= res1 = Integrate[
                   Integrate[{0, -1, 0} . v /. y ->0,
                         {x, 0, 2}],
                        {z, 0, 1}]

              1
Out[5]= -(-)
              2
```

Since the slanted face is part of the plane $y + z = 1$, the unit normal is $\mathbf{n} = (\mathbf{j} + \mathbf{k})/\sqrt{2}$. Noting that $dA = \sqrt{2}\,dx\,dy$ on the slanted face, we can evaluate the surface integral on that face with the following *Mathematica* expression:

```
In[6]:= res2 = Integrate[
                   Integrate[Sqrt[2](({0, 1, 1} / Sqrt[2]) . v
                                     /. z -> 1 - y),
                         {x, 0, 2}],
                        {y, 0, 1}]

              3
Out[6]= -
              5

In[7]:= res1 + res2

              1
Out[7]= --
              10
```

and the result is seen to be $1/10$, the same as obtained above.

21.3   STOKE'S THEOREM

Let $\mathbf{v}$ be a continuously differentiable vector field defined in a region $\mathcal{R}$ of three-dimensional space. Let $\mathcal{S}$ be a piecewise-smooth surface in $\mathcal{R}$ and suppose that the edge of $\mathcal{S}$ is a piece-wise smooth simple close curve $\mathcal{C}$. Then Stoke's theorem says that

$$\int_{\mathcal{S}} \mathbf{n} \cdot \nabla \times \mathbf{v}\, dA = \oint_{\mathcal{C}} \mathbf{v} \cdot d\mathbf{r}, \qquad (21.2)$$

where **n** is the unit normal to the surface $\mathcal{S}$. For example, suppose that $\mathcal{S}$ is the portion of the paraboloid $z = 1 - x^2 - y^2$ which lies in the octant bounded by $0 \le x$, $0 \le y$, and $0 \le z$. As suggested in Fig. 21.2, the curve $\mathcal{S}$ will be the edge of the paraboloid $ABCA$. Let $v = yz\mathbf{k}$.   We will use *Mathematica* to evaluate

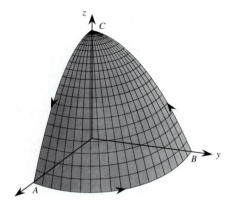

FIGURE 21.2
The paraboloid $z = 1 - x^2 - y^2$ in the first octant. Note the orientation of the boundary $\mathcal{C} = ABCA$.

both sides of Eq. (21.2). First, we determine $\nabla \times \mathbf{v}$:

```
In[8] := v = {0, 0, y z}

Out[8]= {0, 0, y z}

In[9] := curlv = Curl[v]

Out[9]= {z, 0, 0}
```

Now we compute the unit normal vector **n**. If the surface is written as $f(x, y, z) = z + x^2 + y^2 - 1$, then $\mathbf{n} = \nabla f / |\nabla f|$. Thus

```
In[10] := f = z + x^2 + y^2 - 1

              2    2
Out[10]= -1 + x  + y  + z

In[11] := nn = Grad[f] / Sqrt[Grad[f] . Grad[f]]
```

```
                     2 x                         2 y
Out[11]= {-----------------------, -----------------------,
                    2       2                  2       2
           Sqrt[1 + 4 x   + 4 y ]   Sqrt[1 + 4 x   + 4 y ]


                     1
           ---------------------}
                    2       2
           Sqrt[1 + 4 x   + 4 y ]
```

If we write the equation for the paraboloid as $z = g(x, y) = 1 - x^2 - y^2$, then the area element is expressed as $dA = \sqrt{1 + g_x^2 + g_y^2}\, dx\, dy$. The coefficient here is found as follows:

```
    In[12]:= g = 1 - x^2 - y^2

                  2    2
    Out[12]= 1 - x  - y

    In[13]:= acoeff = Sqrt[1 + D[g, x]^2 + D[g, y]^2]

                        2     2
    Out[13]= Sqrt[1 + 4 x   + 4 y ]
```

Finally noting that in xy-plane, the limits of integration are $0 \le x \le \sqrt{1 - y^2}$ and $0 \le y \le 1$, we can evaluate the left-hand side of Eq. (21.2) as an iterated integral:

```
    In[14]:= Integrate[Integrate[(nn . curlv /. z -> g) acoeff,
                        {x, 0, Sqrt[1 - y^2]}],
                        {y, 0, 1}]

              4
    Out[14]= --
             15
```

Now to evaluate the right-hand side of Eq. (21.2), note that

$$\oint_C \mathbf{v} \cdot d\mathbf{r} = \oint_C yz\, dz. \tag{21.3}$$

Along CA, $y = 0$, and along AB, $z = 0$. On BC, $z = 1 - y^2$. Thus

$$\oint_C \mathbf{v} \cdot d\mathbf{r} = \int_{BC} yz\, dz. \tag{21.4}$$

We evaluate this last result as follows:

```
In[15]:= Integrate[y (1 - y^2) D[1 - y^2, y], {y, 1, 0}]

                4
Out[15]= --
               15
```

The two computations agree as they should.

EXERCISES

21.1. Verify the divergence theorem by working out both sides for $\mathbf{v} = x^2 z\mathbf{i} + 3y(z + 1)\mathbf{j} + z^2\mathbf{k}$ for the triangular prism discussed in Section 21.2.

21.2. The following result can be derived from the divergence theorem:

$$\int_{\mathcal{V}} \nabla^2 u \, dV = \int_{\mathcal{S}} \frac{\partial u}{\partial n} \, dA,$$

where $\partial u/\partial n$ denotes the normal derivative of u along the surface $\mathcal{S}$. Let $u = z\cos(xy + z)$. Verify this result for the unit cube.

21.3. Verify Stoke's theorem by working out both sides for $\mathbf{v} = e^{-x}y\mathbf{i} + e^{-y}\mathbf{j} + ze^z\mathbf{k}$ for the unit cube, but excluding the face $y = 1$.

21.4. Let $\mathbf{v} = [y^2 + x^2\cos(yz)]\mathbf{i} - y^2\mathbf{k}$. Evaluate $\int_{\mathcal{S}} \mathbf{n} \cdot \nabla \times v \, dA$ where $\mathcal{S}$ is the surface $z = 1 - x^4 - y^4$ with $0 \leq z$.

CHAPTER
22

MULTI-VARIABLE OPTIMIZATION

22.1 LABORATORY GOALS

a. To use *Mathematica* to solve multi-variable optimization problems.
b. Use the `Plot3D[]` function to visualize solutions to optimization problems.

22.2 DESCRIPTION OF THE TROUGH

It is desired to determine the cross-sectional shape of a long strip of sheet metal which is to be used as a trough. The shape of the trough is shown in Fig. 22.1. The width of the sheet metal piece is L units and two ends of equal length y are bent upward at equal angles θ, measured from the vertical.

We seek to determine the values of y and θ that will maximize the cross sectional area of the trough. The area A is given by the following expression:

$$A = y\cos\theta(L - 2y) + y^2\cos\theta\sin\theta, \tag{22.1}$$

subject to the constraints that $0 < \theta < \pi/2$ and that $0 < y < L/2$. In *Mathematica*, we express the area as

```
In[1]:= A = y Cos[t] (L - 2 y) + y^2 Cos[t] Sin[t]

                          2
Out[1]= (L - 2 y) y Cos[t] + y  Cos[t] Sin[t]
```

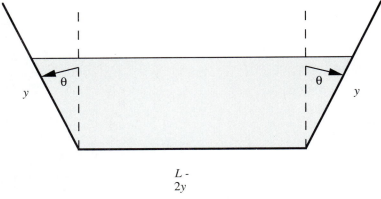

FIGURE 22.1
Cross-sectional view of a symmetric trapezoidal trough. The end-to-end length is L.

where t is used to represent θ.

22.3   LOCATING CRITICAL POINTS

Recall that a maximum point, if it exists, must occur at critical points inside the constraint intervals. Since A is continuously differentiable in both y and θ, we need not be concerned with critical points at which derivatives fail to exist. The most straightforward way to attack the problem, then, is to set $\partial A/\partial \theta = \partial A/\partial y = 0$ and solve for θ and y. This can be set up in *Mathematica* by combining the D[] function and Solve[] function:

```
In[2]:= Solve[{D[A, t] == 0, D[A, y] == 0}, {y, t}]

        Solve::ifun:
            Warning: Inverse functions are being used by Solve, so
            some solutions may not be found.

Out[2]= {}
```

Unfortunately, *Mathematica* does not handle this direct approach very well—indeed, the empty brackets returned indicate that *Mathematica* could find no solutions.

When the direct approach fails, results may often be obtained through intermediate manipulation of the computations. For example, we can simplify the two derivatives which we are setting equal to zero and try again. To illustrate this alternative, we first determine $\partial A/\partial y$:

```
In[3]:= D[A, y]
```

```
Out[3]= (L - 2 y) Cos[t] - 2 y Cos[t] + 2 y Cos[t] Sin[t]
```

We then factor out the $\cos\theta$ term (because we set this derivative equal to zero) and assign the symbolic name **eq1** to the resulting expression:

```
In[4]:= Apart[%, Cos[t]]

Out[4]= Cos[t] (L - 4 y + 2 y Sin[t])

In[5]:= eq1 = %[[2]]

Out[5]= L - 4 y + 2 y Sin[t]
```

We now compute the other partial derivative:

```
In[6]:= D[A, t]

          2      2                  2       2
Out[6]= y  Cos[t]  - (L - 2 y) y Sin[t] - y  Sin[t]
```

and simplify it by eliminating a y from each term:

```
In[7]:= Simplify[% / y]

Out[7]= y Cos[2 t] - L Sin[t] + 2 y Sin[t]
```

We now solve **eq1** for y:

```
In[8]:= ysub = Solve[eq1 == 0, y]

                     -L
Out[8]= {{y -> ---------------}}
                2 (-2 + Sin[t])
```

and then substitute this result into previous result:

```
In[9]:= %% /. %

               -(L Cos[2 t])                 L Sin[t]
Out[9]= {--------------- - L Sin[t] - -----------}
              2 (-2 + Sin[t])              -2 + Sin[t]
```

We eliminate the curly brackets and simplify the result as follows:[1]

```
In[10]:= %[[1]]

               -(L Cos[2 t])                 L Sin[t]
Out[10]= --------------- - L Sin[t] - -----------
              2 (-2 + Sin[t])              -2 + Sin[t]

In[11]:= Simplify[%]

             L (-1 + 2 Sin[t])
Out[11]= -----------------
              2 (-2 + Sin[t])
```

We now ask *Mathematica* to solve this expression for θ:

```
In[12]:= tsub = Flatten[Solve[% == 0, t]]

          Solve::ifun:
                Warning: Inverse functions are being used by Solve, so
                some solutions may not be found.

                  Pi
Out[12]= {t -> --}
                   6
```

Despite the warning message,[2] *Mathematica* determined the root $\theta = \pi/6$. This is now used to obtain the value for y at which the critical point occurs:

---

[1] We are still going to solve two equations in two unknowns. We have explicitly substituted one equation into the other before asking *Mathematica* to go to work.

[2] You may see another warning message:

```
    General::spell:
  Possible spelling error: new symbol name "tsub"
  is similar to existing symbols {Stub, ysub}.
```

This message can also be ignored.

```
In[13]:= ysub = Flatten[ysub  /. %]

                L
Out[13]= {y -> -}
                3
```

22.4   THE SECOND DERIVATIVE TEST

We must now determine the nature of the critical point, noting that if $A_{yy} < 0$ and $A_{yy}A_{\theta\theta} - A_{y\theta}^2 > 0$, then A will have a local maximum at that point.

First, we set up an expression to evaluate A_{yy}:

```
In[14]:= D[A, {y, 2}] /. Join[tsub, ysub]

                3/2
            -3
Out[14]= -----
            2
```

which is evidently negative. Now we compute the second test expression:

```
In[15]:= % D[A, {t, 2}] - D[D[A, y], t]^2 /. Join[tsub, ysub]

            2
           L
Out[15]= ---
           2
```

which is clearly positive. We conclude that a local maximum occurs at this critical point. By inspection we observe that no global maximum can occur at the limits of the constraints and so we have determined the optimal shape of the trough.

22.5   DISCUSSION

The maximum cross-sectional area of the trough is given by this expression:

```
In[16]:= A /. Join[tsub, ysub]

                 2
                L
Out[16]=     ---------
             4 Sqrt[3]
```

In order to more clearly see that this is the maximum point, we examine a surface plot of the area. In order to set this up, we need to assign a numerical value to L. Thus for this example, we let $L = 1$:

```
In[17]:= A1 = A /. L -> 1

                                     2
Out[17]= (1 - 2 y) y Cos[t] + y  Cos[t] Sin[t]
```

and we use the `Plot3D[]` function to examine A over the admissible ranges of

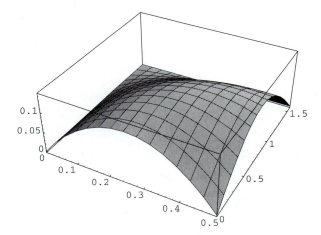

FIGURE 22.2
Surface corresponding to the cross-sectional area of the trough as a function of leg length and leg angle.

both y and θ:

```
In[18]:= Plot3D[A1, {y, 0, 1/2}, {t, 0, Pi/2}]
```

```
Out[18]= -SurfaceGraphics-
```

with the result shown in Fig. 22.2   In order to see more clearly where the

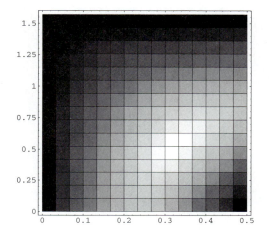

FIGURE 22.3
Density plot corresponding to the cross-sectional area of the trough as a function of leg length and leg angle.

maximum value of A occurs, we employ the **DensityGraphics[]** function. In order to yield an adequate aspect ratio for viewing, we set the **AspectRatio** option to **1** within the **Show[]** function:

```
In[19]:= Show[DensityGraphics[%], AspectRatio -> 1]

Out[18]= -DensityGraphics-
```

From Fig. 22.3 it can be seen that the lightest area, which corresponds to the maximum value of the area, occurs when y is a little bigger than 0.3 and θ is about 0.5. These values correspond to the solution obtained in the previous section.

EXERCISES

22.1. Determine the dimensions of a right circular cylinder of volume V such that the surface area is minimized.

22.2. Determine the dimensions of a right circular cylinder of surface area A such that the volume is maximized.

22.3. Re-do the previous two problems for a right circular cone.

22.4. Suppose that the trough design specification is changed to require that one of the two angles must be 90 degrees, with the height of each lip remaining equal. Determine the shape of maximum cross-sectional area.

CHAPTER
23

VISUALIZING FIELDS

23.1 LABORATORY GOALS

a. To plot the gradient field of a scalar function of two variables and to compare it to the contour plot of that function.

b. To plot the field of a vector function of two variables and to compare it to the divergence of that function.

23.2 GRADIENT FIELDS

We must first load the two *Mathematica* packages **VectorAnalysis** and **PlotField**:

```
In[1]:= <<Calculus`VectorAnalysis`

In[2]:= <<Graphics`PlotField`
```

Suppose we wish to examine the gradient field for the function $f(x, y) = \sin(x^2 + y^2)$. This field can be visualized with the **PlotGradientField[]** function:

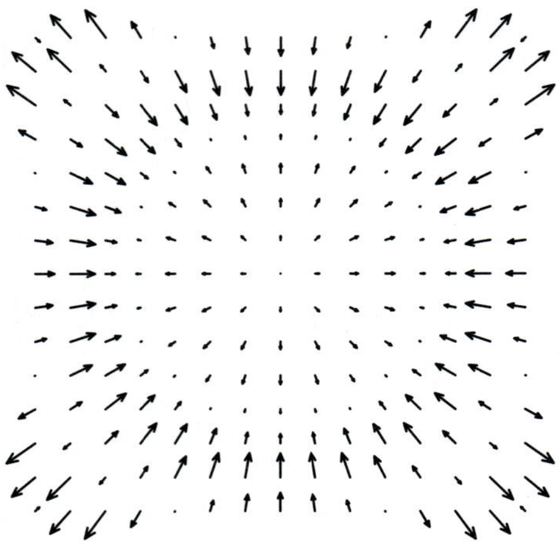

FIGURE 23.1
Gradient field for $f(x, y) = \sin(x^2 + y^2)$ on the domain $-2 \leq x \leq 2$ and $-2 \leq y \leq 2$.

```
In[3]:= f = Sin[x^2 + y^2]

             2    2
Out[3]= Sin[x  + y ]

In[4]:= PlotGradientField[f, {x, -2, 2}, {y, -2, 2}]

Out[4]= -Graphics-
```

In Fig. 23.1, the tail of each arrow is located at the point for which the gradient is evaluated. The direction and length of the arrows correspond to those of the respective gradient. In order to see the relationship between the gradient field and the contours of the surface determined by $f(x, y)$, we first generate a contour plot over the same domain with the `ContourPlot[]` function:

```
In[5]:= ContourPlot[f, {x, -2, 2}, {y, -2, 2},
            PlotPoints -> 30]

Out[5]= -ContourGraphics-
```

Note that we set the `PlotPoints` option to a value of 30. This ensured contour lines that were sufficiently smooth. In Fig. 23.2 the darker areas correspond to the smaller values of $f(x, y)$ while the lighter areas designate the larger values. We can overlay the two illustrations with the `Show[]` function, taking care to place the contour plot first:

```
In[6] := Show[%, %%]

Out[6]= -Graphics-
```

Several important properties of the gradient field can be seen in Fig. 23.3. Note that the gradient arrows are always perpendicular to the contour lines. Further, note that the arrows always point toward lighter regions, that is point in the direction of greatest increase in the function value. Finally, the arrow lengths are proportional to the number of contour lines crossed.

23.3   DIVERGENCE OF A VECTOR FIELD

Mathematica makes it possible to visualize both a given vector field and the divergence of that field. For example, let $\mathbf{g}(x, y) = (\sin xy, \cos xy)$ be a vector function. The vector field formed by $\mathbf{g}$ can be seen with the `PlotVectorField[]` function:

```
In[7] := g = {Sin[x y], Cos[x y]}

Out[7]= {Sin[x y], Cos[x y]}

In[8] := PlotVectorField[g, {x, 0, Pi}, {y, 0, Pi}]
```

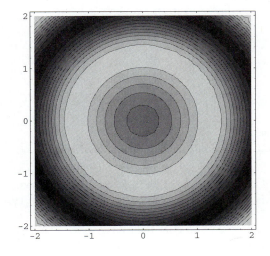

FIGURE 23.2
Contour plot for $f(x, y) = \sin(x^2 + y^2)$ on the domain $-2 \le x \le 2$ and $-2 \le y \le 2$.

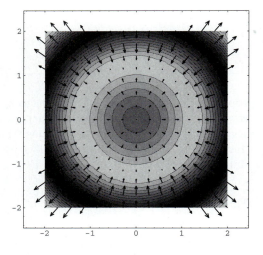

FIGURE 23.3
Superposition of Fig. 23.1 over Fig. 23.2. The domain is as in those figures.

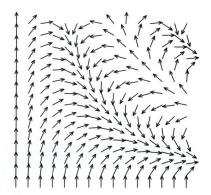

FIGURE 23.4
Vector field plot for $\mathbf{g}(x, y) = (\sin xy, \cos xy)$ on the domain $0 \le x \le \pi$ and $0 \le y \le \pi$.

```
Out[8]= -Graphics-
```

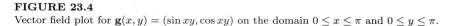

The result of this call to `PlotVectorField[]` is shown in Fig. 23.4. Note that the arrows all have the same length. This follows from the fact that $|\mathbf{g}| = 1$ for x and y.

The divergence of $\mathbf{g}$, $\nabla \cdot \mathbf{g}$ is computed with the `Div[]` function. Note that this function expects a three-dimensional vector for its argument. We use the `Append[]` function to add a third zero component to $\mathbf{g}$, and then take the divergence:

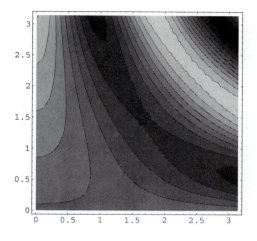

FIGURE 23.5
Contour plot of $\nabla \cdot \mathbf{g}$ on the domain $0 \le x \le \pi$ and $0 \le y \le \pi$.

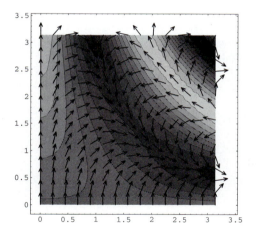

FIGURE 23.6
Superposition of Fig. 23.4 over Fig. 23.5. The domain is as in those figures.

```
In[9]:= divg = Div[Append[g, 0]]

Out[9]= y Cos[x y] - x Sin[x y]
```

Since $\nabla \cdot \mathbf{g}$ is a scalar function of x and y, we can examine its contour plot:

```
In[10]:= ContourPlot[divg, {x, 0, Pi}, {y, 0, Pi},
           PlotPoints -> 30]

Out[10]= -ContourGraphics-
```

We again set `PlotPoints -> 30` in order to ensure sufficient smoothness of contour lines in Fig. 23.5. Now we overlay both Figs. 23.5 and 23.4 with the `Show[]` function:

```
In[11]:= Show[%, %%%]

Out[11]= -Graphics-
```

Figure 23.6 provides some useful insights into the nature of the divergence. Note that $\nabla \cdot \mathbf{g}$ achieves its largest and smallest values (in the regions of lightest and darkest shading respectively) at regions where the arrows are spreading outward or inward respectively.[1] In the regions of intermediate gray shading, $\nabla \cdot \mathbf{g}$ is nearly zero and it is in precisely these locations that the gradient vectors are more or less parallel.

EXERCISES

23.1. Plot the gradient field for $f(x, y) = xy$. Overlay it with the contour plot of $f(x, y)$.

23.2. Plot the gradient field for $f(x, y) = \sin(x \cos y)$. Overlay it with the contour plot of $f(x, y)$.

23.3. Plot the vector field for $\mathbf{g}(x, y) = (\exp(-x^2), x+y)$. Overlay it with the contour plot of $\nabla \cdot \mathbf{g}$.

23.4. Plot the vector field for $\mathbf{g}(x, y) = (J_0(x), J_1(y))$. Overlay it with the contour plot of $\nabla \cdot \mathbf{g}$.

---

[1]Figure 23.6 provides good geometric motivation for the term *divergence*.

CHAPTER
24

COMPLEX ARITHMETIC

24.1 LABORATORY GOALS

a. To become familiar with the manipulations of complex numbers.
b. To become familiar with the *Mathematica* functions `Re[]` and `Im[]`.
c. To become familiar with the syntax of the elementary complex functions.

24.2 MANIPULATING COMPLEX NUMBERS

Complex numbers are numbers of the form $z = x + iy$ where x and y are real, and $i = \sqrt{-1}$. x is called the *real* part of z and y the *imaginary* part. Complex numbers can be added, multiplied, and divided by performing operation on the real and imaginary part. *Mathematica* can often perform much of this tedious process for you.

Although *Mathematica* has some built-in ability to work with complex numbers, it's facility is greatly enhanced by loading `ReIm`, one of the standard packages that comes with *Mathematica*:

```
<<Algebra`ReIm`
```

In *Mathematica* $i = \sqrt{-1}$ is represented by I. Virtually all functions that can take a complex argument can operate on I or any other number:

```
In[1]:= Sqrt[I]

              1/4
Out[1]= (-1)
```

Note that *Mathematica* returns back an exact symbolic result. The real and imaginary part of $\sqrt{i}$ can be obtained with the Re[] and Im[] functions:

```
In[2]:= Re[%2]

            1
Out[2]= -------
         Sqrt[2]

In[3]:= Im[%2]

            1
Out[3]= -------
         Sqrt[2]
```

Note that *Mathematica* returns the *principal value* of $\sqrt{i}$.

Let $z_1 = 1 + 2i$ and $z_2 = 3 - i$. First we enter

```
In[4]:= z1 = 1 + 2 I

Out[4]= 1 + 2 I

In[5]:= z2 = 3 - I

Out[5]= 3 - I
```

Next, we wish to compute $z_1 z_2$ and z_1/z_2:

```
In[6]:= z1 z2

Out[6]= 5 + 5 I

In[7]:= z1 / z2
```

```
              1     7 I
Out[7]=  --  +  ---
             10    10
```

The modulus and phase (or argument) can be found with the the **Abs[]** and **Arg[]** functions:

```
In[8]:= Abs[z1]

Out[8]= Sqrt[5]

In[9]:= Arg[z2]

Out[9]= ArcTan[3, -1]
```

Mathematica will normally give exact symbolic results. Often, it leaves the result of the argument in the form of the **ArcTan[]** function because no simpler form (say in terms of fractions of π exists or can be found using its internal rules. A numerical estimate of the argument can always be obtained with the **N[]** function:

```
In[10]:= N[%]

Out[10]= -0.321751
```

Note that *Mathematica* returns the principal value of the argument, i.e. $-\pi < \arg(z) \leq \pi$. Finally, we note that complex numbers can be used as exponents:

```
In[11]:= I^I

          I
Out[11]= I

In[12]:= Re[%]

          I
Out[12]= I

In[13]:= Im[%%]

Out[13]= 0
```

Although *Mathematica* did not present a simplified version of i^i, it did recognize that the imaginary part is zero.

24.3   COMPLEX FUNCTIONS

First, define the complex variable $z = x + iy$:[1]

```
In[14]:= z = x + I y

Out[14]= x + I y
```

First we point out what appears to be an anomaly in *Mathematica*. Evaluating the real and imaginary parts of z, we obtain:

```
In[15]:= Re[z]

Out[15]= -Im[y] + Re[x]

In[16]:= Im[z]

Out[16]= Im[x] + Re[y]
```

At this point, *Mathematica* has no way of knowing whether x and y are purely real or possible complex-valued. With no other information at hand, it makes the safest possible assumption, which accounts for the form of the results above. This situation can be improved by using the tag /: operator. This operator allows you to give *Mathematica* specific information about a symbol. Here, we use it to explicitly tell *Mathematica* that x and y are real, i.e. that their imaginary parts are zero:

```
In[17]:= x/: Im[x] = 0

Out[17]= 0

In[17]:= y/: Im[y] = 0

Out[17]= 0
```

Now, the **Re[]** and **Im[]** functions work as expected:

---

[1] The space between the I and the y is critical. Without the space, *Mathematica* interprets Iy as the name for a new variable, one which will rarely behave as expected!

```
In[18]:= Re[z]

Out[18]= x

In[19]:= Im[z]

Out[19]= y
```

Mathematica correctly handles complex inputs to most functions. For example the complex exponential is evaluated with

```
In[20]:= Exp[z]

             x + I y
Out[20]= E

In[21]:= Re[%]

             x
Out[21]= E   Cos[y]

In[22]:= Im[%%]

             x
Out[22]= E   Sin[y]
```

which is easily seen to be a commonly-appearing form for this function. *Mathematica* becomes even more useful when real and imaginary parts of more complicated functions are required. For example, suppose we need to determine the real and imaginary parts of $f(z) = \sin(z^2 + 1)$.

```
In[23]:= f = Sin[z^2 + 1]

                          2
Out[23]= Sin[1 + (x + I y) ]

In[24]:= Re[f]

                        2     2
Out[24]= Cosh[2 x y] Sin[1 + x  - y ]

In[25]:= Im[f]

                  2     2
Out[25]= Cos[1 + x  - y ] Sinh[2 x y]
```

The inverse trigonometric and hyperbolic functions also handle complex arguments.

EXERCISES

24.1. Determine the real and imaginary parts of $d^2[e^{z^2}]/dz^2$.

24.2. Let $f(z) = e^{(z-1)}$. Show that $\mathrm{Re}\,[f(z)]$ is an harmonic function, i.e. show that if $u(x, y) = \mathrm{Re}\,[f(z)]$, then $u_{xx} + u_{yy} = 0$.

24.3. Use the `Plot[]` function to sketch the graphs of the real and imaginary parts of $f(z) = \cos^{-1} z$ along the three lines $y = 0$, $y = 1/2$, and $y = 1$ for $0 \le x \le 1$.

24.4. Write the given complex number in both polar form and in the form $a + ib$:
   (a) $[\cos(\pi/12) + i\sin(\pi/12)]^9\{3[\cos(\pi/9) + i\sin(\pi/9)]\}^6$
   (b) $\{2[\cos(2\pi/15) + i\sin(2\pi/15)]\}^7/\{6[\cos(4\pi/9) + i\sin(4\pi/9)]\}^{12}$.

24.5. Determine all zeroes of the polynomial $f(z) = z^7 + 3z + 1$.

24.6. Let $g(z) = \bar{z}$. Let the real and imaginary parts of $g(z)$ correspond to the x and y components of a vector at the point z. Plot the resulting vector field on the domain $-3 \le x \le 3$ and $-3 \le y \le 3$.

24.7. Use the `Solve[]` function to determine the three *third* roots of 1. Show that this set of roots is closed under multiplication. [This set, the three cube roots of one, forms a cyclic group of order 3.]

TAYLOR AND LAURENT SERIES

25.1 LABORATORY GOALS

a. To expand functions in Taylor series about arbitrary points in the complex plane.

b. To use the `TaylorRatioTest[]` function to estimate the radius of convergence of a Taylor Series.

c. To expand functions in Laurent series about arbitrary points in the complex plane.

25.2 TAYLOR SERIES

Portions of Taylor Series are easy to find with *Mathematica*. The `Series[]` function takes two arguments. The first is the function for which the expansion is sought, and the second is a list specifying the expansion variable, the point about which the series is to be expanded, and the number of terms in the expansion.[1] For example to find the first five terms of the Taylor series of $f(z) = \sin z$ about the point $z = 0$, we issue the following:

---

[1]This is not the number of *non-zero* terms.

```
In[1]:= Series[Sin[z], {z, 0, 5}]

            3     5
           z     z         6
Out[1]= z - -- + --- + O[z]
           6     120
```

The expression in Out[1] displays only three terms. Five terms were actually computed, but the even powers of z all have zero coefficients for this example. The term O[z]^6 is *Mathematica*'s way of indicating that the remainder of expansion begins with that power of the expansion variable.[2]

As another example, the expansion about the point $z = i$ is given by

```
In[1]:= Series[Sin[z], {z, I, 5}]

                                                 I                   2
Out[2]= I Sinh[1] + Cosh[1] (-I + z) - - Sinh[1] (-I + z)  -
                                                 2

            3
   Cosh[1] (-I + z)     I                       4
   ----------------- + -- Sinh[1] (-I + z)  +
           6            24

            5
   Cosh[1] (-I + z)          6
   ----------------- + O[-I + z]
          120
```

Note that *Mathematica* preserves exact results for all coefficients.

The Series[] function is very powerful, permitting the determination of Taylor coefficients for many complicated functions. For example, the ten-term Taylor series of $g(x) = \tan^{-1}(\sin z)$ about $z = 0$ is generated by this call to Series[]:

```
In[3]:= Series[ArcTan[Sin[z]], {z, 0, 10}]

             3      5       7         9
            z    3 z    83 z    8375 z          11
Out[3]:= z - -- + ---- - ----- + ------- + O[z]
            2     8      240     24192
```

[2]This is not unlike the Landau notation $O(z^6)$.

Mathematica permits operations on series and will preserve accuracy up to the order of term retained. For example, consider the seven-term Taylor series for $f(z) = e^z$ and $g(z) = \sin z$:

```
In[4]:= f = Series[Exp[z], {z,0,7}]

                  2    3    4     5     6      7
             z    z    z    z     z     z                8
Out[4]= 1 + z + -- + -- + -- + --- + --- + ---- + O[z]
                 2    6    24   120   720   5040

In[5]:= g = Series[Sin[z], {z,0,7}]

             3    5     7
        z    z    z                8
Out[5]= z - -- + --- - ---- + O[z]
            6    120   5040

In[6]:= h = f g

              2    3    5    6    7
             z    z    z    z    z              8
Out[6]= z + z  + -- - -- - -- - --- + O[z]
                 3    30   90   630
```

Compare this with the result obtained by computing the seven-term Taylor series directly:

```
In[7]:= Series[Exp[z] Sin[z], {z, 0, 7}]

              2    3    5    6    7
             z    z    z    z    z              8
Out[7]= z + z  + -- - -- - -- - --- + O[z]
                 3    30   90   630
```

`Out[6]` and `Out[7]` are identical.

Mathematica can also generate the Taylor series for a large family of special functions. For example, the ten-term Taylor expansion of $f(z) = J_0(z)$ about $z = 0$ is given by:

```
In[8]:= Series[BesselJ[0,z], {z,0,10}]

             2    4    6      8        10
            z    z    z      z        z              12
Out[8]= 1 - -- + -- - ---- + ------ - -------- + O[z]
            4    64   2304   147456   14745600
```

The radius of convergence of a Taylor series for the function $f(z)$ is the radius of the largest circle about the point $z = z_0$ in which the function is analytic. The radius of convergence can be estimated from the Taylor series in several ways. For example, if the symbolic form of the Taylor coefficients is known, then the ratio test can usually be applied to yield the radius of convergence. Unfortunately, *Mathematica* does not yield the symbolic form of the Taylor coefficients when giving the n-term Taylor expansion of $f(z)$. *Mathematica* can be used to apply the ratio test through the use of a function called `TaylorRatioTest[]`. The *Mathematica* source code for this package is given below:[3]

```
BeginPackage["EngineeringMath`TaylorRatioTest`"]
TaylorRatioTest::usage = "TaylorRatioTest[f[z], z0] estimates
the radius of convergence of the Taylor series for f[z]
expanded about the point z0"
Options[TaylorRatioTest] = {LastTerm ->10}
Begin["EngineeringMath`TaylorRatioTest`Private`"]
TaylorRatioTest[f_, z0_, opts___Rule] :=
               Module[ {z, i, k, n, g, h, lt},
lt = LastTerm /. {opts} /. Options[TaylorRatioTest];
g[0] = f[z];
g[n_] := g[n] = D[g[n - 1], z];
k = 0;
h[n_] := h[n] = Module[ {a},
               For[k++; a = (g[k] / k!) /. z -> z0,
               a == 0,
               k = k + 1,
               a = (g[k] / k!) /. z -> z0];
               Return[a];
             ];
Table[Abs[N[h[i]/h[i+1]]], {i, 1, lt}]
]
End[]
EndPackage[]
```

Assuming that this package has been placed in a file called `TaylorRatioTest.m`, it is loaded with the following command:

```
In[9]:= <<Miscellaneous`TaylorRatioTest`
```

Recall that the radius of convergence $\rho = \lim_{n \to \infty} |a_n/a_{n+1}|$ where a_n is the Taylor coefficient of the nth *non-zero* term of the Taylor expansion. The function `TaylorRatioTest[]` returns a list containing the first ten terms of this sequence.

---

[3]This package is a very simple example of the power of procedural programming available through *Mathematica*. Readers interested in the details of this aspect of *Mathematica*, which is beyond the scope of this book, should consult *Programming in Mathematica*.

Examination of these terms will almost always suggest the correct value of the radius of convergence. For example, Let $F(z) = \sin z/(2-z)$. The Taylor expansion of $F(z)$ about $z = 0$ is given by

```
In[10]:= F[z_] := Sin[z] / (2 - z)

In[11]:= Series[F[z], {z,0,10}]

              2    3     4     5      6       7        8
         z    z    z     z    7 z    7 z    143 z    143 z
Out[11]= - + -- + -- + -- + ---- + ---- + ------ + ------ +
         2    4    24   48    480    960    40320    80640

                    9           10
             1289 z      1289 z             11
             ------- + -------- + O[z]
             1451520    2903040
```

The **TaylorRatioTest[]** returns the following list:

```
In[12]:= TaylorRatioTest[F, 0]

Out[12]= {2., 6., 2., 1.42857, 2., 2.05594, 2., 1.9969, 2., 2.00011}
```

This result confirms that known result that $\rho = 2$.

25.3   LAURENT SERIES

Consider the function:

$$f(z) = \frac{7z - 2}{(z+1)z(z-2)}, \qquad (25.1)$$

and the annulus shown in Fig. 25.1.   First we enter $f(z)$ into *Mathematica*:

```
In[13]:= f = (7 z - 2) / ((z + 1) z (z - 2))

              -2 + 7 z
Out[13]= -------------------
         (-2 + z) z (1 + z)
```

We seek Laurent series which converge in the three regions shown in Fig. 25.1. That is, series converging in the disk $0 < |z+1| < 1$, in the annulus $1 < |z+1| < 3$ and in the region $3 < |z + 1|$.

To find the series within the region $0 < |z+1| < 1$, we simply expand $f(z)$ about the point $z = -1$ with the **Series[]** function (we will take the first 5 terms):

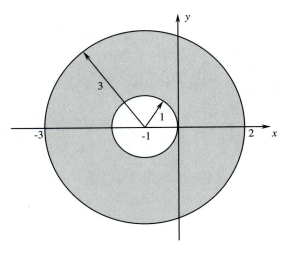

FIGURE 25.1
Regions of convergence for the three Laurent series represented by Eq. 25.1.

```
In[14]:= L1 = Series[f, {z, -1, 5}]

                                    2            3
            -3     5    11 (1 + z)   29 (1 + z)   83 (1 + z)
Out[14]= ----- + -(-) - ----------- - ----------- - ----------- -
         1 + z    3          9            27           81

                       4             5
          245 (1 + z)    731 (1 + z)            6
          ------------ - ------------ + O[1 + z]
              243            729
```

Note that this series contains only one negative power of $(z + 1)$. Next, we seek the series which converges for $3 < |z + 1|$. First, we use the **Apart**[] function to separate the various factors of $f(z)$:

```
In[15]:= ff = Apart[f]

            2      1    3
Out[15]= ------ + - - -----
         -2 + z   z   1 + z
```

Before we can do the expansion, we need to change variables, letting $z = 1/y + 1$. This substitution is made and we obtain

```
In[16]:= fff = ff /. z -> 1/y - 1

               2          1
Out[16]= ------   +   ------  - 3 y
              1          1
          -3 + -    -1 + -
              y          y
```

Now we expand this result using the **Series**[] about the point $y = 0$:

```
In[17]:= L2 = Series[fff, {y, 0, 5}]

              2       3       4        5        6
Out[17]= 7 y   + 19 y  + 55 y  + 163 y  + O[y]
```

Now we change variable back to z:

```
In[18]:= L2 = L2 /. y -> 1/(z+1)

            7           19          55          163         1   6
Out[18]= --------  +  --------  +  --------  +  --------  + O[-----]
             2            3            4            5       1 + z
         (1 + z)      (1 + z)      (1 + z)      (1 + z)
```

This Laurent series converges for $3 < |z + 1|$. By changing variables, we force *Mathematica* to perform the correct manipulations. This approach is evident when we generate the expansion in the annular domain $1 < |z + 1| < 3$.

First, we decompose $f(z)$ into three fractions as before:

```
In[19]:= fff = Apart[f]

            2      1    3
Out[19]= ------ + - - -----
         -2 + z   z   1 + z
```

Now, we change variables, letting $z = y - 1$:

```
In[20]:= fff = fff /. z -> y - 1

            2        1      3
Out[20]= ------  + ------  - -
         -3 + y    -1 + y    y
```

Now we need to separately treat the first term $2/(y-3)$ in order to ensure that it is expanded properly. We perform another change of variables for just this term, letting $y = 3w$:

```
In[21]:= fff[[1]] /. y -> 3 w

                2
Out[21]= --------
            -3 + 3 w
```

We now expand this term in a series about the point $w = 0$:

```
In[22]:= L3a = Series[%, {w, 0, 5}]

                         2      3      4      5
             2    2 w   2 w    2 w    2 w    2 w         6
Out[22]= -(-) - --- - ---- - ---- - ---- - ---- + O[w]
             3    3      3      3      3      3
```

We then change variables back to y:

```
In[23]:= L3a = L3a /. w -> y / 3

                    y        y 2      y 3      y 4      y 5
                2 -      2 (-)    2 (-)    2 (-)    2 (-)
             2      3        3        3        3        3          y 6
Out[23]= -(-) - --- - ------ - ------ - ------ - ------ + O[-]
             3    3      3        3        3        3          3
```

and then restore this result to our original variable, z:

```
In[24]:= L3a = L3a /. y -> z + 1

                        1 + z        1 + z 2      1 + z 3      1 + z 4
                    2 -----    2 (-----)    2 (-----)    2 (-----)
             2          3            3            3            3
Out[24]= -(-) - ------- - ---------- - ---------- - ---------- -
             3      3            3            3            3

                    1 + z 5
                2 (-----)
                      3            1 + z 6
             ---------- + O[-----]
                  3                3
```

We now restore z to the second term of the partial fraction decomposition and then let $z = 1/w - 1$:

```
In[25]:= (fff[[2]] /. y -> z + 1 ) /. z -> (1/w - 1)

                1
Out[26]=      ------
                 1
             -1 + -
                  w
```

Now we expand this result about the point $w = 0$:

```
In[26]:= Series[%, {w,0,5}]

               2    3    4    5       6
Out[26]= w + w  + w  + w  + w  + O[w]
```

We revert to the variable z, and obtain the correct expansion for the second term of the partial fraction expansion:

```
In[27]:= L3b = % /. w -> 1 / (z + 1)

              1               -2          -3          -4          -5
Out[27]=   ----- + (1 + z)  + (1 + z)  + (1 + z)  + (1 + z)   +
           1 + z

                   1   6
                O[-----]
                  1 + z
```

The third term is straightforward to expand, since, when it is re-expressed in terms of z, it has the correct form:

```
in[28]:= L3c = Series[fff[[3]] /. y -> z + 1, {z, -1, 5}]

             -3          6
Out[28]=   ----- + O[1 + z]
           1 + z
```

The full Laurent expansion is then obtained by adding the three individual results just obtained:

```
In[29]:= L3 = L3a + L3b + L3c

                          1 + z         1 + z 2        1 + z 3
                       2 -----      2 (-----)       2 (-----)
              -3    2     3             3              3
Out[29]= ----- + -(-) - ------- - ---------- - ---------- -
          1 + z    3     3             3              3


                1 + z 4       1 + z 5
             2 (-----)     2 (-----)
                  3             3          1 + z 6       1
             ---------- - ---------- + O[-----]   + ----- +
                  3             3             3       1 + z


                  -2           -3           -4           -5        1   6
         (1 + z)    + (1 + z)    + (1 + z)    + (1 + z)    + O[-----]
                                                              1 + z


                     6
         + O[1 + z]
```

This result is the Laurent expansion which converges in $1 < |z + 1| < 3$. Because of the way that *Mathematica* internally stores series, the `Simplify[]` function will not have any effect on a series expansion. Assuming we have all the terms we need, we can force *Mathematica* to truncate the series and treat it as a normal expression. This is done with the `Normal[]` function, which does this by removing the term of the form `O[]`:

```
In[30]:= Normal[%]

                      1
          General::ivar: ----- is not a valid variable.
                      1 + z

             2          -5           -4           -3           -2
Out[30]= -(-) + (1 + z)    + (1 + z)    + (1 + z)    + (1 + z)    -
             3


                            2            3
                 2    2 (1 + z)   2 (1 + z)   2 (1 + z)
             ----- - --------- - ---------- - ---------- -
             1 + z       9           27           81


                    4           5
             2 (1 + z)   2 (1 + z)
             ---------- - ----------
                243          729
```

In the course of normalizing the series, *Mathematica* has simplified numerators and combined terms in the obvious way. The warning message returned can safely be ignored.

EXERCISES

25.1. Use the twelve-term Taylor expansions of $f(z) = e^z$ and $g(z) = \cos z$ to form the twelve-term composition $f[g(z)] = e^{\cos z}$. Also determine the composite series directly and verify that the results match.

25.2. The *error function* erf z is defined by

$$\operatorname{erf}/, z = \frac{2}{\sqrt{\pi}} \int_0^z e^{-s^2} ds.$$

Determine the first ten terms of the Taylor expansion for erf z using the definition given above. Repeat the calculation using the *Mathematica* function Erf []. Compare your results.

25.3. Determine the ten-term Taylor expansion of $f(z) = z^2/(z^2 + 4i)$ about the point $z = 2i$. What is the radius of convergence?

25.4. Determine two distinct Laurent expansions (five terms) for $f(z) = (3z+1)/(z^2 - 1)$ around $z = -1$ and determine where each converges.

25.5. Determine two distinct Laurent expansions (five terms) for $f(z) = 1/[z(z + 1)(z - 2)]$ around $z = 0$ and determine where each converges.

25.6. The Taylor expansion of $f(z) = z/(e^z - 1)$ is used to define the *Bernoulli numbers B_n* as follows:

$$\frac{z}{e^z - 1} = 1 + B_1 z + \frac{B_2}{2!} z^2 + \frac{B_3}{3!} z^3 + \dots$$

Use this definition to determine the first ten Bernoulli numbers.

CHAPTER
26

RESIDUES

26.1 LABORATORY GOALS

a. To evaluate residues at isolated singularities in the complex plane.

b. To evaluate certain real integrals with residues.

26.2 DETERMINING RESIDUES

The residue of a function of a complex variable $f(z)$ is defined to be the coefficient of $(z - a)^{-1}$ in the expansion of $f(z)$ around an isolated singular point. Consequently, if all such singularities can be identified and the Laurent expansions determined, the residues can be found. Determining residues by hand can be a laborious process. Fortunately, *Mathematica* has a function called `Residue[]` which substantially simplifies this process.

For example, let $f(z) = (-3z + 4)/[z(z - 1)(z - 2)]$. By inspection, we see that $f(z)$ has singular points at $z = 0$, $z = 1$, and $z = 2$. We first determine the residue at $z = 0$. The `Residue[]` function is called with two arguments. The first is the function, and the second is a list which specifies the independent variable and the point at which the residue is desired. Thus:

```
In[1]:= f = (-3z + 4)/(z(z-1)(z-2))


        4 - 3 z
```

```
Out[1]=  -------------------
             (-2 + z) (-1 + z) z

In[2]:= Residue[f, {z, 0}]

Out[2]= 2
```

and so the residue is 2. The other two residues are found as follows:

```
In[3]:= Residue[f, {z, 1}]

Out[3]= -1

In[4]:= Residue[f, {z, 2}]

Out[4]= -1
```

Residues of more complicated functions can be found using the **Residue[]** function. For example, let $g(z) = (1 + z)/(1 - \cos z)$. The residue at $z = 0$ is found
by:

```
In[5]:= g = (1 + z) / (1 - Cos[z])

            1 + z
Out[5]= ----------
          1 - Cos[z]

In[6]:= Residue[g, {z, 0}]

Out[6]= 2
```

As a final example, let $h(z) = z/[(z - \sin z)(\cosh z - \cos z)]$. We seek the residue
of $h(z)$ at the origin.[1] We use *Mathematica* to define $h(z)$ and then take the
residue:

```
In[7]:= h = z /((z - Sin[z])(Cosh[z] - Cos[z]))

                          z
Out[7]= -------------------------------------
            (-Cos[z] + Cosh[z]) (z - Sin[z])

In[8]:= Residue[h, {z, 0}]
```

[1] Computing this residue by hand would be a formidable task.

```
Out[8]= 0
```

26.3   INTEGRATING WITH RESIDUES

The residue theorem tells us that, if $f(z)$ is a analytic within and on a closed curve C except at a finite number of singular points within C, then

$$\int_C f(z)\,dz = 2\pi i[\text{Res}\,(z_1) + \text{Res}\,(z_2) + \ldots + \text{Res}\,(z_n)], \qquad (26.1)$$

where $\text{Res}\,(z_k)$ denotes the residue of $f(z)$ at its k-th singular point. To use this theorem, we first determine the singular points within the contour, determine the residues and then compute the integral. For example, let C be the contour $|z| = 4$ and $f(z) = 1/[z(z-2)^3]$. We seek $\int_C f(z)\,dz$. Note that $f(z)$ has two singular points: at $z = 0$ and $z = 2$. We proceed as follows:

```
In[9]:= f = 1 / (z(z - 2)^3)

                 1
Out[9]= -----------
               3
        (-2 + z)  z

In[10]:= result = 2 Pi I ( Residue[f, {z, 0}] +
                           Residue[f, {z, 2}] )

Out[10]= 0
```

Thus this particular integral is zero. As another example, let C be the contour $|z| = 2$ and $g(z) = \tan z$. This function has two singularities within C: one at $z = \pi/2$ and the other at $-\pi/2$. The computation is set up in the following manner:

```
In[11]:= result = 2 Pi I (Residue[Tan[z], {z, Pi / 2}] +
                          Residue[Tan[z], {z, -Pi / 2}])

Out[11]= -4 I Pi
```

Thus $\int_C g(z)\,dz = -4\pi i$.

26.4 EVALUATING REAL INTEGRALS

Residues can be used to determine a wide class of integrals that *Mathematica* cannot directly handle. For example, suppose we wish to evaluate

$$\int_{-\infty}^{\infty} \frac{\cos mx}{1 + x^2} \, dx.$$

Setting this up directly in *Mathematica* with the `Integrate[]` function gives the following result:

```
In[12]:= Integrate[Cos[m x] / (1 + x^2), {x, -Infinity, Infinity}]

          SeriesData::csa:
             Argument 0 in ComposeSeries[0, ComplexInfinity]
                is not a power series.

          SeriesData::csa:
             Argument 0 in ComposeSeries[0, ComplexInfinity]
                is not a power series.

          SeriesData::csa:
             Argument 0 in ComposeSeries[0, ComplexInfinity]
                is not a power series.

          General::stop:
             Further output of SeriesData::csa
                will be suppressed during this calculation.

Out[12]= 0
```

The sequence of ominous warning messages suggests that we should be very careful about believing the answer. In fact, it is incorrect.[2]

A result from residue theory says that if $Q(z)$ is analytic in the upper half of the z-plane except at a finite number of poles none of which falls on the real axis, and if $zQ(z)$ converges to zero uniformly as $z \to \infty$, then

$$\int_{-\infty}^{\infty} \cos mx \, Q(x) \, dx = -2\pi \sum \operatorname{Im}\left[\operatorname{Res}\left(e^{imz}Q(z)\right)\right], \qquad (26.2)$$

and

$$\int_{-\infty}^{\infty} \sin mx \, Q(x) \, dx = 2\pi \sum \operatorname{Re}\left[\operatorname{Res}\left(e^{imz}Q(z)\right)\right], \qquad (26.3)$$

where the sum in both instances is taken over all the residues of $e^{imz}Q(z)$ in the upper half-plane, and Re and Im denote the real and imaginary part, respectively.

---

[2]If m is explicitly set to an integer value, *Mathematica* performs the integration correctly.

In our example, there is one pole of $Q(z)$ at $z = i$. Thus the integral is found by:[3]

```
In[13]:= -2 Pi Im[ Residue[ Exp[I m z] / (1 + z^2), {z, I}]]

                -I
                --
                2
Out[13]= -2 Pi Im[--]
                 m
               E
```

and so the the result is πe^{-m}.

As a rule, these types of integrals should be tried first with the **Integrate[]** function. The many methods provided by residue theory may then be used if *Mathematica* finds the integral intractable.

EXERCISES

Note: In these exercises, try and compute the integral directly with *Mathematica* and with residues. Other residue integration theorems may be helpful!

26.1. Determine the residue of $f(z) = 1/J_0(z)$ at the smallest real zero of $J_0(z)$.

26.2. Evaluate
$$\int_0^{2\pi} \frac{d\theta}{1 - 2p\sin\theta + p^2}, \quad -1 < p < 1.$$

26.3. Evaluate
$$\int_{-\infty}^{\infty} \frac{\cos mx}{(x-a)^2 + b^2}\,dx.$$

26.4. Evaluate
$$\int_{-\infty}^{\infty} \frac{\cos mx}{(a^2 + x^2)^2}\,dx.$$

26.5. Evaluate
$$\int_{-\infty}^{\infty} \frac{x\sin mx}{1 + x^4}\,dx.$$

26.6. Evaluate
$$\int_0^{\infty} \frac{x^{a-1}}{1 + x^3}\,dx, \quad 0 < a < 3.$$

---

[3]Note that we used the **Im[]** function in **In[13]**, but did not load the **ReIm** package. *Mathematica* actually has functions **Re[]** and **Im[]** built in, but their capabilities are limited. The package **ReIm** provides enhanced versions of those functions. Since the enhancements were not needed here, the package was not loaded.

VISUALIZING COMPLEX MAPPINGS

27.1 LABORATORY GOALS

a. To use the `CartesianMap[]` and `PolarMap[]` functions to map certain plane regions under complex mappings.

b. To obtain the parametric equations for images of curves under complex mappings.

27.2 MAPPING RECTANGULAR REGIONS

Many applications of complex analysis are built around the shapes that regions in the z-plane assume in the w-plane under mappings by analytic functions. The `ComplexMap` package provides a way to visualize these mappings under certain conditions. This and the `ReIm` package are both loaded with the following commands:

```
In[1]:= <<Algebra`ReIm`

In[2]:= <<Graphics`ComplexMap`
```

In addition, we will define x and y to be *real* variables with the tag operator $/:$, as discussed in Chapter 24:

```
In[3]:= x/: Im[x] = 0

Out[3]= 0

In[4]:= y/: Im[y] = 0

Out[4]= 0
```

The `CartesianMap[]` function will generate the shape of any *rectangular* region in the z-plane under a given mapping. The syntax of this command is unusual: The first argument is the function name *without* an argument. This is followed by the ranges of the x- and y-coordinates given as a pair of lists.

27.3   THE EXPONENTIAL MAP

For example, consider, the image of the rectangle $0 \le x \le 1$ and $0 \le y \le \pi$ under the mapping $w = e^z$:

```
In[5]:= CartesianMap[Exp, {0,1}, {0,Pi}]

Out[5]= -Graphics-
```

The image under this mapping is shown in Fig. 27.1. The mapping e^z takes the

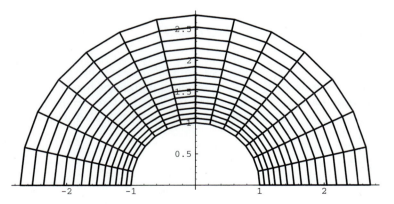

FIGURE 27.1
Image of the rectangle $0 \le x \le 1$ and $0 \le y \le \pi$ under the mapping e^z.

rectangle into a half-annulus. In order to better understand the detailed behavior of e^z, separate the real and imaginary parts of e^z:

```
In[6]:= z= x + I y

Out[6]= x + I y

In[7]:= u = Re[Exp[z]]

            x
Out[8]= E   Cos[y]

In[9]:= v = Im[Exp[z]]

            x
Out[9]= E   Sin[y]
```

Note that these expressions for u and v form a pair of parametric equations in the w-plane. When y is held fixed, they represent rays in the w-plane, while when x is held fixed, they correspond to circular arcs centered at the origin. Thus the rays seen in Fig. 27.1 are the images of the horizontal line segments in the rectangle and the semi-circles are images of the vertical line segments.

27.4   THE SINE MAP

As another example, consider the region $0 \leq x \leq \pi$ and $0 \leq y \leq 1$ under the mapping $w = \sin z$:

```
In[10]:= CartesianMap[Sin, {0,Pi}, {0,1}]

Out[10]= -Graphics-
```

As shown in Fig. 27.2, the images of the horizontal and vertical line segments in the z-plane appear to be a family of confocal ellipses and hyperbolas in the w-plane. To verify this, we proceed as before:

```
In[11]:= u = Re[Sin[z]]

Out[11]= Cosh[y] Sin[x]

In[12]:= v = Im[Sin[z]]

Out[12]= Cos[x] Sinh[y]
```

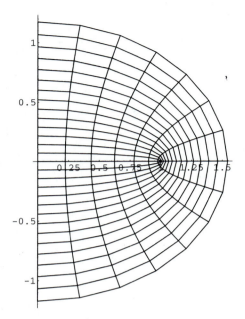

FIGURE 27.2
Image of the rectangle $0 \le x \le \pi$ and $0 \le y \le 1$ under the mapping $\sin z$.

Note that for fixed y,

$$\frac{u^2}{\cosh^2 y} + \frac{v^2}{\sinh^2 y} = 1, \tag{27.1}$$

which is the equation for an ellipse, while for fixed x,

$$\frac{u^2}{\sin^2 x} - \frac{v^2}{\cos^2 x} = 1, \tag{27.2}$$

which is the equation of a pair of hyperbolas. Therefore, vertical line segments map to branches of an hyperbola, while horizontal line segments map to portions of an ellipse. Suppose now we divide the rectangle in the z-plane in two by the line $y = x/\pi$. What would be the image of the diagonal line under our mapping and the images of each of the triangles thus formed? To answer this question, we use the `ParametricPlot[]` function, considering u and v as parametric equations. We also substitute x/π for y in u and v:

```
In[13]:= ParametricPlot[Evaluate[{u, v} /. y -> x / Pi ],
                {x, 0, Pi}]

Out[13]= -Graphics-
```

The result of this call to `ParametricPlot[]` is shown in Fig. 27.3. Having

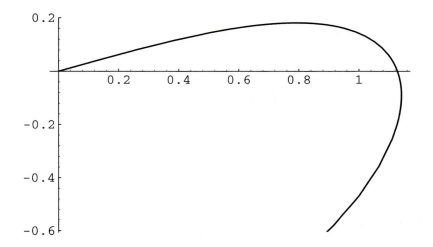

FIGURE 27.3
Image of the linear segment $y = x/\pi$ with $0 \le x \le \pi$ under the mapping $\sin z$.

obtained this result, we can overlay the two graphs and determine the images of each triangle:

```
In[14]:= Show[%, %%%]

Out[14]= -Graphics-
```

As shown in Fig. 27.4, the image of the diagonal segment divides the image in the w-plane into two regions. One conforms to the upper triangle, while the other conforms to the lower as suggested in the figure.

27.5   THE LOGARITHM MAP

For some mappings, the natural coordinates with which to work are polar coordinates. The `PolarMap[]` function performs essentially the same function as the `CartesianMap[]` function, except that the variable lists apply to the radial and angular ranges respectively. Suppose, for example, we wish to examine the image of the unit circle under the map $w = \log z$. [1] For this domain, $0 \le r \le 1$ and $-\pi < \theta \le \pi$. The *Mathematica* input line is given below:

---

[1] We are thinking of the principal value of the logarithm in this example.

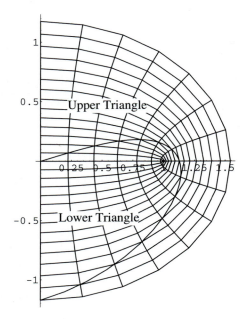

FIGURE 27.4
Overlay of Fig. 27.2 and Fig. 27.3.

```
In[15]:= PolarMap[Log, {0,1}, {-Pi , Pi}]

Out[15]= -Graphics-
```

The result of this call to `PolarMap[]` is shown in Fig. 27.5. To see the images of the circular arcs and rays, we first define two new variable to be purely real:

```
In[16]:= r/: Im[r] = 0

Out[16]= 0

In[17]:= th/: Im[th] = 0

Out[17]= 0
```

We then proceed to determine the real and imaginary parts of the mapping log z:

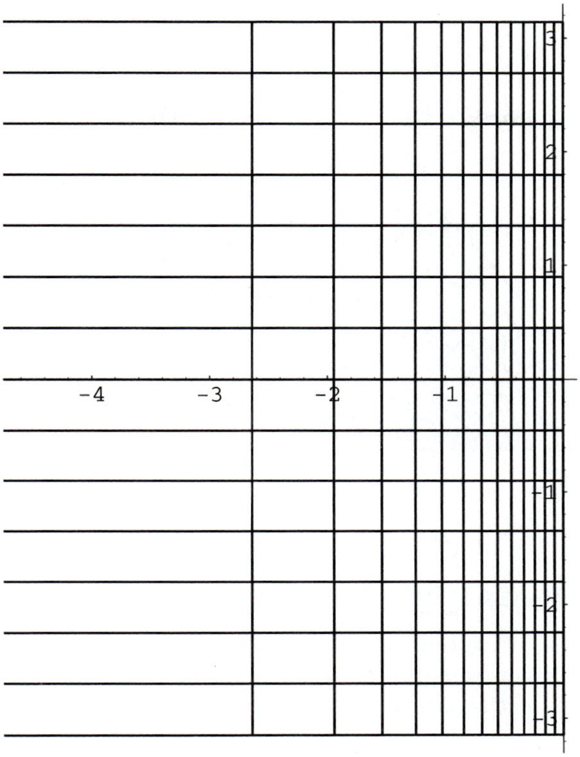

FIGURE 27.5
Image of the unit disk (cut along the negative x-axis) under the mapping $\log z$.

```
In[18]:= z = r Exp[I th]

                I th
Out[18]= E      r

In[19]:= u = Re[Log[z]]

Out[19]= Log[Abs[r]]

In[20]:= v = Im[Log[z]]

Out[20]= th + Arg[r]
```

Note that $\arg r = 0$ since r is a positive real number. For a fixed value of r, the image of the circle with that radius will be a vertical line segment, while the image of a ray (constant θ) would be a horizontal line segment. This accounts for the appearance of Fig. 27.5.

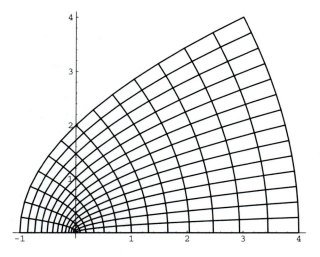

FIGURE 27.6
Image of the square $0 \leq x \leq 1$ and $0 \leq y \leq 1$ under the mapping z^2.

27.6   OTHER MAPPINGS

Because of the way that both the `CartesianMap[]` and `PolarMap[]` functions accept their first arguments, functions like $w = z^2$ cannot be used directly as parameters to either *Mathematica* function. Instead, we must first define a symbolic form of the function:

```
In[21]:= F[z_] := z^2
```

The image of the unit square can now be found with the following call to `CartesianMap[]`

```
In[22]:= CartesianMap[F, {0, 1}, {0, 1}]

Out[22]= -Graphics-
```

The image of the unit square is shown in Fig. 27.6. The images of both vertical and horizontal line segments are parabolas.

EXERCISES

27.1. Determine the parametric equations for the parabolas shown in Fig. 27.6.

27.2. What is the image of the unit circle under the mapping $w = \cosh^{-1} z$? [Hint: Use `ArcCosh[]`.]

27.3. What is the image of the unit square under the mapping $w = \tan z$?

27.4. Determine the parametric equations for the images of the lines $y = x$ and $y = -x$ under the mapping $w = z + 1/z$.

CHAPTER
28

CONFORMAL
MAPPINGS

28.1 LABORATORY GOALS

a. To determine the form of linear fractional transformations satisfying given conditions.

b. To evaluate and plot two-dimensional equilibrium temperatures.

b. To evaluate and plot stream functions for two-dimensional incompressible fluid flow.

28.2 LINEAR FRACTIONAL TRANSFORMATIONS

We begin this laboratory by loading in the `ComplexMap` and `ReIm` packages, and by define x and y to be *real* variables:

```
In[1]:= <<Algebra`ReIm`

In[2]:= <<Graphics`ComplexMap`

In[3]:= x/: Im[x] = 0

Out[3]= 0

In[4]:= y/: Im[y] = 0
```

```
Out[4]= 0
```

Linear fractional transformations , or LFTs, are used extensively in mapping applications.[1] LFTs have the following form:

$$w = \frac{az + b}{cz + d} \qquad (28.1)$$

One way to define an LFT in *Mathematica* is with the following statement:

```
In[5]:= LFT[z_, a_, b_, c_, d_] := (a z + b)/(c z + d)
```

It is well-known that LFTs map circles and straight lines into either circles or straight lines. The particular image of either a circle or line can be obtained with this definition of the LFT. For example, suppose we seek parametric equations for the image of the line $y = x + 1$ under the mapping $w = 1/z$. We express the mapping in terms of its real and imaginary parts:

```
In[6]:= w = LFT[z, 0, 1, 1, 0]

          1
Out[6]= - -
          z

In[7]:= w = w /. z-> x + I y

            1
Out[7]= -------
        x + I y

In[8]:= u = Re[w]

           x
Out[8]= -------
         2    2
        x  + y

In[9]:= v = Im[w]

            y
Out[9]= -(-------)
          2    2
         x  + y
```

---

[1]They are also called bilinear transformations or Möbius transformations.

Now suppose we parameterize $y = x+1$ as $x = t$ and $y = t+1$, with $-\infty < t < \infty$. This leads immediately to parametric equations for u and v:

```
In[10]:= u = u /. {x -> t, y -> t + 1}

                 t
Out[10]= -------------
          2         2
         t  + (1 + t)

In[11]:= v = v /. {x -> t, y -> t + 1}

               1 + t
Out[11]= -(-------------)
          2         2
         t  + (1 + t)
```

Note that this form is not unique since the parameterization of x and y by t is not unique.

This form of the LFT can also be used to establish the fixed point result for LFTs which states that every LFT has at most two fixed points (unless it is the identity transform $w = z$). Since a fixed point is a value of z for which $f(z) = z$, we can use the Solve[] function and our LFT definition as follows:

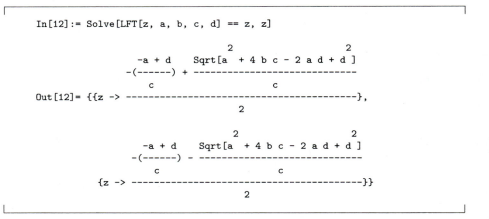

```
In[12]:= Solve[LFT[z, a, b, c, d] == z, z]

                                  2                    2
              -a + d     Sqrt[a  + 4 b c - 2 a d + d ]
             -(------) + -----------------------------
                 c                    c
Out[12]= {{z -> ------------------------------------------},
                                   2

                                  2                    2
              -a + d     Sqrt[a  + 4 b c - 2 a d + d ]
             -(------) - -----------------------------
                 c                    c
         {z -> ------------------------------------------}}
                                   2
```

From this result, we see that the condition for a single fixed point is that $a^2 + 4bc - 2ad + d^2 = 0$.

We often seek an LFT which maps three distinct points in the z-plane into three distinct points in the w-plane. The form to be satisfied is

$$\frac{(w - w_1)(w_2 - w_3)}{(w - w_3)(w_2 - w_1)} = \frac{(z - z_1)(z_2 - z_3)}{(z - z_3)(z_2 - z_1)} \tag{28.2}$$

First we define a *Mathematica* function which has this form:

```
In[13]:= LFT3[z_, z1_, z2_, z3_] := (z - z1)(z2 - z3) /
                                    ((z - z3)(z2 - z1))
```

Now suppose we seek an LFT that maps 0 into -1, 1 into $-i$ and 2 into 1. We use the form just described to form the left and right sides of an equation for w in terms of z and then use the Solve[] function:

```
In[14]:= Solve[LFT3[w, -1, -I, 1] == LFT3[z, 0, 1, 2], w]

                 1 + I - z
Out[14]= {{w -> -(-----------)}}
                 1 + I - I z
```

The desired transformation is evidently

$$w = \frac{-z + 1 + i}{-iz + 1 + i}. \tag{28.3}$$

Suppose instead that we require the point 2 to map into the point at infinity in the w-plane. Determining the transformation now involves two steps. First, require the point 2 to map into an arbitrary point, say a:

```
In[15]:= Solve[LFT3[w, -1, -I, a] == LFT3[z, 0, 1, 2], w]

                 -2 I - 2 a + I z + (2 - I) a z
Out[15]= {{w -> -(-----------------------------)}}
                 -2 I - 2 a + (-1 + 2 I) z + a z
```

Now use the Flatten[] function to remove curly braces, and the substitution operator /., together with the Limit[] function, and let $a \to \infty$:

```
In[16]:= Limit[w /. Flatten[%], a -> ComplexInfinity]

             -2 + (2 - I) z
Out[16]= -(--------------)
               -2 + z
```

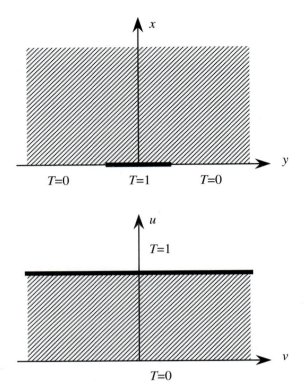

FIGURE 28.1
The mapping $w = \log[(z-1)/(z+1)]$ takes upper half of the z- plane into the infinite strip $0 \le v \le \pi$. The temperature is $T = 1$ along the segment $-1 \le x \le 1$. This boundary maps to the top edge of the strip.

28.3   EQUILIBRIUM TEMPERATURES

An important application of complex mappings is to the solution of Laplace's equation. For example, consider the semi-infinite plate shown in the top half of Fig. 28.1. The temperature T is held at zero everywhere along the lower portion of the plate, except along the segment $-1 \le x \le 1$, where the temperature is 1. The temperature satisfies Laplace's equation

$$T_{xx} + T_{yy} = 0,$$

subject to the indicated boundary conditions. It can be shown that the mapping

$$w = \log\left(\frac{z-1}{z+1}\right), \tag{28.4}$$

maps the half-plane to the semi-infinite strip shown in the lower half of Fig. 28.1. The segment maps to the upper boundary of the strip which is π units wide in the

w-plane. We know that the temperature also satisfies Laplace's equation in the strip. Further, owing to the simple geometry, the solution to Laplace's equation in the strip is $T = v/\pi$. By substituting the imaginary part of w into this result, we can obtain an expression for the temperature in the z-plane. Thus

```
In[17]:= v = Im[Log[(z - 1)/(z + 1) /. z -> x + I y]]

Out[17]= Arg[-1 + x + I y] - Arg[1 + x + I y]

In[18]:= T = v / Pi

          Arg[-1 + x + I y] - Arg[1 + x + I y]
Out[18]= -------------------------------------
                          Pi
```

The temperature can now be plotted with the `ContourPlot[]` function:

```
In[19]:= ContourPlot[T, {x, -2, 2}, {y, 0, 2},
                     PlotPoints -> 30]

Out[19]= -ContourGraphics-
```

A contour plot of the temperature is shown in Fig. 28.2. Note that the correct

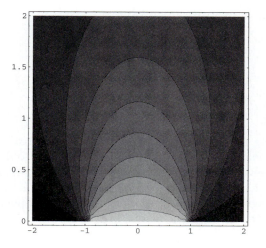

FIGURE 28.2
Contour plot of the temperature distribution in the domain $-2 \le x \le 2$ and $0 \le y \le 2$.

temperatures are attained along the bottom boundary. The contours represent *isothermal* curves.

28.4   FLOW IN A CORNER

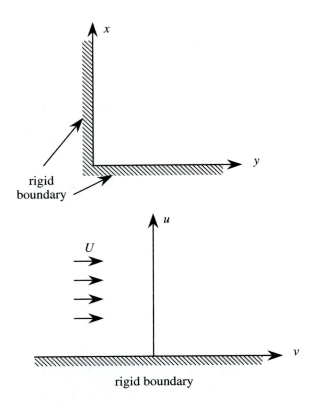

FIGURE 28.3
The mapping $w = z^2$ takes the first quadrant of the z-plane into the upper half-plane. The hatched edges denote a Neumann (or rigid) boundary condition. The flow in the half-plane is uniform.

Complex mapping methods can also be used to solve steady, inviscid, incompressible flow problems. For example, suppose we desire to describe the flow of such a fluid in the vicinity of a corner, suggested in the top-half of Fig. 28.3. The boundaries of the corner are impenetrable, and so satisfy the Neumann boundary condition. This region can be mapped into the upper half-plane by the mapping $w = z^2$ as suggested in the lower half of Fig. 28.3. In this domain, the solution is trivial to obtain. Recall that the velocity field is described in the w-plane by the expression

$$\frac{d\Phi}{dw} = \phi_u + i\psi_u, \tag{28.5}$$

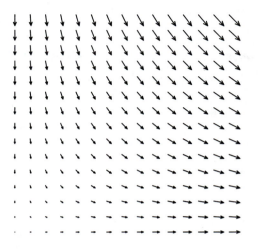

FIGURE 28.4
Hamiltonian field of the stream function for ideal flow in a corner. The arrows are parallel to the stream line. Note that the origin (lower-left) is a stagnation point.

where $\Phi = \phi + i\psi$ is the complex velocity potential. Since the flow in the w plane is uniform and steady, $\phi_u + i\psi_u = U$. Thus $\Phi = Uw$. In the z-plane, the velocity potential is therefore $\Phi = Uz^2$. Thus velocity potential in the corner is described by the following:

```
In[20]:= velx = Re[U z^2 /. z -> x + I y]

                          2    2
Out[20]= -2 x y Im[U] + (x  - y ) Re[U]

In[21]:= vely = Im[U z^2 /. z -> x + I y]

                2    2
Out[21]= (x  - y ) Im[U] + 2 x y Re[U]
```

The imaginary part of the velocity potential is the stream function. The flow in the corner will follow level curves of this function. These curves can be plotted with the `ContourPlot[]` function, but an alternative view can be had by examining the *Hamiltonian* field of the stream function. This vector field is everywhere orthogonal to the gradient of the stream function, and so in a visualization of this field, the vectors will be parallel to the streamlines. First, we load the `PlotField` package:[2]

---

[2]See Chapter 23.

```
In[22]:= <<Graphics`PlotField`
```

Now we invoke the `PlotHamiltonianField[]` function, which uses the same syntax as the `PlotGradientField[]` function, discussed in Chapter 23:

```
In[23]:= PlotHamiltonianField[(vely /. U -> 1), {x, 0, 2},
                                              {y, 0, 2}]

Out[23]= -Graphics-
```

The result is depicted in Fig. 28.4. In addition to indicating the direction of the flow, the magnitude of each arrow also suggests the flow speed. Note the flow is stationary at the point in the lower-left corner of the figure. This is called a stagnation point.

EXERCISES

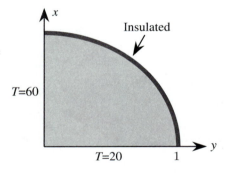

FIGURE 28.5
Cross section of a solid cylinder. The circular edge is insulated.

28.1. Find two distinct LFTs that map $x \le 0$ onto $|w| \ge 2$.

28.2. Determine the image of the annulus $1 \le |z| \le 2$ under the mapping $w = (z+1)/z - i$.

28.3. Determine the equilibrium temperature in the plates discussed in the laboratory. In this case, let the segment $-1 \le x \le 1$ be insulated. Sketch the resulting temperature field.

28.4. The corner flow found in Section 28.4 is not the only one. Determine two other possible flows which satisfy Laplace's equation and the rigid boundary conditions.

28.5. The complex potential $F(z) = \log(z - 1) - \log(z + 1)$ generates a flow in the upper-half plane with a *source* at $z = 1$ and a *sink* at $z = -1$.
(*a*) Plot this flow on the domain $-2 \leq x \leq 2$ and $0 \leq y \leq 4$.
(*b*) Show that the streamlines are the family of circles $x^2 + (y - c)^2 = 1 + c^2$.

28.6. Consider the solid cylinder whose cross section is shown in Fig. 28.5. The horizontal boundary is held at a temperature of 20 degrees, while the vertical boundary is held at 60 degrees. The outer edge is insulated. Determine the temperature inside the cylinder. Plot the isothermal lines.

APPENDIX
A

SUMMARY OF FUNCTIONS AND OPERATORS

This appendix contains a brief tabular summary of the *Mathematica* functions, operators, and keywords used in this book.[1] In addition to the discussions in the text, the *Mathematica* book[2] and *Guide to Standard Packages*[3] should be consulted for detailed usage and syntax information. A quick-reference guide to functions, operators, and symbols is in Table A.1. Each subsequent table contains the name of the function, operator, or keyword and a very brief remark about it. Every table entry is also listed in the Index, and page number references can be obtained from there.

---

[1] Excepting those appearing in Appendix B.

[2] Wolfram, *op. cit.*

[3] Boyland, *op. cit.*

TABLE A.1
Quick Reference Guide

Category	Table	Category	Table
Algebraic Functions	A.2	Lists	A.8
Elementary Function	A.3	Graphics	A.9
Special Functions	A.4	Miscellaneous	A.10
Vectors and Matrices	A.5	Operators	A.11
Calculus	A.6	Keywords	A.12
Solvers	A.7		

TABLE A.2
Algebraic Functions

Mathematica **Name**	**Function Effect**
`Apart[]`	Factor Expression
`Coefficient[]`	Manipulate Coefficients
`Expand[]`	Expand Expression
`Factor[]`	Factor Expression
`N[]`	Convert to Numerical Value
`Numerator[]`	Gets Numerator
`Simplify[]`	Simplifies Expression

TABLE A.3
Elementary Functions

Mathematica **Name**	**Function Effect**
Abs[]	Absolute Value
ArcCos[]	Inverse Cosine
ArcCosh[]	Inverse Hyperbolic Cosine
ArcTan[]	Inverse Tangent
Arg[]	Argument
Cos[]	Cosine
Cosh[]	Hyperbolic Cosine
Csc[]	Cosecant
Exp[]	Exponential
Im[]	Imaginary Part
Log[]	Natural Logarithm
Mod[]	Modulo
Re[]	Real Part
Sec[]	Secant
Sech[]	Hyperbolic Secant
Sin[]	Sine
Sinh[]	Hyperbolic Sine
Sqrt[]	Square Root
Tan[]	Tangent

TABLE A.4
Special Functions

Mathematica **Name**	**Function Effect**
Ai[]	Airy Function of the First Kind
Bi[]	Airy Function of the Second Kind
BesselJ[]	Bessel function of the First Kind
BesselY[]	Bessel function of the Second Kind
Bi[]	Airy Function of the Second Kind
Delta[]	Dirac Delta
EllipticK[]	Complete Elliptic Integral
Erf[]	Error Function
Erfi[]	Imaginary Error Function
HermiteH[]	Hermite Polynomials
JacobiSN[]	Jacobi Elliptic Sine
LegendreP[]	Legendre Polynomials
SinIntegral[]	Sine Integral

TABLE A.5

Vector and Matrix Functions

Mathematica **Name**	**Function Effect**
`Biharmonic[]`	Biharmonic Operator
`Cross[]`	Cross Product
`CrossProduct[]`	Cross Product
`Curl[]`	Curl Operator
`Det[]`	Determinant
`Div[]`	Divergence Operator
`DotProduct[]`	Dot Product
`EigenValues[]`	Matrix Eigenvalues
`EigenVectors[]`	Matrix Eigenvectors
`Inverse[]`	Matrix Inverse
`Laplacian`	Laplacian Operator
`MatrixExp[]`	Matrix Exponential
`MatrixPower[]`	Matrix Power
`ScalarTripleProduct[]`	Scalar Triple Product
`Transpose[]`	Matrix Transpose

TABLE A.6

Calculus Functions

Mathematica **Name**	**Function Effect**
`C[]`	Integration Constants
`ComplexToTrig[]`	Convert Complex Exponential to Trigonometric Form
`D[]`	Take Derivative
`FourierTrigSeries[]`	Determine Fourier Coefficients
`Integrate[]`	Evaluate Integral (symbolic)
`Interpolation[]`	Generates an Interpolating Function
`InverseLaplaceTransform[]`	Inverse Laplace Transform
`LaplaceTransform[]`	Laplace Transform
`NIntegrate[]`	Evaluate Integral (numerical)
`Normal[]`	Normalize Series
`O[]`	Tail of Power Series
`Residue[]`	Determines Residue
`Series[]`	Generates Taylor expansion

TABLE A.7
Symbolic and Numerical Solvers

Mathematica **Name**	**Function Effect**
DSolve[]	Differential Equation Solver (Symbolic)
FindRoot[]	Numerical Equation solver
NDSolve[]	Differential Equation Solver (Numerical)
NSolve[]	Algebraic Equation Solver (Numeric)
Solve[]	Algebraic Equation Solver (Symbolic)

TABLE A.8
List Manipulation Functions

Mathematica **Name**	**Function Effect**
Append[]	Add item to list
AppendTo[]	Add item to list
Flatten[]	Strip braces from list
Length[]	Length of list
ReadList[]	Read data into a list
Table[]	Generate a list

TABLE A.9
Graphical Functions

Mathematica **Name**	**Function Effect**
CartesianMap[]	Complex Map in Cartesian Coordinates
CylindricalPlot3D[]	Three-dimensional Plot in Cylindrical Coordinates
ContourGraphics[]	Converts Graphic Form
ContourPlot[]	Contour Plot
DensityGraphics[]	Converts Graphic Form
DensityPlot[]	Density Plot
ListPlot[]	Plot a List
ListPlot3D[]	Plot a List as a surface
ParametricPlot[]	Two-dimensional Parametric Plot
ParametricPlot3D[]	Three-dimensional Parametric Plot
Plot[]	Two-dimensional plot
Plot3D[]	Three-dimensional plot
PlotGradientField[]	Two-dimensional gradient field plot
PlotHamiltonianField[]	Two-dimensional hamiltonian field plot
PlotVectorField[]	Two-dimensional vector field plot
PointSize[]	Change Point Size
PolarMap[]	Complex Map in Polar Coordinates
Show[]	Redisplay Graphics
SphericalPlot3D[]	Three-dimensional Plot in Spherical Coordinates
Thickness[]	Change Line Thickness

TABLE A.10
Miscellaneous Functions

Mathematica **Name**	**Function Effect**
CForm[]	Output C Code
Clear[]	Undefine a Symbol
ColumnForm[]	Output a Vector in Column Form
CoordinateRanges[]	Determine Coordinate Ranges
Coordinates[]	Determine Coordinate System
CoordinatesFromCartesian[]	Change From Cartesian Coordinates
CoordinatesToCartesian[]	Change to Cartesian Coordinates
Do[]	Iterate a Set of Commands
Evaluate[]	Force Evaluation of an Expression
FortranForm[]	Output FORTRAN Code
If[]	Conditional Statement
In[]	Holds Input Statements
InterpolatingFunction[]	Function Approximation
Out[]	Holds Output Statements
SetCoordinates[]	Change Coordinate System
Short[]	Outputs Short Form
Sum[]	Iterate a Sum

TABLE A.11

Mathematica operators used in the text.

Mathematica **Symbol**	**Effect**
"	String delineation
%	Previous output
%%	Next-to-previous output
^	Exponentiation
*	Multiplication
−	Subtraction
−>	Substitution
+	Addition
=	Assignment
==	Logical comparison
{}	Makes lists
[[]]	Makes lists
>>	Write to file
.	List multiply
;	Suppress output
??	Get brief help message
'	Derivative
/	Division
:=	Delayed assignment
/.	Tag set

TABLE A.12
Mathematica keywords used in text.

Mathematica **Symbol**	**Use**
`AspectRatio`	Aspect Ratio for Graphics
`Automatic`	Forces Default Choice
`AxesLabel`	Label for Coordinate Axes
`ComplexInfinity`	For Limits with Complex Functions
`CoordinateSystem`	Value of Current Coordinate System
`Cylindrical`	Cylindrical Coordinates
`DefaultFont`	Name and Size of Default Font
`E`	e
`FaceGrids`	Grids on Boxes in 3D Plots
`Frame`	Turns Frame On or Off
`FrameLabel`	Label for Frame
`GridLines`	Places Grid Lines
`I`	$i = \sqrt{-1}$
`Infinity`	∞
`InterpolatingOrder`	Sets Order of Interpolating Function
`$MachinePrecision`	Hardware Accuracy for Floating Point Operations
`Pi`	π
`PlotLabel`	Label for Plot
`PlotPoints`	Plotting Resolution
`PlotStyle`	Plot Drawing Options
`RecordLists`	Defines Records in Lists
`Spherical`	Spherical Coordinates
`True`	Boolean Switch
`ViewPoint`	Coordinates of Viewpoint
`ViewVertical`	Which Axis is Up
`WorkingPrecision`	Effective Precision of Computation

APPENDIX
B

UNIT
CONVERSIONS
AND CONSTANTS

This appendix describes the ability of *Mathematica* to perform unit conversions
and other useful scientific and engineering data conversion calculations. We first
load the **Units** package:

```
In[1]:= <<Miscellaneous'Units'
```

Units are always spelled out and capitalized. The **Units** package is familiar with
all common (and many unusual) units of measurement. The **Convert**[] function
will provide the necessary conversion factor for change units. For example, to
convert meters per second into miles per hour, we give the following command:

```
In[2]:= Convert[Meter/Second, Mile/Hour]

          2.23694 Mile
Out[2]= ------------
            Hour
```

If just the coefficient is needed for use in a subsequent *Mathematica* expression, it can be picked off by multiplying the result by the reciprocal units:

```
In[3]:= % Hour/Mile

Out[3]= 2.23694
```

As another consider the conversion factor taking miles per hour into yards per day:

```
In[4]:= Convert[Mile/Hour, Yard/Day]

          42240. Yard
Out[4]= -----------
             Day
```

Attempts to convert between incompatible units will fail with an obvious message:

```
In[5]:= Convert[Amp, Volt]

          Convert::incomp: Incompatible units in Amp and Volt.

Out[5]= Amp
```

The `ConvertTemperature[]` function is especially designed to convert specified temperatures from one system to another:

```
In[6]:= ConvertTemperature[-40, Fahrenheit, Celsius]

Out[6]= -40.

In[7]:= ConvertTemperature[273, Celsius, Rankine]

Out[7]= 983.07
```

The functions `MKS[]`, `SI[]`, and `CGS[]` provide conversion of the given units to the appropriate units in those respective systems:

```
In[8]:= MKS[Feet / Second]

        0.3048 Meter
Out[8]= ------------
           Second

In[9]:= SI[Knot]

        0.514444 Meter
Out[9]= --------------
            Second

In[10]:= CGS[Acre]

                     7         2
Out[10]= 4.04686 10   Centimeter
```

B.1 PHYSICAL CONSTANTS

A companion package called PhysicalConstants provides a handy way of recalling all manner of important scientific and engineering constants:

```
In[11]:= <<Miscellaneous'PhysicalConstants'

In[12]:= SpeedOfLight

                    8
         2.99792 10  Meter
Out[12]= -----------------
              Second

In[13]:= SpeedOfSound

         340.292 Meter
Out[13]= -------------
            Second
```

Note that the speed of sound provided is at 1 standard atmosphere.

The physical constants can be combined with the Convert[] and other functions in many useful ways:

```
In[14]:= Convert[SpeedOfSound, Foot / Second]
```

```
            1116.44 Foot
Out[14]= ------------
             Second

In[15]:= Convert[SpeedOfLight, Furlong / Week]

                      11
           9.01309 10    Furlong
Out[15]= --------------------
                 Week

In[16]:= Convert[EarthMass, Ton]

                      21
Out[16]= 5.88162 10    Ton
```

B.2 CHEMICAL DATA

Another package, called `ChemicalElements` provides information about the nuclear, physical, and atomic properties of elements of the periodic table.

```
In[17]:= <<Miscellaneous'ChemicalElements'

In[18]:= Abbreviation[Iron]

Out[18]= Fe

In[19]:= AtomicWeight[C]

Out[19]= 12.011

In[20]:= StableIsotopes[Technetium]

Out[21]= {}
```

All isotopes are radioactive. It does not occur in nature.

```
In[21]:= MeltingPoint[W]

Out[21]= 3680. Kelvin

In[22]:= BoilingPoint[Titanium]

Out[22]= 3560. Kelvin

In[23]:= Density[Iodine]
```

```
            4930. Kilogram
Out[23]= --------------
                 3
            Meter
```

```
In[24]:= ThermalConductivity[Strontium]
```

```
            35.3 Watt
Out[24]= ------------
            Kelvin Meter
```

Naturally, these results can be converted into different units by using some of the other functions described in this appendix:

```
In[25]:= CGS[HeatOfFusion[Gallium]]
```

```
                  10
            5.59 10    Erg
Out[25]= -------------
                Mole
```

```
In[26]:= Convert[Density[Nickel], Slug / (Foot^3)]
```

```
            17.2727 Slug
Out[26]= ------------
                 3
             Foot
```

C

In order to simplify things, most graphics functions in this book were called with their many different options set to default values. From time to time, more elegant plots are required, say, for projects, special assignments, or classroom presentations. This appendix includes a short discussion of many plotting options that users might find useful in these situations.

C.1 TWO-DIMENSIONAL PLOTS

Consider the following graph comparing $\sin x$ and $J_0(x)$ on the same axes:

```
In[1]:= Plot[{Sin[x], BesselJ[0, x]}, {x, 0, 4Pi}]

Out[1]= -Graphics-
```

Figure C.1 is similar in appearance to most of the two-dimensional plots used throughout this book. Now consider the same plot, but with the following options invoked:

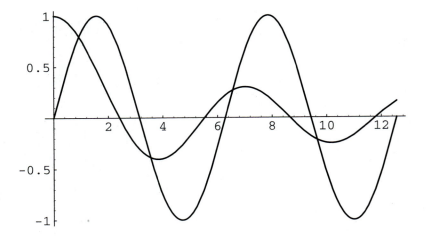

FIGURE C.1
Comparison of $\sin x$ and $J_0(x)$ on the interval $0 \leq x \leq 4\pi$. No special plotting options were used.

```
In[2]:= Plot[{Sin[x], BesselJ[0, x]}, {x, 0, 4Pi},
           PlotStyle -> {{}, {Thickness[0.01]}},
           GridLines -> {{0, Pi, 2Pi, 3Pi, 4Pi}, Automatic},
           Frame -> True, FrameLabel -> {"x", "y"},
           PlotLabel -> "Comparison of Sin[x]
           and BesselJ[0, x]", DefaultFont -> {"Helvetica", 10}]

Out[2]= -Graphics-
```

The **PlotStyle** option takes a list of lists as an argument. If only one list is given, the plotstyle of all curves is affected. In our example, the first list was null, indicating that the first curve, corresponding to the call to **Sin[]** would be plotted normally. The second list includes a call to the **Thickness[]** function. This function sets the thickness of the drawn line to the specified value. Note in Fig. C.2 the increased thickness of the curve corresponding to the call to **BesselJ[]**.

The **GridLines** option also takes a list as argument. The first component of the list is another list indicating the placement of the *vertical* gridlines. Here, we wanted them placed at intervals of π along the x-axis. The second argument is the keyword **Automatic**, which instructs *Mathematica* to use its own standard way of determining the number and placement of grid lines in the *horizontal* direction.

The next option we used was **Frame**. By setting this option to the keyword **True**, a frame is drawn around the plot. We proceeded to label portions of the frame with the **FrameLabel** option. This takes a list for an argument. The first

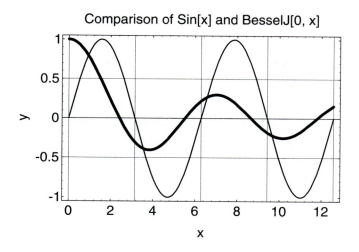

FIGURE C.2
Same basic information as in Fig. C.1 but with numerous options invoked.

and second components of the list in our example wrote the string "x" and "y" in their customary positions. Additional arguments would have caused labeling to be applied to the top and right-hand side of the frame.

The plot itself receives a main label with the `PlotLabel` option. This also takes a string for an argument. Note that the string was split over two lines, meaning that `PlotLabel` parses out extra spaces and centers the result automatically. Finally, the last option called, `DefaultFont`, changes the font used by *Mathematica* to both the screen and the output device. In this example, the font was set to `Helvetica` and scaled to a 10 point size. Thus all the text and labeling on the plot match the font used elsewhere.[1]

C.2   THREE-DIMENSIONAL PLOTS

Now we take a brief look at some options that can enhance the appearance of three-dimensional plots. Consider the surface generated by the function $\cos(x + \cos y)$, shown plotted in Fig. C.3 with no options invoked.

```
In[3]:= Plot3D[Cos[x + Cos[y]], {x, 0, 4Pi}, {y, 0, 4Pi}]

Out[3]= -SurfaceGraphics-
```

---

[1]Font availability is highly system-dependent. Most PostScript printers support Courier, Helvetica, and Times-Roman, so these are probably available in a variety of sizes. More exotic fonts *may be* available, depending on how you (or your system administrator if you are using a laboratory computer) configured your machine.

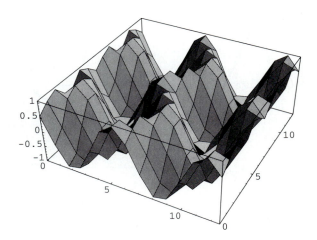

FIGURE C.3
Surface generated by $f(x, y) = \cos(x + \cos y)$ on the domain $0 \le x \le 4\pi$ and $0 \le y \le 4\pi$. No special plotting options were used.

We now re-draw this figure with the following call to `Plot3D[]` accompanied by

```
In[4]:= Plot3D[Cos[x + Cos[y]],
            {x, 0, 4Pi}, {y, 0, 4Pi}, PlotPoints -> 30,
            ViewVertical -> {1, 0, 0},
            FaceGrids -> {{0, 0, 1}, {0, 0, -1}},
            AxesLabel -> {"x", "y", "z"},
            PlotLabel -> "Cos[x + Cos[y]]",
            DefaultFont -> {"Helvetica", 10}]

Out[4]= -SurfaceGraphics-
```

The result is shown in Fig. C.4.

The first option called is `PlotPoints` which changes the resolution used in rendering the plot. In this case, 30 points are sampled in each coordinate direction. The default is 15 in each direction. Experience shows that 30 will often generate a very attractive plot. By passing a list as the argument, separate control of the resolution in each direction can also be obtained.

Next we invoke the `ViewVertical` option with a list as argument. All but one component of the list should be set to 0, with one set to 1. The first position is set to on, which tells *Mathematica* to draw the figure with x-axis as the vertical axis. The effect is to draw the figure "sideways". When combined with the

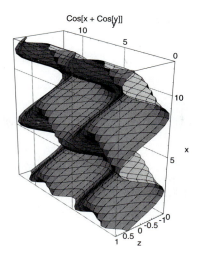

FIGURE C.4
Same basic information as in Fig. C.3 but with numerous options invoked.

`ViewPoint` option, many useful perspectives can be obtained. This can greatly enhance the visualization of complicated surfaces.

The `FaceGrids` option is called with a list of two arguments. Each argument tells the `Plot3D[]` function to place a grid at that location. The format for these lists is the same as that for the `ViewVertical` option. Our example places a grid at the top and bottom of the displayed z-axis. These grids can be useful for studying the location of surface textures.

The `AxesLabel`, `PlotLabel`, and `DefaultFont` options work just as they did in the previous section. Note that the argument to `AxesLabel` now takes *three* strings.

We close this appendix by noting that there are many additional and very elaborate graphics capabilities built into *Mathematica*.[2] The interested reader should refer to the *Mathematica* book for additional details on the many powerful graphics abilities available to those who might need them.

---

[2]The ability to manipulate the color and placement of simulated lighting when rendering three-dimensional graphics would take a whole book in itself!

GENERATING
FORTRAN
AND C CODE

Mathematica contains features which allow its output to be easily used by other types of software that often find use in engineering mathematics. This appendix briefly explains how to use *Mathematica* in this fashion with both the FORTRAN and C programming languages.

D.1 FORTRAN EXAMPLE

Let $f(x) = x \sin x$ with $x \in [-\pi, \pi]$. Suppose we require a FORTRAN function which computes the ten-term Fourier series for this function. First, we load the `FourierTransform` package:

```
In[1]:= <<Calculus'FourierTransform'
```

Now compute the Fourier series:

```
In[2]:= F = FourierTrigSeries[x Sin[x], {x, -Pi, Pi}, 10]
```

```
              Cos[x]     2 Cos[2 x]     Cos[3 x]     2 Cos[4 x]
Out[2]= 1 -  ------  -  ----------  +  --------  -  ----------  +
                2          3              4             15

              Cos[5 x]     2 Cos[6 x]     Cos[7 x]     2 Cos[8 x]
             --------  -  ----------  +  --------  -  ----------  +
                12           35             24             63

              Cos[9 x]     2 Cos[10 x]
             --------  -  -----------
                40            99
```

The `FortranForm[]` function can be used to express this result as the right-hand side of a valid FORTRAN expression:

```
In[3]:= FortranForm[F]

Out[3]= 1 - Cos(x)/2 - 2*Cos(2*x)/3 + Cos(3*x)/4 - 2*Cos(4*x)/15 +
         -   Cos(5*x)/12 - 2*Cos(6*x)/35 + Cos(7*x)/24 -
         -   2*Cos(8*x)/63 + Cos(9*x)/40 - 2*Cos(10*x)/99
```

This result can be placed in a file for external editing using the *Mathematica* symbol for output redirection >>:

```
In[4]:= FortranForm[F] >> "scratch"
```

The file with name `scratch` now contains the Fourier expansion in FORTRAN format. This may then be included in a FORTRAN source file for use as appropriate.

D.2 C EXAMPLE

Suppose we are writing a C function which will compute the first two terms of the asymptotic expansion of $J_0(x)$ for $x \gg 1$. This expansion can be obtained be expanding $J_0(x)$ about the point at infinity. Thus,

```
In[5]:= G = Series[BesselJ[0, x], {x, Infinity, 2}]

                         1           Pi           9          1 3
Out[5]= Sqrt[2] Sqrt[----] (Cos[-- - x] (1 - ------ + O[-] ) +
                      Pi x        4                 2       x
                                               128 x
```

```
     -1        1 3       Pi
    (--- + O[-] ) Sin[-- - x])
     8 x       x         4
```

This can be converted into C code with the **CForm[]** function. Note that we first normalize the series expansion with the **Normal[]** function. We should also convert integer and rational expressions into floating point form, in order to avoid the later problem of data type conflicts. The result is

```
In[6]:= CForm[N[Normal[G]]]

Out[6]= 0.797885*Sqrt(1/x)*((1. - 0.0703125/Power(x,2))*
            Cos(0.785398 - 1.*x) - 0.125*Sin(0.785398 - 1.*x)/x)
```

Note that **Power(x,2)** is a C library function which the user must usually supply. This output can be captured in a file for later use with output redirection:

```
In[7]:= CForm[N[Normal[G]]] >> "scratch"
```

Since *Mathematica* also can generate the polynomial expansions for many special polynomials—such as those of Legendre and Chebyshev—it can be used as a convenient tool for writing FORTRAN and C code fragments which require the use of these polynomials.

BIBLIOGRAPHY

Anderson, Dale A., John C. Tannehill, and Richard H. Pletcher: *Computational Fluid Mechanics and Heat Transfer*, Hemisphere Publishing, Washington, 1984, p. 155.

Bertin, John J.: *Engineering Fluid Mechanics*, Prentice-Hall, Englewood Cliffs, 1984.

Boyland, Phil: *Guide to Standard Mathematica Packages*, Wolfram Research, Champaign, Ill., 1991.

Boyland, Phil et al.: *Guide to Standard Mathematica Packages Supplement V2.2*, Wolfram Research, Champaign, Ill., 1993.

Greenberg, Michael D.: *Advanced Engineering Mathematics*, Prentice-Hall, Englewood Cliffs, 1988.

Kreyszig, Erwin: *Advanced Engineering Mathematics*, Seventh Edition, Wiley, New York, 1993.

Maeder, Roman E.: *Programming in Mathematica*, Second Edition, Addison-Wesley, Boston, 1991.

Oneil, Peter V.: *Advanced Engineering Mathematics*, Wadsworth, Belmont, CA, 1991.

Wolfram, Stephen: *Mathematica: A System For Doing Mathematics By Computer*, Addison-Wesley, Redwood City, CA, 1991.

Wiley, C. Ray and Barrett, Louis C.: *Advanced Engineering Mathematics*, McGraw-Hill, New York, 1982.

Zill, Dennis G. and Cullen, Michael R.: *Advanced Engineering Mathematics*, PWS-Kent, Boston, 1992.

INDEX

', 59, 145
->, 8, 39, 66
., 98, 178, 194
/., 39, 45, 50, 83
/:, 222, 242, 250
:=, 52
;, 40, 182
=, 52
==, 50
>>, 279
??, 2, 116
[[]], 15, 52, 66
&&, 122
{}, 15
%, 3, 50
%%, 5
*, 28
., 38

Abs[], 221, 246
Airy's equation, 115
amplitude, 73, 75
annulus, 229
Apart[], 74, 207, 230
Append[], 94, 216
AppendTo[], 157

arc length, 194
ArcCos[], 17, 186
ArcCosh[], 249
ArcSin[], 90
ArcTan[], 77, 80, 186, 221, 226
Arg[], 221, 246, 255
argument, 221
art, 63
ASCII, 44
AspectRatio, 211
asymtotic expansion, 279
Automatic, 274
AxesLabel, 277

bar
    cantilevered, 144
    clamped, 144
    hinged, 144
Bernoulli numbers, 235
Bernoulli's equation, 61
Bessel functions, 80, 115, 161, 163, 183,
        218, 227, 240, 279
Bessel's equation, 115
BesselJ[], 80, 115, 163, 165, 227, 273,
        274, 279
BesselY[], 115, 163, 165

`Biharmonic[]`, 180
biharmonic, 180
biharmonic equation, 191
bilinear transformations, 251
boundary conditions, 144
   clamped, 144
   free, 144
   hinged, 144
   homogeneous, 54
   Neumann, 256
Burger's equation, 12

`C[]`, 59, 66, 145
C language, 50, 122, 278
`CartesianMap[]`, 242
Cauchy-Euler equation, 112
`CForm[]`, 280
`CGS[]`, 269
change of variables, 230–233
chaos, 111
`Characters[]`, 46
Chebyshev's equation, 120
`Clear[]`, 172, 181
`Coefficient[]`, 75, 146, 150
`ColumnForm[]`, 16
complementary solution, 68
complete elliptic integral, 91
complex argument, 220
complex exponential, 67, 223
complex exponents, 221
complex functions, 223
complex mappings, 241–249
   exponential, 242
   logarithm, 245
   sine, 243
complex numbers, 219
complex velocity potential, 257
`ComplexInfinity`, 253
`ComplexToTrig[]`, 67, 147, 151
conditions
   boundary, 135, 143, 161
   initial, 69
cone, 212
contemplation, 63
contour integrals, 238

contour plot, 9, 214, 255
`ContourGraphics[]`, 9
`ContourPlot[]`, 214, 255, 257
conversion factor, 269
`Convert[]`, 268
`ConvertTemperature[]`, 269
coordinate systems
   table of, 186
`CoordinateRanges[]`, 185
`Coordinates[]`, 185
coordinates
   cylindrical, 161, 185
   polar, 245
   spherical, 185
`CoordinatesFromCartesian[]`, 186
`CoordinatesToCartesian[]`, 186
`CoordinateSystem`, 184
`Cos[]`, 6, 77, 165, 192, 205, 207, 215, 223, 237
`Cosh[]`, 183, 223, 237, 243
critical damping, 72
critical points, 206
`Cross[]`, 195, 196
cross product, 17, 18, 182
`CrossProduct[]`, 18, 182, 187, 188, 195
`Csc[]`, 113
`Curl[]`, 179, 182, 189, 202
curl, 179
curvature, 196
`Cylindrical`, 185
`CylindricalPlot3D[]`, 165, 190

`D[]`, 4, 146, 193, 196, 203, 206, 207
dashpot, 70
data types, 28
default coordinates, 185
`DefaultFont`, 275, 277
`Delta[]`, 81
delta function, 81
density plot, 8
`DensityGraphics[]`, 8, 211
`DensityPlot[]`, 9
`Det[]`, 38, 147, 151, 163, 170, 197
determinant, 38, 147
difference equations, 168

difference quotient, 169
differential equation
  Airy's, 115
  Bernoulli's, 61
  Bessel's, 115
  Cauchy-Euler, 112
  Chebyshev's, 120
  Duffing, 110
  first-order
    homogeneous, 61
    homogeneous systems, 93
    linear, 58
    separable, 60
  fourth-order, 143
  Hermite's, 116
  Laguerre's, 120
  Legendre's, 115
  Lorenz's, 111
  nonhomogeneous, 66
  nonhomogeneous systems, 96
  parametric Bessel's, 120, 162
  Ricatti's, 62
  second-order, 65
  Van der Pol's, 108
Dirac delta function, 81
DiracDelta[], 81
direction cosines, 18
directional derivatives, 178
Div[], 179, 189, 199, 216
divergence, 179, 215
divergence theorem, 199
Do[], 157
dot product, 17, 38, 178, 194
DotProduct[], 17, 187, 188
DSolve[], 58–63, 66, 69, 94, 96, 99,
    101, 105, 112, 117, 145
Duffing's equation, 110

E, 6
eigenfrequency, 162
eigenmode, 162
EigenValues[], 40
eigenvalues, 54, 156
EigenVectors[], 41
elliptic amplitude function, 90

elliptic functions, 87
elliptic modulus, 90
EllipticK[], 91
equations
  difference, 168
  inconsistent, 51
  nonlinear, 52
  overdetermined systems, 51
  simultaneous linear, 49
  transcendental, 54
  underdetermined systems, 51
equidimensional equation, 112
equilibrium temperature, 254
Erf[], 235
Erfi[], 116
error function, 235
Evaluate[], 31, 73, 107
Exp[], 79, 138, 177, 179, 223, 227, 242
Expand[], 3
exponential decay, 74
exponentiation, 3

FaceGrids, 277
Factor[], 3
fields
  scalar, 183
  vector, 183
FindRoot[], 55, 118, 153, 157, 164
fixed points, 252
Flatten[], 33, 94, 99, 208, 253
flow
  inviscid incompressible, 256
FORTRAN language, 278
FortranForm[], 279
Fourier coefficients, 123
Fourier cosine series, 126
Fourier series, 278
Fourier sine coefficients, 137
Fourier sine series, 123
FourierTrigSeries[], 129
Frame, 159, 274
FrameLabel, 274
free boundary, 167
FromCharacterCode[], 47
fundamental matrix, 97

Gibb's phenomenon, 126
Grad[], 177, 182, 188, 202
gradient field, 213
gravitational acceleration, 87
GridLines, 159, 274
group, 224
guess
  blind, 63

Hamiltonian field, 257
heat equation, 135
heated bar, 136
Heaviside function, 81
helix, 193
Hermite polynomials, 116
Hermite's equation, 116
HermiteH[], 117
hyperbolic functions, 224

I, 6, 220
IBM, 2
If[], 81, 122, 168, 171
Im[], 220, 222, 223, 240, 243, 246, 250,
  255, 257
implied multiplication, 3
In[], 3, 66, 73
Indeterminate, 27
Infinity, 185, 239, 279
integral
  definite, 4
  indefinite, 4
Integrate[], 4, 97, 123, 137, 194, 200,
  201, 203, 239, 240
InterpolatingFunction[], 105
Interpolation[], 31, 33
interpolation, 31
Inverse[], 38, 97
inverse Laplace transform, 79
inverse matrix, 38
inverse trigonometric functions, 224
InverseLaplaceTransform[], 80
isothermal curves, 256
iterated integral, 200, 203

Jacobian elliptic function

sine, 90
JacobiSN[], 90

Korteweg-deVries equation, 57

Laguerre's equation, 120
Laplace transform, 79
  operational properties, 83
Laplace's equation, 191, 254
LaplaceTransform[], 79
Laplacian, 180
Laplacian[], 180
Laurent series, 229
Legendre polynomials, 116
Legendre's equation, 115
LegendreP[], 116
Length[], 16
Limit[], 102, 253
limitations
  computer algebra systems, 148
linear fractional transformations, 251–
  259
list, 15, 25
  components of, 15
  manipulation of, 26, 66
  multidimensional, 32
  reading data into, 27
  warnings about, 27
list of lists, 37, 147
ListPlot[], 28, 30, 158, 159
ListPlot3D[], 32
local variables, 138
Log[], 4, 89, 113, 245, 246, 255
logistics equation, 64
Lorenz attractor, 111
Lorenz's equation, 111

$MachinePrecision, 56
Macintosh, 1, 42, 140
matrix
  eigenvalues, 40
  eigenvectors, 40
  powers, 42
  probability transition, 43
matrix exponential, 95
matrix multiplication, 38

matrix powers, 40
matrix transpose, 38
MatrixExp[], 95–97
MatrixForm[], 38
MatrixForm, 172
MatrixPower[], 42
membrane, 161
  annular, 161
  half-annular, 167
  rectangular, 167
MicroSoft Windows, 140
MKS[], 269
Möbius transformations, 251
Mod[], 122
modulus, 221

N[], 5, 53, 91, 102, 131, 171, 221
natural frequency, 87
NDSolve[], 105, 106
NeXT, 140
NIntegrate[], 5, 120, 128
Normal[], 234
NSolve[], 76, 172
Numerator[], 151
numerical accuracy, 56
numerical evaluation, 5
numerical methods, 104

O[], 226, 234
optimization, 205
  second-derivative test, 209
Out[], 3, 50, 59, 69, 105, 179, 226
overlaying graphics, 7, 214, 245
overlaying surfaces, 10, 127

package
  ChemicalElements, 271
  ComplexMap, 241, 250
  CrossProduct, 195
  FourierTransform, 128, 278
  LaplaceTransform, 79
  ParametricPlot3D, 165, 189
  PhysicalConstants, 270
  PlotField, 213, 257
  ReIm, 219, 240, 241, 250

TaylorRatioTest, 228
Trigonometry, 147
Units, 268
VectorAnalysis, 14, 177, 184, 199, 213
packages, 14, 67, 79
  enhancements to built-in functions, 240
parametric equations, 243, 251, 252
ParametricPlot[], 109, 244
ParametricPlot3D[], 111, 193
Part[], 74
partial differentiation, 179
partial fractions, 233
particle motion, 192
particular solution, 68
pentadiagonal matrix, 176
periodic table, 271
phase, 73, 75
  complex, 221
phase plane, 109
Pi, 6, 38
Plot[], 5, 31, 69, 72, 73, 76, 81, 90, 101, 105, 107, 108, 113, 127, 136, 149, 155, 163, 273
Plot3D[], 8, 138, 165, 210, 275, 277
PlotGradientField[], 213, 258
PlotHamiltonianField[], 258
PlotLabel, 275, 277
PlotPoints, 8, 165, 190, 214, 218, 276
PlotStyle, 158, 274
PlotVectorField[], 215, 216
PointSize[], 158
PolarMap[], 245
polynomial
  roots, 52
position vector, 192
principal value, 220, 221
procedural programming, 228
procedures, 157

quantum harmonic oscillator, 116

radius of convergence, 228
radius of curvature, 197

Re[], 220, 222, 223, 240, 243, 246, 257
ReadList[], 27
RecordLists, 28
relativity, 13
Residue[], 236, 237
residue, 236
residue theorem, 238
resolution, 10
resonance, 69
Ricatti's equation, 62

scalar multiplication, 15
scalar triple product, 17, 18
ScalarTripleProduct[], 18
Sec[], 88
Sech[], 57
separation of variables, 144, 162
Series[], 225–227, 229, 231, 279
series
    Laurent, 229
    Taylor, 225
SetCoordinates[], 185
Short[], 40
shortening expressions, 40
Show[], 7, 125, 159, 211, 214, 218
SI[], 269
simple pendulum, 87, 104, 110
    nonperiodic solutions, 89
Simplify[], 69, 99, 148, 151, 182, 194,
    196, 207, 234
Sin[], 5, 77, 113, 123, 127, 129, 137,
    188, 192, 205, 207, 213, 215, 223,
    226, 237, 243, 273
Sinh[], 183, 223, 243
SinIntegral[], 81
soliton, 57
solutions
    nonuniqueness of, 62
Solve[], 45, 48, 50, 59, 66, 83, 89, 99,
    147, 148, 154, 170, 172, 206, 224,
    253
Sort[], 171, 172
spectrum, 150, 167
spelling errors, 181
Spherical, 185, 188

SphericalPlot3D[], 190, 191
spring-mass
    damped, 70, 78
    nonlinear, 110
    undamped, 67
Sqrt[], 17, 18, 75, 186, 196, 202, 203,
    220
stability, 110
steady-state solution, 73
Stoke's theorem, 201
stream function, 257
Sturm-Liouville equation, 117, 169, 172
substitution, 40
Sum[], 124, 127, 138
superscripts
    parenthesized, 179
surface contours, 214
surface integral, 201
surface plot, 8
Sutherland's formula, 11
symbolic equation, 50, 60, 65, 93, 96

Table[], 32, 45, 72, 73, 106, 124, 137,
    146, 150, 158, 164, 168, 171, 174
tables
    algebra functions, 261
    calculus functions, 263
    elementary functions, 262
    graphics functions, 264
    keywords, 267
    list functions, 264
    miscellaneous functions, 265
    operators, 266
    solver functions, 264
    special functions, 262
    vector and matrix functions, 263
Take[], 46
Tan[], 54, 89
Taylor series, 225
    operations on, 227
TaylorRatioTest[], 228, 229
Thickness[], 274
TNB coordinates, 195
ToCharacterCode[], 46
torsion, 197

transformations
  bilinear, 251
  linear fractional, 251
  Möbius, 251
transient solution, 74
transition probabilities, 42
`Transpose[]`, 29, 38
tridiagonal matrix, 171
`Trigonometry`, 67
`True`, 274

unit binormal vector, 195
unit conversions, 268
unit normal vector, 195, 202
unit tangent vector, 195
Unix, 2, 140

Van der Pol's equation, 108
variation of parameters, 97
vector addition, 15
vector differentiation, 177
vector field, 215
vector identities, 181
vector norm, 17
vibrating bar, 143
vibrating rope, 176
vibrating string, 150, 173
vibration frequencies, 145
vibrations
  nonlinear, 108
`ViewPoint`, 11, 139, 166, 277
`ViewVertical`, 276, 277
viscosity, 11

warning message, 193, 208, 235, 239
`WorkingPrecision`, 55